THE HERO TRILOGY

~

WHEN YOU COMIN BACK, RED RYDER?
THE HEART OUTRIGHT
THE MAJESTIC KID

THE HERO TRILOGY

~

WHEN YOU COMIN BACK, RED RYDER?
THE HEART OUTRIGHT
THE MAJESTIC KID

MARK MEDOFF

PEREGRINE SMITH BOOKS

SALT LAKE CITY

This is a Peregrine Smith Book
Published by Gibbs Smith, Publisher, P.O. Box 667, Layton, UT 84041

Manufactured in the United States of America

Design by J. Scott Knudsen

Front cover: *The Heart Outright,* by George Wooliver
Back cover photo of Mark Medoff by Jodie Schwartz

Lyrics for *The Majestic Kid* are by Mark Medoff and Jan Scarbrough

93 92 91 90 89   7 6 5 4 3 2 1

Library of Congress Cataloging-in-Publication Data
Medoff, Mark Howard.
     The hero trilogy / Mark Medoff.
          p. cm. — (Peregrine plays)
     When you comin back, Red Ryder? — The heart outright — The Majestic Kid.
     ISBN 0-87905-319-4
     I. Title. II. Series.
PS3563.E27H4   1989
812'.54 — dc20   89-8706
                                                                                                        CIP

The paper used in this publication meets the minimum requirements of American National Standard for Information Sciences — Permanence of Paper for Printed Library Materials, ANSI Z39.48-1984. ⊚

CONTENTS

~

INTRODUCTION: ADIOS, OLD WEST

~

I LIVE IN THE NEW WEST, but growing up in Miami Beach, Florida, in the fifties, I was a child of the Old West.

Never mind that until I was thirteen I was allergic to horses, that I never hunted the land for anything more treacherous or romantic than frogs, that I did not visit so important a piece of the West as California until I was twenty-four, that when I first contemplated accepting a job in New Mexico, I mistook it—in the geographic morass of my mind—for Utah. And that I didn't own a gun until I was forty and a local policeman urged me to arm myself against lunatics.

At the end of the tumultuous sixties, I wrote a play called *When You Comin Back, Red Ryder?*, about the death of the American heroic myth. In *Red Ryder*, the protagonist, Teddy, a Vietnam vet who grew up against a glorious western backdrop, who was weaned on American western heroes, who grew to know them as brethren, worship them as Gods . . . this very angry young man wonders, "Where did all those people get to so fast?" And laments: "Somebody pulled a fast one."

In remembering my own relationship to those western heroes, I wrote this in 1974 as part of the introduction to the published version of *Red Ryder:*

In 1948 I am eight, my brother six, and we meet the Durango Kid for the first time at the Airway Theater in Louisville. I remember the Kid as the Superman of cowboys, changing his clothes in a cave rather than a cramped phone booth or closet.

A mild-mannered rancher until trouble hits, the Kid then trans-mogrifies into a scourge in black mask and tight black togs who rides a white horse to ninety minutes of rectified wrongs . . . I believe in the Durango Kid, as I come to believe in Cisco and Red and all the others. The Saturday matinee is an institution of my childhood, a schoolroom as surely as the one I attend at I. M. Bloom School Monday through Friday.

How many western movies have there been since *The Outlaw Josie Wales* in 1976? Less than half a dozen? How many western movies on television in the last decade in the tradition of "Cheyenne" or "Paladin" or "The Lone Ranger"? None?

Why is the Old West out of favor? What happened to our faith in heroic intervention, our hope of salvation in the face of peril?

Beginning with the assassination of JFK, followed by those other assassinations — Malcolm X, Bobby Kennedy, Martin Luther King — with Vietnam, the counterculture, the new morality, Watergate, dollar gas and ten-thousand-dollar Volkswagens, America lost its innocence. It was virtually impossible to pretend that some individual wearing a pearl-handled six-gun and riding a handsome horse could gallop into American life *anywhere* and save *anyone,* to say nothing about shooting guns out of hands and beating up ten or fifteen bad guys in a saloon single-handedly and walking away without a scratch.

Where the tube used to be full of western series, now it's sitcoms; however silly, they're very aware. Whereas the old westerns and western TV series gave us "men," the sitcoms today tend to give us buffoonlike "adults" and a great many knowledgeable and enormously glib children; other series, such as "Dallas" and "Dynasty," give us adult protagonists who are extremely cynical.

Today's teenagers and college students, the top of the movie-going market, know virtually nothing about westerns, have little experience in them. The prime movie-going audience has been weaned on TV sitcoms and MTV; heroism is centered in rock stardom and outer space.

It's a fascinating sign of our times that the only way anything of substance seems to be getting done about world hunger is for the world of rock and roll to do it. Our ostensible leaders, political leaders, have done, been willing, able to do very little. In a curious way, the people we admired of old — those political leaders, our mythical western and soldier heroes — have been replaced by media superstars. It is the rare person anymore who doesn't yearn at least secretly to be a rock or movie or television superstar, even though so much of what so many of those stars transmit is anarchic and hedonistic in the extreme.

We have come a long way from the Code of the West conveyed by those old western heroes who kissed the woman only reluctantly and who might occasionally imbibe a shot of whiskey but were more likely to ask for milk or sarsaparilla to the elitist society of today's superstars, for whom, generally, only their own rules apply. Whereas those old cowboy heroes embodied the very essence of the notion of law and order, today we live in a society in which the desire — and the ability — to live outside the law is becoming pandemic.

The pre-assassination, pre-Vietnam generations didn't fear the future the way the present generation seems to. We could revel in the mythology of the past as we adapted it to the present — the old western movie hero become World War II hero become TV series western hero — with us nightly, every week, all year — a constant reminder of American heroic mythology. Beside that we had all those family series — "Father Knows Best," "Ozzie and Harriet," "The Donna Reed Show," "My Three Sons," "Stu Erwin," "Leave It to Beaver" — in which what we thought of as traditional values were reaffirmed by the half-hour weekly. And even though we thought these families were too good to be true, we still respected the point of view they represented. We still wanted to *try* to be a society like that, to *aspire* to values like that.

Perhaps the greatest irony of the so-called revolution of the sixties and early seventies is that all of us who were young then, we children of the Old West, actually thought for a while we could, through righteous thinking, through a summoning up of those values we'd been weaned on . . . we actually thought for a while we could stop that war, stop the deterioration of our society and make love and peace the cornerstones of our future. The naivete of that belief was surely as great as any example in history. It's no wonder, now that we're in charge of the entertainment industries in this country, we've turned with a vengeance on the genres that formed us.

As a nation, after the sixties, we had little egocentrism left, little of our old confidence left. Our men, our gunslingers, had been defeated, and our youth, who had grown up on those cowboy movies, on the heroism they espoused, who thought they could change the world, could engage the world to live by the Code of

the West, found that the realities of the times—political and social
realities—were much stronger than their ability to resist them.
Whereas we believed in this country for two hundred years that we
could make our own destiny, suddenly we seemed to be living in
a highly deterministic world. The shock produced a lot of nihilism—
highlighted by that philosophy's cornerstone: destruction for the sake
of destruction, with no obligation to offer viable replacements for
what's destroyed. Anarchy. Hedonism. Massive self-absorption, self-
indulgence. Say hello to the new morality and the drug culture with
their attendant rending of the American fabric.

Youth, whatever their age, weren't young anymore. Entertainment began to mirror that lack of youth. My younger children have
at nine and twelve, if not social, at least sexual awareness—garnered
from prime-time television—that I didn't have until I was in high
school. And unfortunately, TV and film don't make sex very attractive; there's very little truly romantic about it. And there is about
it a fierce anti-feminism, despite all the yahooing about women's
rights.

I've written recently about Stephen Ryder, the callow young man
in *When You Comin Back, Red Ryder?* who has the audacity to name
himself after one of those mythological western heroes of yore.
Stephen was humiliated by Teddy, that disillusioned Vietnam vet
in that diner in New Mexico in 1969. Since then he's been to Vietnam himself and come back. He's lost a hand and he's lost a lot of
naivete like a lot of American boys weaned on John Wayne, on Lash
LaRue and Roy and Hoppy and Red Ryder himself. Stephen "Red"
Ryder manages a pornographic movie house now in Austin, Texas—
once an historical part of the Old West. He has this to say about
the movies:

> Took me awhile to figure out what I figured the problem to be . . .
> they've ruined sex. Now hear me out. Started in about 1969
> when jist about ever' movie that they made hadda have some
> woman's naked bosoms up there on the screen. I mean, there's
> no movies for kids anymore. I mean, once in while there's a PG
> with jist a lotta cussin and maybe a touch a what they call your
> "brief nudity." It's like a movie ain't worth makin, it don't have
> any value, unless there's naked lady bosoms in it. But naked lady
> bosoms, ya see, don't necessarily make a movie good, and there's
> so many naked-lady-bosom movies around by now, people don't

jist go to the movies anymore to see naked lady bosoms. You don't gotta pay four bucks to see a pair on screen. Walk down a street in any town in summer and look for ladies in your tank-top T-shirt affair. Go to the topless bars. Go to a nudist beach. Join a motorcycle club. Git married.

There is very rarely male genitalia on screen, as if to do so would . . . *what?* Admit we'd reach a nadir we dare not admit we've reached. Or might the absence of male genitalia on the screen sug-gest somehow, in the wide realm of unconscious symbolism, that there *is* no male genitalia anymore. Our male protagonists — you can't really call them heroes anymore — have lost their manhood. Or is it as simple as: We've always exploited women, what's gonna stop us continuing? Though there are a lot of women in executive positions in the entertainment industry, the studios and networks and produc-tion companies are for the very most part still run by men. Their articulate disclaimers and even decent intentions aside, most of them are still hopeless male chauvinist pigs.

This is not to say that our view of women hasn't changed a good deal from the old westerns. The sixties and seventies to some extent really did liberate the woman from the insularity and narrow point of view we insisted on for her. For one thing, many claim not to want to be rescued anymore and you can be sure there's a lot of pres-sure brought to bear within the studios and networks not to make movies or TV shows in which this happens. And what would the western be without the little gal to rescue?

One of my post-*Red Ryder* plays in called *The Majestic Kid.* It involves an idealistic young lawyer from Chicago who moves out west and finds a very different west than he learned about as a child through those old movies. Finding himself frightened and confused, he calls up the memory of those old western heroes — embodied in the play by an old, singing cowboy hero named the Laredo Kid. At the end of the play, after the Old West and the New West have but-ted heads and the Old West has suffered heavy losses, Laredo has this speech:

> It was just all wrong out there, pard . . . I was scared fer you 'n them gals, pard, cuz I knew I couldn't do nothin to help ya. . . . Pard, 'pears maybe you kin, but me, I don't know if I kin live in a world where folks don't seem to know or care whut's right 'n

whut ain't, maybe even includin folks in the government of the
republic out in Washington. I don't know if I *wanna* live in a
world where the good guys and the bad guys are the same guys.

Let's talk about the embarrassment of the President of the United
States of America resigning from office, stigmatized as a crook, all
too reminiscent of those bad judges and sheriffs and high-rollers who
ran towns and were obsessed with greed in most of those old western movies and one of whom showed up each and every week on
those old TV western series . . . *and was defeated* — a constant reminder
of what happened on celluloid and tape — and what was *supposed* to
happen in real life — when the forces of evil were confronted by the
forces of good.

In the seventies we came to deify the bad guys in some very
stunning, serious work: *Bonnie and Clyde, The Wild Bunch, The God-
father,* and the Jack Nicholson characters in such movies as *Five Easy
Pieces* and *Carnal Knowledge.* It was as if the best of current moviemakers were saying there's no morality left, so let's not idealize what
ought to be; let's mirror what *is,* unattractive as it is.

In *Butch Cassidy and the Sundance Kid* we had two guys who were
anything but heroic; for me, they were the death knell for the old
western hero, those two rather charming but not terribly bright,
unheroic guys who ended up getting themselves killed for their lack
of heroism. If not played by Newman and Redford, those guys
wouldn't have been much different from you and me. A lot of people realized that. Demystification was in full flower. The movie star
who *didn't* look like Alan Ladd or John Wayne or dress in those fab-
ulous outfits like Roy and Hoppy and Lash came to the fore. Just
regular guys with not necessarily great bodies or noses or hair or
voices. A lot of short guys who — in this era of telling it like it is —
we were *told* were short. Nicholson and Hoffman and Redford and
Newman and Pacino and Dreyfuss. A few people, a mere handful
of insiders, knew Alan Ladd was short, but not the general movie-
going public, for Godsake. Shortness wasn't permitted in the
mythology.

Then there was *The Wild Bunch,* directed by Sam Peckinpah,
another seminal western. In the old westerns, in the series on TV,
there was no blood. In *The Wild Bunch* we saw real blood and we
saw death at 96fps — slow motion. People didn't shoot the guns out
of other people's hands; they shot them in the back and in the face

and death was ugly. Peckinpah had learned from watching Vietnam on TV, perhaps, what death looked like before the camera, and doing his part for demystification, he showed us what it really looked like in the movie theaters, in case we didn't watch the news. We could never go back to "pretend" from there unless we were being satiric, making fun of ourselves, of our old innocence—as happened at the end of the western's heyday with *Blazing Saddles* and as recently happened with *Rustler's Rhapsody*—which died quickly at the box office from lack of interest. The fifties generation isn't quite ready yet to yak it up about our fall from grace. And the kids didn't get what that movie was all about.

It was Peckinpah who gave us in *Straw Dogs* the amalgamation of the old and new western hero in Dustin Hoffman. Hoffman plays a mathematician living in England. Very much like *Shane,* he's driven finally to defend what he cares about, in this case mainly himself, his manhood. In Shane's case, we know all along that he's struggling within himself *not* to fight because he knows he'll kill whomever he fights. With Hoffman, we're dealing with a very ordinary guy in macho terms. When he fights, he doesn't walk into town and face the bad guys down; he fights on their terms, he resorts to every bit of trickery he can design, he fights frantically for *survival.* It's also notable of that movie that it's his wife, dispirited by his obsession with numbers rather than things masculine, who sets the gory ending in motion by tempting the "bad guys"—who aren't really bad until she tempts them. The movie displays a very angry view of women, almost as if Peckinpah were punishing them for having the audacity to want to be different from the traditional role we'd stuffed and crushed them into in the old western and just about every other literary form during the past six thousand years. It was almost as if *Straw Dogs* was saying: Men would be basically good if it weren't for women, who are bad and therefore make men bad by making them crave women. Which brings us to the major problem with many of the old western heroes, the part many of us under their spell still struggle to disavow.

In *The Majestic Kid* it crystallizes for the young lawyer, Aaron Weiss, in the realization that, as he says to the Laredo Kid, "he lurched into adolescence steeped in the male-male and the male-horse relationship . . . And shallow dipstick that I was, I failed to comprehend the obdurate indifference all you guys displayed toward women."

LAREDO: We weren't indifferent to them gals! We put 'em on a pedestal!

AARON: You never got near 'em.

LAREDO: We worshipped 'em from afar. And I saved one from disaster in ever' last dang pi'ture I as in!

AARON: What good is that to someone like me who just wanted to learn to . . . to touch and be touched?

LAREDO: *Don't touch 'em!*

AARON: What?

LAREDO: Well, I mean with all the rectifyin of wrongs I was doin, all the disasters I was savin 'em from, when did I have time to go on a date?

AARON: No—oh, no. No, no, no—they scared the crap out of you. All you "kids." The Durango Kid, Ringo Kid, Cisco, Sundance, Billy *the* Kid. The Laredo and Majestic Kids. Little boys scared to death of having to meet a woman face to face and deal with her, not as a *gal* but as a woman, and protected from her by a hundred and nine scripts with the same plot . . .Whadduya know . . . I don't have to be a hero.

What Aaron wants to be is just a regular guy—a responsible but wholly contemporary and regular guy—wife, kids, job, hobby. And he wants to learn to deal with women as they want to be dealt with.

What's replaced the Old West and the old western hero more recently? Anything? Yes. Some fifties nostalgia—*Raiders of the Lost Ark, Romancing the Stone, Jewel of the Nile*—and a lot of fantastical and futuristic stuff. This young generation is the first that can't seem to generate much faith out of the past, doesn't find a great deal to recommend the present, and so is hooked more resolutely, perhaps, than earlier generations on the future.

Close Encounters, Star Wars, Starman, The Last Starfighter, E.T., Cocoon, Explorers. A lot of wishful thinking about heroics and especially a sensibility that hopes there's another better world somewhere out there and that that other, better world will get in touch with us soon and take some of us away from here to there. And, of course, there's *Splash,* where Tom Hanks escapes this world by heading underwater for the rest of his life with a mermaid. In a way, this

young man heading off with his fish to live underwater is a heading
back to the fantastical heroics of those old westerns. We know you
can't live like a fish underwater if you're really a human, but it's nice
to see humans again indulging respectfully in fantasy, in contem-
plations of better worlds, better ways, beginning to balance mega-
doses of cynical reality with other points of view. It stimulates the
senses, even the intellect, and may even engender some fresh hope
for the future of the species before we're so utterly convinced hope
is ridiculous that we stop fighting the decline altogether and let true
and utter anarchy reign, as it does in the futuristic movies featuring
the new western hero, Mad Max, a character out of the Eastwood-
Man-With-No-Name mold.

The old Clint Eastwood-Man-With-No-Name character has also
become Rambo, a character operating outside the law in a world
where the law seems to hold no sway.

Veterans' groups suggest that Rambo is paving the way for other
Vietnams. Whether that's true or not, one thing is certain: In the
Rambo movies, Rambo is revising history; he's winning the war we
lost or weren't able to win, depending on your point of view. Rambo
tries in a two-hour explosion of vengeance to give us back the dignity, confidence, heroic faith and posture we've lost over the last two
decades. I think much of the anger that so many people in the country displayed toward returning Vietnam vets had less to do with the
fact that many people thought they were fools for attending that war
than it had to do with some subconscious anger that they lost it,
disgracing the legacy of soldier John Wayne, disgracing the legacy
of the Pilgrims, the Revolution, the pioneers, and those character
apotheosized by Hollywood on celluloid, beginning with William
S. Hart and Bronco Billy Anderson and coming forward through
Tom Mix and Hoot Gibson to Marshall Dillon and Paladin.

A couple of summers ago, we had two straight westerns, *Pale
Rider* and *Silverado,* out of the old mold except that the death and
violence in them are from the Peckinpah school. We're so used to
Peckinpah violence, though, that we're unfazed by it. We have car
bombings and suicide bombings and airplane bombings and airport
bombings and hijackers throwing dead bodies out of airplanes to keep
us mindful of what *real* violence is like. In *Silverado* and *Pale Rider*
again we have the forces of good defeating the forces of evil in the
Old West. It's almost as if these moviemakers are saying: Let's go
back, let's change the future, very much like the movie *Back to the*

Future, in which a young man returns to the youth of his parents and through his own personality and will, changes the present he left, a present that was unpleasant, that was not good, that was— most of all—without heroic faith in grown-ups, parent figures.

I think back to a time just a short decade after the time that young man returns to in *Back to the Future,* to 1966. The Old West I encountered then was like this: I pulled off the road into the Ag school ranch of New Mexico State University. It was just what I expected. There was wide open space and cattle and the smell of manure and mountains and pick-up trucks and lots of people in jeans and boots and straw cowboy hats. I quickly found that people were polite but strong, folksy but wise, steeped in traditions that were visible, still in vogue, still being accepted by the next generation. The College of Agriculture was the biggest then. The main throughway between the university and downtown—a mile and a half stretch of two-lane blacktop—was farmland on both sides. Now it's all fast food joints, discount and car part stores. A very ugly street. It has no respect for itself.

Farmland in Las Cruces is being sold as fast as developers will buy it, to build on and resell to mainly eastern people (an easterner being anyone who lives east of Texas or west of New Mexico). These easterners grew up on western movies and TV series and are moving "out West" from back East. In many cases the easterners do not come gracefully. They seem to resent the desire on the part of any of the natives to preserve *anything* of what was. The easterners bring many of their acquired incivilities with them and I've noticed a change in what was once an almost unerring politeness among many people out here in New Mexico. Needless to say, more and more out West is starting to resemble back East. I think in a curious way many of the people moving out West feel that out West *should* resemble back East, that we have no right not to suffer what they've suffered. Tucson and Phoenix, for example, remind me in temperament of nothing so much as midtown Manhattan.

The most elemental image of the "real westerner," the rancher-farmer-cowboy is changing too, as he can't make a decent living doing what he's done historically, living the mythology. The romance seems to be off it for him as well as us. The College of Agriculture at NMSU has lost many students. Many kids of the farms and ranches are looking for other ways of life. Computer Science has grown incredibly, as have the Colleges of Engineering and Business

Administration. Enrollment in the arts has decreased notably too. It's a no-nonsense era in education.

While we're at it, let's talk fashion, couture, let's talk western wear. In the late seventies and early eighties, Los Angeles and New York took western wear unto themselves, bastardized it into high fashion and pretty much destroyed by confusion and puffery the authenticity of dress of the westerner. Maybe it was some sort of last gasp effort to keep the faith in the Old West, even though in their trend-setting hearts they knew it was lost. Thankfully, you won't find a Hollywood executive wearing cowboy boots to work today anymore than you'll find him soliciting ideas for western flicks. Of course, that's another way for them to say the Old West is passé: Not even the duds are viable anymore.

And let's not forget that whatever can be said about the unfortunate disaster that was *Heaven's Gate,* reputedly the biggest artistic and financial disaster in movie history, this above all else *can* be said: *It was a western.*

One of several movies I've written on contract that never got made was about the New West, about somebody who moved here and tangled with someone who'd grown up here. I set the movie in New Mexico. The head of the studio wanted it moved to New England, without pick-up trucks. Why? It made perfect sense to set the movie in New Mexico. "No dust," he said. "People don't want to see movies with dust."

I live in the New West on five acres of pasture land with my family, a dog, a couple of horses, a pick-up truck. I harbor a lot of resentment concerning the changes in this part of the country I've lived in almost half my life. I own guns. I own guns because I'm uncertain whether, even in New Mexico, there's anyone to come to my rescue or anyone else's anymore. I can't bet on the police to arrive on time or with sufficient latitude to save me; I don't expect my neighbors to stand by me as they almost inevitably did in every western movie of my childhood with the notable exception of *High Noon.* I'm afraid in the crunch I'd be Gary Cooper, standing alone. And, let me tell you, I don't like the feeling. I'm just a real person. I'm not without fear, lots of people are better shots, physically stronger; my guns are loaded with real bullets; if I ever have to use one and miss my target, I suspect I'll be in a lot of trouble.

And who trusts the government to protect us? Ronald Reagan rode out of all those cowboy and cavalry movies and saved many a day; we expected him to do the same as President, to do what he said he could do—*because* he was Ronald Reagan—that Jimmy Carter, say, *couldn't* do because he *wasn't* Ronald Reagan. But, sad to say, he didn't make many more improvements than any of his merely mortal predecessors did.

I think we've seen that *Pale Rider* and *Silverado,* those recent efforts to resuscitate, resurrect the western movie, proved unsuccessful. The movie-going public—the kids mostly, with their lack of experience or interest in the Old West—told the money moguls in Hollywood that the western is dead, and oughta stay that way.

Rest in Peace, Western Flick.

I don't so much lament the passing of the genre itself as the mythological force it represented in our lives. What does this young generation have to believe in, from which it can take strength and hope, out of which it can establish a faith that comforts and guides? The likelihood of visits from and transportation to other planets, better worlds? I don't suppose, really, it's any more ridiculous than the western mythology I believed in.

Yet, how about this: The worse this world seems to become, the more inhospitable, the less there seems to be to believe in, the more I feel disposed to escalate my efforts to find something. Not for the world per se, but for three people specifically: Debra, Rachel, and Jessica—ages nineteen, twelve, and nine. It was easy for me to be a nihilist, to be irremediably and unequivocally cynical before I had children. Though I still want to write the most dramatic, the most powerful material I can fathom, sense, feel; though I have to exorcise my own demons through my writing, I find myself wanting desperately to discover out of the difficulties I put my characters through some positive possibility to hold out for those characters in the end. *For* those characters, yes, but more for my children. And by association, other children—their peers, the generation upcoming, my children's generation and beyond that, their children's generation.

Jean-Paul Sartre said all literature should be aimed at changing the world. I think a writer can't sit down to do that; but, I think as a by-product of the passion to write characters through turmoil to the best they're capable of, large-size understanding and comprehension are possible, and therefore change is not impossible.

I want to do what I can to leave a world in which *my* children will be able and want to have children of their own. And I want them to have what I had — the luxury of bearing a mythology out of the past into the present which they can respect, a tradition of heroism to which they can aspire, from which they can take hope in the present and conjure a future worth living. If they can't, then we — as parents, real and figurative, and I as an artist, as a recorder, a crystalizer and synthesizer, an interpreter of the past and present — will have failed.

At the end of *The Majestic Kid,* Aaron Weiss, the young easterner weaned on the Old West, has outgrown his need to have The Laredo Kid define him and show him the way; he has discovered that what Laredo had to offer him as a child has to be tempered for a world in which people are unaligned and largely without hope of heaven, but no less — in fact, perhaps *more* — responsible for their conduct and moral choices than the Good Ole Days when it was pretty widely agreed God and the Forces of Good were on our side. What Laredo taught Aaron has to be, not discarded, but adapted for a new age, a new manhood. And Laredo, a simpler, less complex man than Aaron requires today, says: "Whut's gonna happen to me, pard? You don't need me no more."

Aaron says, "Time for both of us to get on to other dreams, Laredo."

But Laredo asks: "Whose? L'il fellers today, they don't even know who I was — I mean, who I am. I mean . . ." And he stands there, seeming to be just what he says: "I'm lost, pardner."

And Aaron tells him: "But thanks to you, pardner, I'm not."

Finally Laredo understands that he has served, has taught, he has helped make a better, a stronger, a worthier, a more complete man, if not the man he thought he was intended to make. And though cut loose, he knows he isn't being obliterated.

And as he prepares to take his leave, his last words, indeed the last of that play and of this prologue, are these:

"Which way," he asks, "is that sunset?"

1988
Las Cruces, New Mexico

WHEN YOU COMIN BACK, RED RYDER?

A Play in Two Acts

For Stephanie

The rust consumes the buds and fruits of the earth;
The herds are sick; children die unborn,
And labor is vain. The God of plague and pyre
Raids like detestable lightning . . .
SOPHOCLES

Where have you gone, Joe Dimaggio?
A nation turns its lonely eyes to you.
PAUL SIMON

HOME MOVIE

~

IT HAS BEEN a long time since I have been afraid of anything but madmen with guns. The rest, however threatening, can be challenged and dealt with.

In 1948 I am eight, my brother six, and — though twenty-six years later when I remind him he will not remember — we meet the Durango Kid for the first time at the Airway Theater in Louisville. I remember the Kid as the Superman of cowboys, changing his clothes in a cave rather than a cramped phone booth or closet. A mild-mannered rancher until trouble hits, the Kid then transmogrifies into a scourge in black mask and tight black togs who rides a white horse to ninety minutes of rectified wrongs. He is accompanied on the road to righteousness by the loyal, if porcine and unresplendent, Smiley Burnett. All those top boys of yore, it seems, are companioned by another guy, and inevitably that other guy is afflicted with a pox, ranging from obesity (Pancho) to age (Gabby Hayes), from the curse of grunting American Indianhood (Tonto, Little Beaver) to imbecility (Pat Brady, who talks to Jeeps). Nevertheless, I believe in the Durango Kid, as I come to believe in Cisco and Red and all the others. I'm not concerned that my heroes surround themselves with lepers and idiots, that they seem to have an abiding lack of interest in women — except as objects to save from other guys — or that their lives are as simply and cleanly plotted as my own. The Saturday matinee is an institution of my childhood, a schoolroom as surely as the one I attend at I. M. Bloom School Monday through Friday. My brother and I learn about justice and re-enact what we learn in back of our apartment. We charge down

*the hill on our bikes, I the Durango Kid, the principal player (and to this
day I cannot stand it otherwise), my brother and our cronies my assistants —
pedaling hell-bent-for-leather to the rescue of a girl whose name I cannot remember, from whom I accept a brief thank you for all of us, if I am feeling beneficent,
before leading my forces off to gun down her defilers with loaded fingers or
cap pistols.*

*Why would I suspect then, when I am eight, that when I return to Louis-
ville for the first time in twenty-five years the Airway Theater will house
a furnace company?*

It was August 1, 1971, and I was thirty-one, disillusioned of
my ideals into compatible rage and equanimity. (I imagined a sce-
nario in which *TIME* or *Newsweek* did a cover story on me entitled
"The Marriage of Genius and Rage." Nice.) My wife Stephanie and
I entered a Toddle House in Albuquerque out of nostalgia: I remembered my father telling me when I was a boy that Toddle Houses
served up terrific eggs.

We were in Albuquerque to see two one-act plays I'd written.
It was to have been three, but the director couldn't flush out an actor
who was willing at one point to put his hands to his groin and squeeze
his own genitalia. I had been trying with kamikaze concentration
to write not merely good plays, but a Good play. Neither of the two
we were to see (or the pariah third) was better than good. Sometimes I drove myself to such artistic frustration that I believed I *should*
have become a doctor. I would have today been in practice with my
father in Miami, young Dr. Medoff rather than Assistant Professor
of English Medoff, one of New Mexico's most minor writers.

We found ourselves alone in the diner with two kids in the last
of their teens — an obese waitress and a greasy twig of a boy who
had worked the night shift and lingered now to play his part in an
illusive love affair with her.

*I am nine, writing my first book. It is about a boy and a donkey and
is based on the hardbound volume sitting in front of me. I am changing
conjunctions.*

A crippled young man came into the Toddle House, sat in a
booth, read his newspaper.

Stephen and Nancy — their names — continued their tender, abu-
sive dance.

I was sure that they were a play about themselves. I told Stephanie to remember what she could.

As for the eggs . . . the stench of Drano in the stopped-up sink directly under our noses took care of that. So much for nostalgia.

When I am fifteen my beloved Dodgers beat the goddamn Yankees in the World Series at last, healing the stigmata of those earlier wounds. Around World Series time my tenth grade English teacher has his classes write a short story. Mine is about a teenager who kills someone and goes to prison. (I can only conjecture at how much the domination of the Yankees over the Dodgers in my boyhood and early teens has to do with the development of my obdurant hostility toward anything that seeks to dominate me.) My story is called "He Was Only A Kid." I receive an A + on it. The teacher tells the class he has never given an A + on anything before and he asks me to read the story to the class. I am, perhaps, never prouder in my life.

He instructs me to send the story to COLLIERS . . .which sends it back with blinding speed. Bastards! I had typed "Age 15" right there on the title page — some second-string reader could have at least written a little encouragement on the lousy rejection form. ("Dear Mr. Medoff: Whew! — what a story. I'm afraid, however, it doesn't QUITE fit our present needs.") Should have sent the damn thing to ARGOSY anyway.

Reeling from the agony of that rejection, I become a closet writer, turning out the stuff in my room at night and stashing it under my stroke books and SPORT magazines in the closet.

Usually we made the two hundred and twenty-five mile drive from Albuquerque to Las Cruces, where we lived, in three hours, sometimes a minute or two under. We had an old Porsche C then which we loved to drive fast around corners and down highways. It took longer that morning because Stephanie wrote on the "Parade" section of Sunday's Albuquerque *Journal* everything we could remember about the two kids in the Toddle House and what they had to say to each other.

I am seventeen and, in my main occupation, a jock — although one who will never fulfill his dream of quarterbacking the University of Miami Hurricanes on the floor of the Orange Bowl, a failure I will never quite forgive myself. Because I am an athlete and a member of Student Council, I figure I won't be bombed with cries of "Fairy!" if I submit a short story to the

Embryo, the literary magazine at Miami Beach High School. The faculty advisor tells me it's a fine story but that he wonders if my mother or father has not written it for me.

I dive headlong back into the closet.

Armed hungrily with the notes on the Albuquerque *Journal* "Parade" section, I sat down the next morning to write a one-act play about a greasy counterman named Stephen Castle and a fat waitress named Nancy. They worked in a run-down diner in a small town in my mind somewhere between Deming and Lordsburg, N.M. By the time I had finished the one-act play the next day, the young crippled man who read his newspaper had become a crippled man in his sixties who owned a motel and service station next door and Stephanie and I had become a textile importer and his wife. She, oddly, came out of my head carrying a Guarnerius violin.

An Interstate bypass had opened. Hints of things dying under the heels of "progress."

The play ended with Stephen Castle walking out of the diner with the importer and his wife. They were going to drive him on the new superhighway to Baton Rouge; there, he insisted, he had a great future in a restaurant where the waiters wore tuxedos. . . . He returned moments later, unable to make the break.

Or not permitted to by the playwright.

In my freshman year at the University of Miami I am taking Advanced Comp from an elderly, distant woman named Dr. Grace Garlinghouse-King. I'm bored with writing advanced compositions and with almost everything else. I ask her if I may write a short story. I can't read what she thinks of my request or of me. She gives me A's on my advanced compositions — perhaps she has suspected me all along of something like this.

The play about Stephen and Nancy was about more than whether or not a nineteen-year-old boy broke away from a life leading nowhere, but I didn't happen to know what else it wanted to deal with. Confused, I put the play away and wouldn't touch it, as it happened, for a year. When I returned to it, a number of my demons synthesized in the character of Teddy, who walked into that diner and exhumed and buried bodies of my child- and young manhood, blessing me with the purgation of glorious and bitter tears for the six days it took to draft the whole play.

I was never happier with the experience of *Red Ryder* (or *Ryder* as, I'm told, it's known in the theatrical lexicon of New York) than I was during those six days. It is the dizzying intimacy of discovering a play in my own head in the privacy of my own den that is orgasmic. The rest—the collaboration of the business of Show Biz, the audiences—about all of that there is something else, steeped in a terrible and delicious ambivalence.

At two in the morning several days after I have given her a short story called "One Blind Mouse" (in this one two guys kill six people), Dr. Grace Garlinghouse-King awakens me to say that there is nothing more she can teach me about writing. It is an extraordinary thing for her to say to someone desperately in the market for words even half as strong. She has awakened the man who teaches Creative Writing at the University of Miami, she tells me, a man of local legend named Fred Shaw, and I am to see him that afternoon. He will have read my story by then. If he feels as strongly as she about my prospects, I will do my time in her class writing for him.

January, 1972. Gloria in Excelsis: My first play, *The Wager*, was to be done at the HB Playwrights Foundation Theatre in Greenwich Village. Greenwich Village—that place of mythic proportions I dreamed of being a dissipated part of in my quaintly, safely rebellious college days. Something called an Equity Showcase. Also something called a miracle.

I had known from the beginning that Albuquerque and Denver, San Antonio, Palo Alto, and Las Cruces meant nothing until you had been in New York City. (The Apocrypha have not endured the ages because they are apocryphal.) But how in hell did a lad writing plays in Las Cruces, N.M., get someone in New York City to do anything about his work, other than, say, ignore it.

Some of our local cognoscenti assured me that what I needed was an agent. But that, on the other hand, most agents—your top boys—wouldn't touch you until you'd "done something." *But* that, on the other hand, nobody would "do anything" unless you had an agent. All of the "on the other hands" struck me as ballbreakers.

Others who knew as little as I said I had to move to New York and "go see people." Move to New York? Did they have any idea how long it would take me to work myself into a starting quarterback slot in those Central Park games that have been going on for years?

My dentist in Miami Beach, a friend since childhood, kept sticking his fingers into my mouth, and telling me to write to his cousin Kenneth in Cleveland, who was "in the theater."

I was cynical and frightened; I, who had "heard stories" and read *The Season,* scoffed at my dentist: Everybody knew somebody "in the theater." Dr. Marchand should keep his cousin to himself and stick to teeth.

I was a desperate man. Past thirty now and no more than a whisper of my *least* acceptable literary intentions. A wagon train of suicide notes rolling through my fantasies of failure as I sat at my stool each morning before I launched another attack against my demons.

I had to get rolling!

All right. I sent my dentist's cousin *The Wager.* If, as I was sure, he was merely another poseur, who would be the wiser? Four days after Cousin Kenneth should have received the manuscript in Cleveland, I received a telegram from New York. (I had an unlisted phone number, not in preparation for my eventual fame, but so that my first wife could not call me.) As Stephanie and I drove down to the Western Union office, I said theatrically to this beautiful woman I felt compelled to become immortal for, and whom I would shortly marry for Love: "This is it!"

The telegram said that Cousin Kenneth could do an immediate reading production of *The Wager.* The telegram said to call him. I did and he and I were wed in an extension of the old mail order bride routine: immaculate conception. We were pregnant.

"Tell us, Mr. Medoff, what is your advice to the young playwright?" "Have your teeth cleaned regularly."

I spent three and a half years writing stories and a "novel" for Fred Shaw. Master of prolepsis, he prescribes a ten-year apprenticeship to discipline and dedication. He flagellates and strokes me. He is, next to my father and a head counselor at the camp my brother and I attended through most of the fifties, the only "real" man I ever love and respect. Real in the sense that there were others, not real but "heroic" in the tradition of the American myth that died its grotesque death in the late sixties when our revolution failed utterly, punctuated for emphasis by the third coming of Richard Nixon. "Heroes" like the glorious Duke of Flatbush, Cousy of the behind-the-back lay-up, Ike of the "good" war, and corrals full of clean livin cowboys who straightened up more little towns and Sodomites than even the America of myth could have cast. Finally, JFK and Sandy Koufax there for a while. But about JFK there were

the nagging rumors of inconstancy; of Sandy . . . well, what can one say intel-
ligently about the paradoxical lunacy of arthritis of the elbow?

Fred Shaw helps me to learn to write, for he tells me in absolute humil-
ity, I think, that no one can teach me. Read and write, he admonishes me,
and through those three and a half years I do very little else. I am, for the
first time in my life, committed fully to something at which I might fail.

A year and a half before *The Wager* was to get its HB production, Ken Frankel did a reading production of the play at The Cubiculo. I couldn't afford to be there. He told me that the powers at
The Cubiculo said it was the best reading production they'd seen
there and they were definitely interested in the play. My friend Top
Cat saw it, said the reading production stank and that the play had
been injudiciously cut to fill a prescribed space. Tie game, end of nine.

Ken wanted to show the play to a New York Producer he used
to work for, a man with many Big Productions under his belt. I'd
never heard of him, but that was certainly no criterion of anything
except that he wasn't David Merrick, whom I had heard of.

The New York Producer liked the play but wanted to see it done
somewhere before he "optioned" it. (An option agreement is a form
of chattel enslavement of a "property" for a period of months—
usually six—set down in an elaborate denigration of the English language. Decoded, the option agreement buys the right to *consider* doing
a play.)

Incredible. Just like that and I was mere baby steps away from
being the Toast of Broadway. I began working up some snappy pat-
ter so that I could give as good as I got the first time the old Carsoni
dragged me onto "The Tonight Show."

I arranged to have the play done in Miami. Ken would direct.
I would take a leave of absence from the university. Stephanie would
move with her daughter into my house to care for my son the dog.
Her daughter and my dog were the same age. Perfect. This was it.

Ken backed out of leaving his job for certain glory at the last
minute. The hell with him! I wanted to direct the play myself anyway. It got rave notices in a town infamous for its wholesale slaughter
of and malignant indifference to theater. The play ran three months
and earned me in excess of a hundred dollars. Deducted from my
air fare, living expenses, and the salary I had given up at the university, getting the New York Producer a "look" at my play ran me
about six grand.

My mother, father, and brother were delighted though. And I got to lord it over some of my former classmates who were already trudging into the obsequies of their medical and legal practices. The New York Producer was impressed . . . but wanted just *one more* free look at the play before he optioned it. Can't be too careful, what with blah blah blah. Okay. Anything.

A mere year later, the play was done at HB through an arrangement the New York Producer set up with the Foundation, for which I will pay henceforward two percent of my earnings on that play. A careful man, that New York Producer, and one who knew the value of my dollar. But what matter? This was it!

The experience at HB, for our first "professional" outing, was infinitely rewarding to both Stephanie and me. We cared deeply for the people involved in the production. We were totally enamored of "New York Theater," *real theater* . . . despite the fact that the New York Producer disliked the production. He still "loved" the play, however, and decided to definitely option it for Off-Broadway production next fall (Jesus, Off-Broadway! This was it!) . . . *following* just ONE MORE FREE LOOK at the "property" at a place called The Manhattan Theatre Club (fleeting visions of hors d'oeuvres being served by a couple of natty old geezers in tattersall vests to a lot of chic New York theater types.) "Important tests," said the N.Y. Producer. "Blah blah blah ensemble. Best to be sure that blah blah blah." I was beginning to suffer attacks of what must have been aphasia. No, no! My educated wife and I battled our distrust of the man gallantly, rationalized brilliantly . . . for, on the very brink of *certain* glory, we saw no present alternative to him. And we were, if nothing else at that point, pragmatists to the core.

To compound the–alternative–to–him–that–I–didn't–see theory, I told the N.Y.P. that I had just finished two other plays: One, *The Kramer,* I had just been informed would be done immediately by the American Conservatory Theatre in San Francisco in their new Plays in Progress series on a grant from the Office for Advanced Drama Research, one of those wonderful but maddeningly rare organizations that gives a damn about new writers; the other play, however, called *When You Comin Back, Red Ryder?* was more or less just sitting around waiting to become the object of further prevarication.

He read it and told me it would never make it as a play. Make a helluva movie, he told me. I was tempted — the house in Bell Air, the pool, Dalmatians, Cy DeVore shirts. . . . I said no, though. I wrote it as a play, I said, and I wanted to try to get it done that way. Foolish, he told me. Come on, whudduya say, let him see if he couldn't find a buyer in television.

Television! That did it. I was too young and far too egotistical to imagine I could write anything inconsequential enough that my only option for it would be television.

Appear at this point Variation II of the dentist with the cousin "in the theater": One of my writing students at New Mexico State University had an aunt who was "in the theater" in New York. I called her. I knew well enough now not to look a gift aunt in the mouth. She was doing sets for a little theater group "uptown" called The Circle Repertory Theater and was playing a bit part in the play they currently had in rehearsal, called *The Hot L Baltimore*.

I met her. She was gracious as all hell and took me to the Circle, there introduced me to the young man in charge, Marshall Mason. He said he would be glad to read my script and that he would try to get someone down to see *The Wager*.

I told him that I'd send the script up with a friend of mine who was anxious to direct it, fella name a Frankel who went to Northwestern when Marshall was there. (Some aphorist told me back about then that there were only ten people in Show Business and if you knew three of them, you'd work forever.)

The summer I graduate college, I park cars in New Rochelle and sell hot dogs at a carnival in Ottawa. I am still under the fringe influence of Jack Kerouac and those boys. Part of me yearns to suffer in filth and squalor, to endure my disaffection in the manner of those wonderful derelicts in On the Road. *I am stymied hopelessly, however, by the Jewish Cleanliness Fetish. I am aimless, though, in the sense that I am armed with no "acceptable" direction to my life. My aimlessness, on the other hand, is slightly complicated by the fact that I want to make a decent living while I wander about "committing experience" (as I enjoyed referring to it) and continuing my quest for literary brilliance. My mother and father are trying to be adult about the whole thing but are terrified. A BA in English, they have counseled me since I gave up pre-med, is worthless. I do not tell them that I agree . . . or that I am terrified too.*

When I am in Ottawa, my mother sends me a telegram telling me that I am one of the winners in the Prize College Stories 1963 contest and that Random House will publish my story in the fall. In HARDBACK.

A heretofore studiously undemonstrative-when-happy individual, I run screaming through the Central Canadian Exhibition, a lunatical ombudsman for The Young Writer With Only A BA In English.

At the end of the summer I land in Washington, D.C., as Assistant Director of Admissions at a technical institute. I envision that I will work at the institute by day, write by night, and within a year or so be rich and famous and playing quarterback for the Kennedys on the weekends.

Ken called to say that Marshall loved *Red Ryder* and that we could do a workshop of the play at the Circle in June. If that went well, they'd open their next season with it.

I was commuting between San Francisco and Las Cruces for *The Kramer.*

The New York Producer caught me in San Francisco, told me CBS had given him the go ahead to negotiate with me for the TV rights to *Red Ryder.* They wanted to make a Movie of the Week out of it. I would write the screenplay. The N.Y.P. waited expectantly for me to be tickled to death. He was not happy that I was not. He told me what I needed was the advice of a good agent—whose advice, I could only presume, would be to accept the grand offices of the N.Y.P.—so he had interested the best he knew in me via *The Wager.* Gilbert Parker and I talked on the phone. He was Vice-President of something called Curtis-Brown Ltd., which sounded suspiciously like a conservative haberdashery, but no matter. I liked him immediately. I liked him even more when he advised me to hold onto all the rights to *Red Ryder* and do it the way I wanted.

I spend a year and a half with the technical institute in Washington. The closest I come to quarterbacking for the Kennedys is a glimpse one Sunday of the President and his wife walking across the Ellipse a couple of months before time changes in America.

As for the rich and famous . . . The institute creates the position of Supervisor of Publications for me. I put out five enormously irrelevant publications for the place and coach the basketball team to an 0–7 record in the City League. I get even with the basketball team for its misuse of my advice by leading the staff team to a 60–point victory over the uncoordinated bastards in the first—and last—Student-Staff game. All of their girlfriends and wives are there. I feel some better.

In March, the team in a sense gets even with me when a kid driving for a liquor store drives his car through the driver's side of mine with me in it. I go home to Miami Beach and into the hospital to see if anyone can figure out how to get rid of this headache I have for three months.

In September I enter graduate school at Stanford, aiming at another "worthless" degree in English. I have not dealt well with the Real World. Do not like it. I am relieved to go back to school for two years — to that sanctuary and safety.

In May, 1973, following a surprisingly unromantic operation on my aging-jock left knee, I whipped to N.Y. for a weekend to hear the first reading of *Red Ryder.* "Whipping" here and there was giving me the sanctimonious feeling that I was much hotter spit than I was. Of the eight people who read that Saturday, two — Brad Dourif and Jim Kiernan — went all the way with us. (Over a year later, Jim and I would stand backstage at the Eastside Playhouse, as the play moved toward its three hundredth performance and I got ready to do my last performance as Teddy, and we would marvel at all of it before we parted and before it ended.)

I met my agent for the first time that day. He was shaped differently than I expected. He sounded shorter on the telephone, was in fact a big guy, sharp dresser, smoker of an obscure brand of cigarettes that lent him an appealing esoteric quality. I was to learn as time went on and he negotiated large pieces of my life that he was, as we used to say, "tough as nails." The New York Producer regretted many times, I suspect, ever bringing me together with him. That first day, most notably, Gilbert told me he wasn't sure the play would work and he introduced me to the spinach, mushroom, and bacon salad, a confection I couldn't fathom having lived without for thirty-two years.

In two years at Stanford I write nothing of value. I remember myself best as someone who accomplishes a year of sincere tennis (the first year) and a year of colitis and psychotherapy (the second). (Anyone who claims to have seen everything there is to see and done everything there is to do but hasn't had colitis is full of crap — Old Confucian proverb.)

I am a gaunt neurotic on the fringe of the revolution that is exploding at Berkeley and sort of festooning at Stanford. As outraged by the war as anyone, I am uninterested in auditioning for the show as all the choice roles seem taken. Or perhaps I am merely afflicted with stage fright.

For my thesis, I write a novel called The Savior. *It has a lot to do with my mind's-eye vision of myself as a bad-faith Christ. It is accepted by the*

Writing Center faculty. However, as I am well aware that it stinks, I assume they are too. I am too busy to care. I am obsessed, as is Bellow's Henderson, with that voice in me that cries, I want, I *want. I want to be a "successful" writer; enough getting ready! I want to be immortal! I want to be able to stomach myself! I want to stop having to eat mashed potatoes every day to help the medication I am taking to stop me from shitting my brains out! My hands and knuckles are bruised and scabbed from the punches I unload on the bathroom door. I punish my hands for the tricks my mind is playing on my gastrointestinal system. Makes sense.*

I want to go to Europe in May when I finish at Stanford. My psychiatrist doesn't seem to think it's a terrific idea but I'm angry at him for helping to make me better by inviting me to experience a lot of truths that make me sick. My parents think I'm planning to freeload the rest of my life and think I ought to get a job and cut the crap (Love to!). But I'm angry at them too because (Who else but!) they're at the root of what I'm trying to get better from that's making me sick. Fred Shaw, however, at whom I am angry only because I have not written a thing of note, tells me flatly that what I should do is take a teaching position somewhere and Persevere. *I know I should take a teaching position, goddamn it, but because I know it I don't want to! It is the end of April, I protest, surely it's too late to find a teaching position for next year. He tells me to write to a friend of his who is head of the English department at New Mexico State University, the school at which he had begun his teaching career years before.*

I go to Las Cruces on my way from Palo Alto to Miami Beach. It is brutally hot and I am driving an un-air conditioned black Volkswagen that continues to vapor lock at regular intervals. I am traveling with the girl who has suffered through my colitis and my psychotherapy with me and whom I am rewarding for her loyalty by tormenting toward madness.

New Mexico State University strikes me on sight as a monument to Demeter, the goddess of agriculture, sculptured in manure. It has cows, for chrissake, right on campus. I am a Jewish boy from Miami Beach, what the hell do I want with cows! I swear a secret oath to myself after having peach cobbler with the Head and his wife: Unlike that great man of my childhood, I shall not return. No sir!

I spend the first several weeks at home looking for another job. Am offered a teaching position at the Hebrew Academy on the Beach but turn it down on the grounds that I could not possibly wear a yarmulka *to class every day. I come, though, within an exhalation of breath ("Yes.") of accepting a job with the Peace Corps as the writer/researcher on a psychiatric team. It's a six-month job, from which I can save three thousand dollars to go to Europe and find Sartre and make him explain the predicament he and I have gotten me into. Maybe the Peace Corps Newsletter will publish a few of my stories. I think constantly of having turned around one way instead of another, and how very different things might have been, would almost certainly have been, and I am enraptured and infuriated by the sense and senselessness of it all.*

In August I pack up and head back to Las Cruces. My first day there I go into a Seven/Eleven store, browse over the paperback rack and am just about to steal a book — a business I honed to a fine science in graduate school — when it comes to me out of the burning bush of my brain that I am twenty-six years old and an Instructor of English at a university, that suddenly I am an adult in some vague technical sense, and that a whole era of my life is irremediably over.

I have been here eight years now. I have not stolen a book. Nor, for that matter, have I had an attack of colitis.

The first rehearsal Gilbert and I saw of *Red Ryder* as it was being prepared for its week long workshop run was a remarkable experience. In short, we were appalled. In long, we were terrified the play was going to meet an undeservedly gruesome stillbirth. I could barely speak to Ken. Gilbert left immediately after the rehearsal without bothering even the "barely" part. The play had been in rehearsal two weeks and made its run in another week. I could not imagine anything but embarrassment. The staging seemed inept, some of the casting improbable, and to my own glaring discredit, the crucial scene in the second act between the husband and wife sucked.

I had been floating on a wave of tenuous elation for months — since *The Wager* at HB and *The Kramer* at ACT; I had *really* begun to think this was it.

That one rehearsal was a lung and a half of water and a stomach-knotting reaffirmation of my obsessive unwillingness to allow others to control my destiny. It is a problematical obsession in the theater.

I love teaching Freshman Composition. I expected at best to tolerate it. I am happy to get up every morning and go to class. I am a very good teacher and my students feed off of me. For years I will break into a sweat every time I walk into class — not from nervousness but from excitement. But I'm also lonely and not meeting girls who are not students (upholding for the moment the ethic that decrees against dating students). I live a monastic life away from the university my first two months. I have a small SONY: I lie on my couch with it on my chest. I do not like Las Cruces now any better than I did last summer. To Las Cruces, an Italian restaurant is a place that serves pizza and ravioli. People drive pick-ups with rifles racked in the back of the cabs. Some of the roads aren't even paved. My novel goes out to publishers; comes back. My year in therapy has not settled; I am erratic and hacking up my few new friends and lovers.

I keep writing though. If nothing else, I can martyr myself to myself, I figure. I begin a short story. The second day I sit down to it I realize on rereading that I have nine pages of dialogue inundating two lines of narrative. Although my mother has insisted for years that I should be writing plays, I decide to try turning the story into a play anyway (Ah, blessed Maturity. At last!) I call it The Wager.

The workshop production of *Red Ryder* opened. The audience at the first performance screamed and whistled. I was stunned: Were they crazy? I knew we'd made impressive headway, but there were things, I felt, for which Ken, the cast, and I were unpardonably guilty. But even Gilbert assured me that it "worked."

Re-enter at this point the New York Producer, who owned for the hard won, really-not-that-exciting-anymore sum of two hundred and fifty dollars the option on *The Wager*. The joys of the Theater, I've found, seem always to come *at least* a month after you've earned them, thereby systematically mitigating your enjoyment of them. In dealing with this man, I found that his hesitancy to make a decision—or "carefulness," why don't we call it to give him the benefit of the doubt—his "carefulness" alleviated the initial rush of a promise time and again. The N.Y.P. said he was wrong about *Red Ryder*. The play "worked," he said. He wanted to option it *immediately*. I resisted both leaping for joy and his throat.

He took Stephanie and me to Sardi's the next afternoon—our first visit there. We felt Show Biz as hell (no matter that we learned afterward we were in the schlock section, packed in with a bunch of rubbernecks who didn't realize they were in the schlock section either). He told us that he wanted to open *Red Ryder* in the fall and *The Wager* in the spring, convinced that *Red Ryder* would have the greater commercial appeal.

Our feelings for this man were very complicated by this time. We felt like young marrieds being hyped on—not life insurance—but snake oil or one of those other questionable elixirs. When we were with him, we couldn't help be attracted to something about him (and *still* find that to be true). When we viewed him from an objective distance, we would have preferred to cut his tongue out and serve it to the dogs outside the saloon.

Gilbert was adamant that I not option *Red Ryder* to the N.Y.P. He had had *The Wager* to deal with for over a year. It had taken him that long just to sign the piddling option agreement. We didn't need him to sit on *Red Ryder* too. We could hire a chicken.

I won't pretend I fully comprehend the perverse notion of loyalty and who knows what else that led me to overrule Gilbert and allow the N.Y.P. to option *Red Ryder*. The play was *set* to open the Circle's season; the Circle was the hottest group in town because of *The Hot L*; if *Red Ryder* did well, any number of producers would be interested in moving the production to Off-Broadway. I have the silly feeling that I didn't want to "hurt" this man who coaxed me over a crock of cheese in Sardi's to give him this play when he had done nothing with the first. Perhaps if not the cut of his jib, the cut of his hair. He had a hairstyle that screamed of competence. Oh hell, I don't know.

The option was signed after weeks of maddening, niggling "carefulness" and a cross contract hacked out in flesh and bone with the Circle. I had a nightmare fantasy in which the play moved to Off-Broadway, under the aegis not of Zeus of course but of the N.Y.P., bearing not the head of Gorgon but a likeness of the Mad Hatter, a comic strip bubble coming out of his mouth crying, "I'm late, I'm late, I'm late."

And now the fun started. Ken, the N.Y.P., and the folks at Circle felt the cast could remain essentially as it was in the workshop for the opening at the end of October — for the "real" thing: a "Welcome to the American theater, Mr. Medoff" . . . or banishment back to the desert of New Mexico, there to draw flies to my carcass. No thanks. I wouldn't have it, and there ensued debate, the seriousness of which was mitigated by the grotesquely humorous undertones (a mere pair of syllables away from undertaker) inherent to dissecting absent human beings in their external roles (actor, writer, so forth). I insisted — as I finally pointed out it said right there in my contract I could — that three of the actors, including the lead, be recast. The N.Y.P., out of fear I think, and Marshall Mason, out of long distance reports, since he was in Los Angeles directing *Hot L* during our workshop run, concluded that I was crazy to want to break up a winning combination, that what "worked" should be left alone.

I couldn't accept that line of thinking—my mind swings to "winning" teams made better, sometimes great by trades and the acquisition of new blood—and, aside from the distastefulness of having to hurt those three actors, I'm glad I couldn't.

The debate raged for months. Let's rejoin it later.

Ken came out to Las Cruces for a week. We ate a lot of Mexican food in a lot of diners, worked on the script and on the directorial concept. (In another debate that was going on, pressure was being applied to me to replace him.) We worked sternly with each other. Parted confidently.

I returned to New York in late August on my way to Los Angeles where The Mark Taper Forum was going to do *The Kramer* in its "New Theatre for Now Festival." We began the task of recasting four of the cast—the fourth being Clarisse, the wife, because the actress who played her in the workshop had taken a position elsewhere. Most important, however, was the casting of the lead, Teddy.

Of the perhaps thirty young men we read for Teddy in those four days, only two seemed right to me, and one, Kevin Conway, seemed the righter of the two once I got past the fact that the other one looked more like the playwright. There was opposition to Kevin, however. Everyone agreed that he did a magnificent reading, that he was a wonderful young actor. The reluctance was based on other things, almost exclusively physical. (It is amusing to note that months later Kevin told me at lunch one day that one of the people involved in this casting fiasco had told him that it was I who opposed him because I didn't think he was sexy enough. Very clever, these Chinese.)

The wars that went on during the next three weeks, the compromises agreed to and backed out of by various factions, the jockeying for historical position . . . culminated with me in a pay phone booth in Westwood, California, and Ken and the N.Y.P. on extensions in the N.Y.P.'s office in New York. I was screaming at them in an apoplectic rage that I was going to make perfectly clear to them for the very last time that the young man who had played Teddy in the workshop—a nice young man, an attractive and talented young man—was *wrong* for the part and would play it over my dead body; that as far as I as concerned, we should have cast Kevin Conway three weeks ago; and that if they didn't go ahead and commit to him and get the goddamn play into rehearsal on time I was coming through the transcontinental wires and I was going to tear both of their tongues right out of their goddamn throats.

Now, deep down inside, I didn't expect my threats and hysteria to have the least affect on these men. But they did. Perhaps I had driven them to exhaustion. How foolish of me to have been trying to sway them with cool verbal imprecations. Threats and hysteria. I'd remember that. They agreed to Kevin Conway.

Not the war, to be sure, but at least a notable skirmish.

The Wager, *when I finish it in early 1967, is a long one-act play in ten scenes. It runs the two nights of the annual Ides of March Festival at the Las Cruces Community Theater. Mentally, I break a bottle of champagne across my bow and launch myself to sea. I have been sailing since.*

The other person who resides in my shell, the one who strives to live a "normal" life, gets married that September, largely, I think, to do penance for real and imagined sins he has committed against the women in his life. My wife directs my second play, another one act, Machinations, *at the next Ides of March Festival. The year after that it's* Doing a Good One for the Red Man, *which I direct.*

In those three years, I get an education in the basic theater as an actor, director, writer. I hesitate to wonder at the quality of life had there been no Las Cruces Community Theater crammed into a moldering adobe building in the old Mexican quarter. (I.O.U. one new theater.)

In the summer of 1969, Doing a Good One for the Red Man *is one of the "featured" plays at the New Playwrights Festival at Trinity University in San Antonio, sponsored by Trinity and the Dallas Theatre Center. Now, by this time I am as confident inside as I appear to be outside about my prospects as a playwright, so the being-chosen is merely another step in the progression toward rich and famous. What happens after the actual presentation of* Red Man *on the final night of the Festival is something else again.*

It is part of the dues for being chosen that following the doing the playwright shall come forward and face his audience, much in the tradition, let's say, of the defendant who is guilty until proven innocent. In the case of all the plays but mine and the one by Mark Berman, the other "featured" playwright, the facing of audiences takes place before the other members of the Festival — other novitiates, the actors, a few administrative types, among them a priest, schooled in gentleness. In Berman's and my cases, however, our audience consists not only of the above-mentioned, but of several hundred of San Antonio's wealthiest theater makers (Remember the Alamo? They do.)

and several "famous" writers, with only one of whom I am even remotely familiar.

Doing a Good One for the Red Man, *as it happens, is a farce about the white man and the Injun, dealt with as indelicately as possible. The audience in San Antonio that evening starts off laughing at the play, following their cue cards smartly. But then, maybe a third of the way through it, they stop. And don't start again. As Lenny says, "It's granite out there."*

I am not pleased to have to go up on stage with those "famous" writers after the last note of the dirge has hit leadenly in the house. The Playwright-from-Texas (a man whose claim to fame, as I recall, is a paean to Texas which is performed religiously each summer somewhere in Texas for bands of heathen tourists) says, and I summarize for him here, that he thinks the content of my play is a lot of commie horseshit and the language reeks. In short, I hit him right where he lives.

In the midst of the ensuing bloodletting, Paul Baker, Director of the Dallas Theatre Center and Head of the Trinity Drama Department, feels compelled to come on stage to remind the audience that the discussion of the play is supposed to be constructive and that the viewpoint should be theatrical rather than political—for, in fact, the "discussion" has turned to disabusing me of my notion that the white man had done quite a number on the ole Injun—at least these white Texas folks didn't have nothin to do with it. We're the good white folks, boy. It was you Jewish people put up all them pawnshops on them reservations.

As the dust settles during the next few hours, I experience as powerful a high from the upset I've created as I would had those people leaped in sympathy to their feet at the end of the performance.

I aggravate the hell out of people in real life, why not in the theater? Rhetorical question, of course.

On October 30, 1973, *When You Comin Back, Red Ryder?* opened at the Circle. Stephanie and Gilbert watched. Ken and I did not. Afterward, a party on stage followed by a pilgrimage to Sardi's to await Mel Gussow's review in *The New York Times.* ("He looked pissed when he left.") Ken and I wear the same calm exterior underlaid with fatalistic hatred.

The early edition arrived, brought to the table in the tradition of the Theater by the maitre d'. The papers were practically torn open. So long, calm exterior.

There was no review. How embarrassing! And here again, the loathsome business of having your destiny in the hands of others.

The memory leaves the taste of something fetid in my mind even today. (This build to nothing is not unlike what happened little more than a month later when, on opening night at the Eastside Playhouse, Kevin reached the climactic moment of the first act, pulled the trigger, and the gun did not fire.)

(We labor to drive our lives to climactic trigger-pullings, and misfires, if you ask me, are a real pain in the ass.)

We disbanded. The *Daily News* was on strike, so there would be nothing from Douglas Watt until the strike was settled — and just as well, it turned out.

The next day, Ken and his roommate, Jacqueline, Stephanie and I drove into Connecticut, trying to keep busy while we waited for Mel Gussow, for the AP, and the suburban papers which, we were assured by someone we assumed didn't know what he was talking about, would be forthcoming beginning at eventide.

It was a day for reflection. Whatever doubts Ken ever had about the play, whatever doubts I had about his direction, we had worked creatively together through hours and days of script and production problems, had worked to a bond of brotherhood, not a relationship without rancor but one strong in empathy and blood. We were proud of what we had wrought together, proud of our cast; and we would know tomorrow, whatever the outcome of the notices, that we had given it a good shot. We reflected on the efficacy of workshop productions — the wonder of the opportunity to "work out" a play relatively inexpensively before a bunch of blessed loonies gambled fifty-six thousand dollars on an Off-Broadway production, more on a Broadway job. It was a day for feeling familial, protectively smug, and insular.

We ate at a wonderful restaurant on a little stream in Westport and drove back into the city. It was midnight when I got out of the silent car to buy *The Times* at Seventy-second and Broadway. I turned coolly to the index in the second section and read "Circle Theatre does it again." I didn't bother to turn to the review before I raised my fist in the air in a gesture of defiance and trotted across the intersection, a primal scream upon my lips.

The year I come up for tenure at the university, the revolution is dead, the war continues, and two of my colleagues decide to have my tenure denied and, in effect, bring about my firing. The grounds they choose are simple:

I am a communist and teach a straight Marxist line in my classes, failing any students who don't adhere to the line. Marvelous!

The essence of the problem, really, is perhaps not so much more than this: I come into "their" department, a rakish, slightly mad young man who, because he has difficulty respecting anyone, does not respect them for a perfectly plausible reason — they simply don't strike him as other than ordinary — and therefore he is in no way deferential toward them. How many people, after all, are worthy of deference?

Several of my colleagues — hardly deferential types themselves — come to my defense with my department head — a confirmed liberal straining at the administrative bit — and after months of details, accusations, and a goodly portion of dated McCarthy clichés, the vote of the Tenure and Promotion Committee is 7–2, my favor. As for my two accusers, one retires quietly, an old warhorse limping off to the seaside in California; the other continues in withered silence, both of them, I expect, eating their livers by the hunk over the developments in my life the past several years. Bon appétit, *boys.*

The Gussow review in hand, others passed to us verbally, Ken, Jacque, Stephanie, and I made several hundred dollars' worth of hyperbolic phone calls from the Medoffs' hotel room, our lives changing even as we spoke.

Though I have the year before San Antonio expanded The Wager *into a full-length play and it has been done twice by The Stanford Repertory Theatre,* The Trial of Myles Fife, *based on my tenure experience, is the first play I intend from the beginning to be full length. The university's Drama Division offers to do the play and it is directed by my wife.*

By the time the play is mounted, much of the conspicuous self-indulgence is gone and the play, about a fifty-year-old English professor on trial in his mind for real and imagined crimes, is roundly well received by students, faculty, and administration. (Actually I am a bit put off that the play generates no trouble.) The playwright plays the amalgam character based on his accusers. Very therapeutic.

For a number of reasons, Myles Fife *is the period on a four-year sentence of my life. My wife and I are divorced a month after the play runs — that act in itself a parenthetical exclamation point on the end line of a lot of infantile frailty and stupidity.*

Little more than a year later, Stephanie and I walk into the Toddle House in Albuquerque. When You Comin Back, Red Ryder? *is born and, in many ways, me with it.*

• • •

In my fantasies about artistic success, the fruition was always pure. I had paid my dues, I deserved to enjoy it.

Forget it.

There were two moments of unadulterated purity in the *Red Ryder* experience once it left my typewriter. One was ramming my fist into the air at Seventy-second and Broadway with my first *New York Times* review tucked securely into a paper I had not read but whose content I knew beyond doubt. The second was sitting with my wife on one side of me and my agent on the other in the Blaine Thompson Advertising Agency offices above Sardi's, waiting for Clive Barnes's review of the Eastside Playhouse opening on December 5, 1973. Up and across town at the theater, Ken and the cast, those nine who had invested their hopes and gizzards in this thing too, were waiting for me to get the Barnes review and call them with the word. They didn't want to go to Sardi's again and be embarrassed. If the review was for us, they would descend like locusts. In the meantime they would continue to eat chile on the set and to keep their buttocks squeezed tightly together.

I was very drunk on Jack Daniels, which I had been drinking steadily since early afternoon when there was nothing more to do but wait. (It seemed someone's aberrant, bad joke to have to go through two Critics' Nights with the same show.) Stephanie and Gilbert were sober. Our press people and general manager whipped frantically from phone to phone, getting set to begin tallying the reviews. A TV review, which we would watch and which I would not remember even as I watched it, and the Barnes review would be first. Everything was in readiness. Stephanie and I sat locked hand in hand in identical silence. Gilbert hovered mother-hennishly over us, prepared to deal with the outcome. In retrospect, the idiotic vulnerability of it all is more detestable than words can tell.

Locked in my memory for all time is the picture of Leonard Mulhern, our general manager, standing in the doorway of that conference room at Blaine Thompson, holding a Xerox copy of Clive Barnes's typewritten review, saying with a simplicity that belied itself so wonderfully that I would pinch his cheek still were he here today: "Clive Barnes gave you a . . . *rave.*"

I had wondered for years of course what I would do at that moment. Something *memorable*. Something they'd talk about for a long time downstairs at Sardi's: "Jesus, you think *that* was something? You shoulda seen what Medoff did when *Ryder* opened!"

The time had come to do it—whatever it was to be. So I did it: (Biographers ready?) Nothing.

I sat there.

I had nothing to say. Neither did my wife. Finally we held each other. We had come a great distance to this silence.

The moment—that pure moment—ended with word that Douglas Watt, who had come to review the play a second time, despised it a second time. The vitriol in both of his reviews prompted the side of me that won't permit the other side of me to agonize for more than twenty-four hours over any rejection to conjecture that perhaps I had once beaten him *very* badly at ping-pong in an earlier incarnation. He had been unable to forgive me. Perhaps a girl we were both crazy about witnessed the whole thing. Perhaps I had been a poor winner, rubbing his defeat in his face: "Eleven-nothing, Doug, shutout!" In the interest of fairness—a form of play really not all that interesting when one is on the defensive—let me hasten to note that I don't believe in reincarnation, so it is conceivable that the man simply despised the play and thought he was performing a public service by blasting it twice. On the other hand, perhaps the play threatened him as it does many men. On the other hand, after twenty-four hours, who, hardly, gave a damn.

I read the Barnes review to Jim Kiernan over the phone and he repeated it to the people at the theater. Within fifteen minutes we were all over each other in Sardi's. We were crazy. Delirious. We were going to be a "hit." Incredibly, wonderfully pretentious word to bandy about. We knew it! Forget about the septuagenarian Mr. Watts of the *Post,* whom we were told had napped through the play (hope the gunshot didn't startle him) and whose indecipherable piece of gibberish appeared that afternoon, and the several others, who would at least create their misgivings intelligibly, if incorrectly.

Red honey, welcome home.

The success of Red Ryder *has radically changed my life. Six of my plays have been published by Dramatists Play Service in the last year. The Kramer is being readied for publication by the University of Minnesota Press in its* Playwrights for Tomorrow *series. I am offered films to write; radio and television programs to be on; symposiums to sit on; pieces of paper to write my name on; people wait expectantly to hear what I have to say, as if because I can write I can also speak. Heady stuff.*

I have won the Outer Critics Circle John Gassner Award as Best Playwright for the 1973–74 season, an OBIE for Distinguished Playwrighting, and a Guggenheim Fellowship in Playwrighting. The university last spring presented me its Westhafer Award, the highest honor it has to bestow on one of its faculty and promoted me three years ahead of schedule to Associate Professor (quite a jog down the road from the Army-McCarthy hearings).

I stepped into the lead of the Chicago production of Red Ryder *on two days' notice last May, received embarrassingly good notices, and played the part for six weeks; then, while Kevin did the part in Massachusetts, I played New York for a month, reveling in playing with some of those people who have been so important to me for over a year, who played such roles in the birth of my child.*

But. Thinking about the adulterated purity of it all . . .: Friends have had difficulty dealing with what's happened to me, making me feel as if I am almost expected to apologize for making of myself what I said I would and for having achieved something they have not. A number of my colleagues at the university have displayed little fits of—as one euphemistically calls it—"healthy envy."

The gravest difficulties, though, have to do with the living of these disparate lives: one as husband and father, the other as writer—or "successful" writer, I must say, because when I was having my successes "locally," I was home most of the time or not very far away for very long. I have been gone almost half of this last year. Sometimes my wife goes with me, sometimes our daughter goes with us. None of the configurations is nearly ideal. We love Las Cruces, want to "live" here, but don't. We live several places and, if I am to continue to write for the theater, we must continue to live several places. The problem is insoluble in any simple way because the bottom line is so simple itself: If I don't write, I don't function in any other role. Two disparate lives, then, really dependent on the continuation of the one.

Simple.

When *Red Ryder* opened, General Manager Mulhern bet me it would still be running at the Eastside Playhouse on July 4, 1975. It won't be. It closed two weeks ago today after more than three hundred performances—a lot of performances by anyone's standards. But still a great disappointment. The why of it is, finally, a puzzle. When I was playing Teddy in New York, the cast assured me the reason box office had tailed off months earlier was due to bad management and that for five months management had not seemed to "care." (It must be said, though, that our management *did* keep the show running after another might have closed it.) Others blamed the director and stage manager for letting the show "slip." Others credited Nixon and the economic plight of the country. Others the location of the theater (a very nice, safe neighborhood in the East Seventies but one which is not easily accessible by subway as are most of the other Off-Broadway houses, most of which are in "bad" neighborhoods). Still others felt the play had simply played its audience to depletion quite naturally. And I'm sure the puzzle has even more possible pieces. In what shape and order it should all be put together, I don't know and, in a way, don't care. It's done and I've learned what I can learn. One play, well received or not, long run or short, does not a career make.

The Eastside Playhouse will not be empty for long. *The Wager* goes into rehearsal there in four days (under different management than *Red Ryder*) and opens in four weeks. I leave wife, child, "home" once more tomorrow morning to fly to New York.

A year ago, before *Red Ryder* opened for real, I went looking for Stephen and Nancy, expecting somehow to find them in their places at the Toddle House in Albuquerque, just as Stephen and Angel are in their places each time the play is performed. I wanted to tell them what we had done to each other's lives. The Toddle House, though, was shut down and a couple of tumbleweeds stood sentinel in the overgrown front yard. I felt lonely and I started to cry and took off in a hurry.

I think of them now. I think of Fred Shaw, who died on January 2, 1971, before it all happened. I think of my son the dog, whom we gave to a family in the country who are always home. And I think of something Stephanie said to me once: You live your life, she said, as if you think you're going to die tomorrow and there's not a moment to waste.

I have no intentions of dying tomorrow. In fact, if I can keep the madmen at bay, I'm giving serious thought to living forever.

CHARACTERS

~

STEPHEN

ANGEL

LYLE

CLARK

CLARISSE

RICHARD

TEDDY

CHERYL

Time of Action: The end of the '60s

Place: A diner in southern New Mexico

WHEN YOU COMIN BACK, RED RYDER? was first presented by the Circle Repertory Theatre Company (by arrangement with Elliot Martin) in New York City, in November 1973. It was directed by Kenneth Frankel; the setting was by Bill Stabile; costumes by Penny Davis; and the lighting by Cheryl Thacker.

The Circle Repertory Theatre Company production of *WHEN YOU COMIN BACK, RED RYDER?* was subsequently presented by Elliot Martin at the Eastside Playhouse, in New York City, where it opened officially on December 6, 1973.

ACT I

~

A diner on the desert in southern New Mexico at the end of the sixties. Stools, booths, a chair or two, a jukebox. On one of the windows: FOSTER'S DINERS—ARIZ., N. MEX., TEX. The lettering has begun to chip away and although the diner is clean, its day has gone. A boy nineteen, STEPHEN/RED sits at the far end of the counter reading a newspaper, his back against the partition, his feet propped on the second stool, the newspaper tabled by his thighs and knees. He is plain looking in an obtrusive way—small, his hair slicked straight back off his forehead. He wears a short sleeve sportshirt open one too many buttons at the top, the sleeves rolled several times toward his shoulders—in the last of the sixties, an unconscious parody in his dress of the mid-fifties. He smokes Raleigh cigarettes and has a tattoo, "Born dead," on his forearm.

The clock behind the counter reads 6:05. Stephen glances irritably at it, then out of the window, then at his own watch.

The jukebox plays. Morning lights come through the windows.

Stephen hears someone coming. He knows the steps. He moves to the jukebox, reaches behind it, and rejects the record that's playing. He takes his stool again and raises the newspaper so that it covers his face. ANGEL enters. She is perhaps several years older than Stephen. She is obese, her white uniform stretched across the rolls of her body. She has a pinched face, short hair framed by a bow made of limp, thick pastel yarn, somewhat prominent front teeth. She wears a wedding band on the ring finger of her right hand. She carries a very small purse.

ANGEL: Good mornin, Stephen.

> *(Stephen does not look at her, but glances at the clock and makes a strained sucking sound through his teeth—a habit he has throughout—and flips the newspaper back up to his face. Unperturbed, Angel proceeds behind the counter)*

I'm sorry I'm late. My mom and me, our daily fight was a little off schedule today.

(Stephen loudly shuffles the paper, sucks his teeth)

I said I'm sorry, Stephen. God. I'm only six minutes late.

STEPHEN: Only six minutes, huh? I got six minutes to just hang around this joint when my shift's up, right? This is really the kinda dump I'm gonna hang around in my spare time, ain't it?

ANGEL: Stephen, that's a paper cup you got your coffee in.

(Stephen is entrenched behind his newspaper)

STEPHEN: Clark can afford it, believe me.

ANGEL: That's not the point, Stephen.

STEPHEN: Oh no? You're gonna tell me the point though, right? Hold it—lemme get a pencil.

ANGEL: The point is that if you're drinkin your coffee here, you're s'posed to use a glass cup, and if it's to go, you're s'posed to get charged fifteen instead of ten and ya get one of those five cent paper cups to take it with you with. That's the point, Stephen.

STEPHEN: Yeah, well I'm takin it with me, so where's the problem?

(Stephen has taken the last cigarette from a pack, slipped the coupon into his shirt pocket and crumpled the pack. He basketball shoots it across the service area)

ANGEL: Stephen.

(She retrieves the pack and begins her morning routine: filling salt and pepper shakers, the sugar dispensers, setting out place mats, and cleaning up the mess Stephen evidently leaves for her each morning. Stephen reaches over and underneath the counter and pulls up a half empty carton of Raleighs and slides out a fresh pack. He returns the carton and slaps the new pack down on the counter)

What're ya gonna get with your cigarette coupons, Stephen?

(Stephen reads his paper, smokes, sips his coffee)

Stephen?

(Stephen lowers the newspaper)

STEPHEN: How many times I gotta tell ya to don't call me Stephen.

ANGEL: I don't like callin ya Red. It's stupid — callin somebody with brown hair Red.

STEPHEN: It's my name, ain't it? I don't like Stephen. I like Red. When I was a kid I had red hair.

ANGEL: But ya don't now. Now ya got brown hair.

STEPHEN: *(Exasperated)* But *then* I did, and then's when counts.

ANGEL: Who says *then's* when counts?

STEPHEN: The person that's doin the *countin!* Namely yours truly! I don't call you . . . Caroline or . . . *Madge,* do I?

ANGEL: Because those aren't my name. My name's Angel, so —

STEPHEN: Yeah, well ya don't look like no angel to me.

ANGEL: I can't help that, Stephen. At least I was named my name at birth. Nobody asked me if I'd mind bein named Angel, but at least —

STEPHEN: You could change it, couldn't ya?

ANGEL: What for? To what?

STEPHEN: *(Thinking a moment, setting her up)* To Mabel.

ANGEL: How come Mabel?

STEPHEN: Yeah . . . Mabel.

ANGEL: How come? You like Mabel?

STEPHEN: I *hate* Mabel. *(Stephen stares at her, sucks his teeth)*

ANGEL: Look, Stephen, if you're in such a big hurry to get outta here, how come you're just sittin around cleaning your teeth?

STEPHEN: Hey look, I'll be gone in a minute. I mean if it's too much to ask if I have a cigarette and a cup of coffee in peace, for chrissake, just say so. A person's s'posed to unwind for two minutes a day, in case you ain't read the latest medical report. If it's too much to ask to just lemme sit here in *peace* for two minutes, then say so. I wouldn't wanna take up a stool somebody was waitin for or anything. *(Looking around him)* Christ, will ya look at the waitin line to get on this stool.

ANGEL: *(A beat)* Did you notice what's playin at the films?

STEPHEN: Buncha crap, whudduya think?

ANGEL: *(A beat)* I saw ya circle somethin in the gift book the other mornin.

STEPHEN: What *gift* book?

ANGEL: The Raleigh *coup*on gift book.

STEPHEN: Hey — com'ere.

(Angel advances close to him. He snatches the pencil from behind her ear and draws a circle on the newspaper)

There. Now I just drew a circle on the newspaper. That mean I'm gonna get me that car?

ANGEL: Come on, Stephen, tell me. What're ya gonna get?

STEPHEN: Christ, whudduyou care what I'm gonna get?

ANGEL: God, Stephen, I'm not the FBI or somebody. What are you so upset about? Just tell me what you're gonna get.

STEPHEN: *(Mumbling irascibly)* Back pack.

ANGEL: What?

STEPHEN: Whudduya, got home fries in your ears?

ANGEL: Just that I didn't hear what you said is all.

STEPHEN: Back. Pack.

ANGEL: Who's gettin a back pack?

STEPHEN: The guy down the enda the counter. Chingado the Chicano. He's hitchin to Guatemala.

ANGEL: You're gettin a back pack? How come?

STEPHEN: Whuddo people usually get a back pack for?

ANGEL: Ya gonna go campin.

STEPHEN: No I ain't gonna go *camp*in. I'm gonna go gettin the hell outta this lousy little town is where I'm gonna go *camp*in.

ANGEL: When? I mean . . . when?

STEPHEN: When? Just as soon as I get somethin taken care of.

ANGEL: When will that be?

STEPHEN: When will that be? When I get it taken care of—when d'ya think. Lemme have a donut.

ANGEL: *(Getting him a donut)* Where ya gonna go?

STEPHEN: Where am I gonna go? I'm gonna go hitchin that way *(Pointing left)* or I'm gonna go hitchin that way *(Pointing right)* and when I get to some place that don't still smella Turdville here I'm gonna get me a decent job and I'm gonna make me some bread. *(He picks up the donut and bites into it)*

ANGEL: Rye or whole wheat, Stephen?

STEPHEN: This is some donut. I think they glued the crumbs together with Elmer's.

ANGEL: Rye or whole wheat, Stephen?

STEPHEN: *(With his mouth full)* Believe me, that ain't funny.

ANGEL: Don't talk with your mouth full.

STEPHEN: Christ, my coffee's cold. How d'ya like that?

(He looks at her. She pours him a fresh cup of coffee in a mug. She sets it down by him. He looks at it a minute, then pours the coffee from the mug into his paper cup)

I told ya, I'm leavin in less'n two minutes.

ANGEL: That's right, I forgot.

STEPHEN: Yeah, yeah.

ANGEL: You better let your hair grow and get some different clothes if you're gonna hitch somewhere, Stephen. You're outta style. Nobody's gonna pick up a boy dressed like you with his hair like yours. And with a tattoo on his arm that says "Born Dead." People wear tattoos now that say "Love" and "Peace," Stephen, not "Born Dead."

STEPHEN: Love and peace my Aunt Fanny's butt! And who says I want *them* to pick me, for chrissake? You think I'm dyin for a case a the clap, or what? I got a coupla hundred truck drivers come through here in the middle of the night that said they'd all gimme a ride anytime anywhere they was goin. You think I'm gonna lower myself to ride with those other morons—you're outta your mind.

ANGEL: Two hundred truck drivers? Uh-uh, I'm sorry, I have to call you on that one, Stephen. If it wasn't for Lyle's station and his motel, Lyle'd be our *only* customer.

STEPHEN: You know, right? Cause you're here all night while I'm home sacked out on my rear, so you know how many truck drivers still stop in here, now ain't that right?

ANGEL: In the three weeks since the bypass opened, Stephen, you know exactly how many customers you had in the nights? You wanna know exactly how many, Stephen?

STEPHEN: No Christ, I don't wanna know how many. I wanna have two minutes of peace to read my damn newspaper—if that's not askin too much! Is that askin too much? If it is, just say the word and I'll get the hell outta here and go to the goddamn cemetery or somewhere.

(LYLE STRIKER enters. He is a man in his early sixties. He wears a brace on one leg and uses an aluminum crutch—the type with wrist and forearm supports. In his relationship to Angel there is a distant sexual overtone)

LYLE: Mornin. Mornin.

ANGEL: Good mornin, Lyle.

LYLE: Mornin, Red.

(Stephen stares blankly at Lyle. Lyle to Angel, winking)

Nice to see Red so chipper this mornin. Whatya got stuck in your craw this mornin, Redbird?

(Stephen sucks his teeth, Lyle takes what is evidently his stool. Angel sets a mug of coffee before him and begins to get his breakfast together. She glances meaningfully at Stephen)

ANGEL: How's business, Lyle?

LYLE: All eight rooms full up last night. That's seventeen outta twenty days since the bypass open up. Most of 'em already checked out. Looks like my new sign gonna pay off right handsomely.

STEPHEN: Damn thing's high enough. Ya oughta get yourself some collision insurance in case a coupla airplanes crash into it.

LYLE: Well now, least I don't have billboards strung up and down the highway like dirty underdrawers proclaimin my whereabouts.

STEPHEN: Don't tell me about it.

LYLE: "Steak and eggs our specialty." *(Laughing)* Steak and eggs're ever'body's specialty.

STEPHEN: Yeah, well don't tell me about it. Tell Clark.

LYLE: You tell Clark. I got enough trouble with my gas and oil people.

STEPHEN: Yeah, you got it real tough, Lyle. You lead a real tough life, I'm tellin ya.

LYLE: Well now, if you think it's so easy a life that I lead, Red, I hereby will it to ya for one day and let's see how you like takin care of an eight unit motel and a gas and service station entire by yourself.

STEPHEN: Keep sittin there babblin, Lyle, and you're gonna miss about fifty dollars wortha business from that Cadillac sittin out there for the last half hour waitin for you to quit makin speeches and get off your keister and give 'em some gas.

(Lyle turns his stool, sees that Stephen is telling the truth)

LYLE: Didn't hear 'em pull up.

(Lyle takes a swig of his coffee and hustles up)

STEPHEN: Came right outta room four and drove twenty feet to the premium pump. Been searchin the countryside for somebody to fill that yacht up with about fifty dollars wortha gas.

LYLE: Back shortly. Keep my seat warm. *(Winks at Angel and exits)*

STEPHEN: *(Yelling after him)* Yeah, gonna build a fire under it. *(A beat, to Angel)* Christ, will ya look at that yacht. Looks like the goddamn Queen Mary. Ya wanna bet he clears fifty bucks fillin that tank up?

ANGEL: They don't look like they oughta be stayin at Lyle's, do they?

STEPHEN: What'sa matter, the old Cripple's ain't good enough for ya now that you had your debutante comin out?

ANGEL: Very funny, Stephen.

STEPHEN: Ain't fancy enough for their Cadillac to sit in fronta number four of—that what you're sayin?

(Stephen goes to the window to look toward Lyle's)

ANGEL: Lyle's isn't exactly the Ramada Inn, ya know.

STEPHEN: Yeah? I'll take it. The Crip don't want it, let him give it to me. He ever mentions to ya he's thinkin about givin it away, you toss my name in the hat as a willin benefice'rary. Christ, I could really do somethin with the layout he's got.

ANGEL: Why don't ya ask Lyle to hire ya on? I bet he would. What do you wanna bet if ya asked him to hire ya on to help out at the station and the motel, he'd hire ya.

STEPHEN: *(Returning to his stool)* I told ya, I'm hitchin outta here. And after this deal I'm through workin for the other guy. The next job I get, it's gonna be workin for Number One here.

ANGEL: Oh yeah? What're ya gonna do?

STEPHEN: Don't you worry about me. Okay?

ANGEL: Yeah, but what're ya gonna *do*, Stephen?

STEPHEN: What am I gonna do? I'm gonna come drivin up to your door one day in a Chevrolet Corvette Sting Ray convertible the color of money is what I'm gonna do. Then I'm gonna rev up that four-ten engine through my glass-pack mufflers and I'm gonna lay about four hundred feet a rubber down your street. *(A beat. He looks from a distance to her)* Anybody pull a stunt like that on your street one day, you be sure and tell 'em who it was. You tell 'em it was Red Ryder, everybody, drivin a Chevrolet

Corvette Sting Ray convertible the color of money and livin in his own apartment. You be sure and tell 'em.

ANGEL: I'll tell them, Stephen.

STEPHEN: You tell 'em it was Red Ryder and from now on he's workin for Number One.

ANGEL: What kinda work's Number One gonna be *doin* though, Stephen? —

STEPHEN: And I'll tell ya one thing. When I'm ready to go, I'm gonna write a letter to the goddamn *com*pany tellin 'em what the hell kinda deal I think Clark's givin us out here.

ANGEL: Hey, do me a favor. Never mind the company. Just get Mr. Clark in here when I'm around and tell him off. I'd pay money to see that.

STEPHEN: I ain't gonna waste my time talkin to Clark. He's just runnin a lousy franchise. When I quit, I'm writin a *registered* letter to the *com*pany. I'm writin a registered letter to ole man Foster hisself.

ANGEL: I'd pay twenty bucks to see ya read off Mr. Clark.

STEPHEN: You ain't got twenty bucks.

ANGEL: *(Sticking out her hand)* You wouldn't care to bet on that, would ya?

STEPHEN: How much money you got? *(Angel sticks her tongue into her cheek and takes a crack at a haughty look)* You probably got three, four thousand stored up. Ya never do a damn thing but come to work, watch television with that ole Cripple out there, and go home to get ready to do the same goddamn thing all over again.

(He snaps the newspaper up. His remark is true enough to hurt her just visibly. A beat)

ANGEL: How long you been workin here, Stephen?

STEPHEN: I don't keep tracka time.

ANGEL: You know how long I been workin here?

(Stephen reads his paper)

Fourteen months. Ya know how many times I asked Mr. Clark for a raise?

(Stephen sucks his teeth, reads his paper)

STEPHEN: Your problem is ya shouldn't ask *him* nothin.

ANGEL: He's the *boss*, Stephen—

STEPHEN: What ya should do is write a re*gi*stered letter direct to the company.

ANGEL: What should I tell them?

STEPHEN: Christ, tell 'em you're out here in goddamn New Mexico gettin the royal shaft from Clark and that either they make him cough up that raise or they can do you know what with their lousy job.

ANGEL: I think you're right, Stephen.

STEPHEN: I *know* I'm right.

ANGEL: You should have a raise too. If they think workin the graveyard shift is easy, let 'em try it sometime. Who'd Mr. Clark get if you quit?

STEPHEN: Who? No one, that's who. Ole Clark'd have to work it hisself. *(Laughs)* That'd do my heart good, to see old Clark in here at three A.M. hashin potatoes. I think maybe I'll threaten to quit unless he gives me a raise and see what he says to that.

ANGEL: I'll bet he'll give ya one pretty darn quick, that's what I bet. You should do it, Stephen.

STEPHEN: I just might do it today.

(TOMMY CLARK enters in a big hurry, carrying two plastic bags full of red chile pods)

ANGEL: Good mornin, Mr. Clark.

CLARK: Here's the chile for the enchilada lunch special. Get right on 'em. *(Clark zips into the kitchen area)*

ANGEL: *(To Stephen)* Do it, Stephen.

(Clark dumps the chile, opens the cash register, glances at the drawer, whips it shut, and turns on Stephen)

CLARK: That's a five cent cup ya got your coffee in, Red.

STEPHEN: I was just leavin.

CLARK: Nickels don't grow on trees, boy—leastwise not on one a the ones in the Clark yard.

STEPHEN: Yeah, well—

CLARK: *(To Angel)* Back in about an hour to check the books.

(Stephen has returned to his stool and propped his feet up on the next stool)

Double cut that chile with water. Couldn't get the milder ones. *(To Stephen)* Yore momma let ya stick your feet on her furniture at home, Red?

(Stephen snaps his feet from the stool)

(To Angel) Let's get the Sunday Special sign up. Chop, chop. Be lunch before ya know it. *(Clark glances at Stephen and exits in a hurry)* Back shortly.

(Silence. Angel cannot look immediately at Stephen. Stephen, in pain, slaps his feet back up on the adjacent stool. Angel takes a toothpick from the dispenser and chews on it. After a moment she glances at the clock)

ANGEL: Boy, Mr. Clark was sure in a good mood this mornin, wasn't he? *(A beat)* Isn't your guardian gonna pick ya up this mornin?

STEPHEN: My . . . *what*—?

ANGEL: I don't know. What do you call him? Your stepfather. That's right, you call him your stepfather.

STEPHEN: I call him Ray. I don't call him my stepfather. I call him Ray. Who calls anybody "your *step*father"?

ANGEL: *(Putting up the Sunday Special Enchilada sign)* Well, isn't *Ray* gonna pick ya up?

STEPHEN: Lemme have one a them toothpicks.

ANGEL: *(Getting the toothpick)* Who's pickin ya up?

STEPHEN: *No*body's pickin me up. Somebody gotta pick me up before you're happy?

ANGEL: He just always picks ya up on a Sunday.

STEPHEN: Two Sundays!

ANGEL: Seems like more'n two.

STEPHEN: Two.

ANGEL: *(A beat)* He's not pickin ya up?

STEPHEN: *No,* he ain't pickin me *up.*

ANGEL: *(A beat)* Your mom pickin ya up?

STEPHEN: *No*body's pickin me up. My mom don't got a car in the first place.

ANGEL: She's got Ray's car.

STEPHEN: Ray's on vacation.

ANGEL: Where'd they go?

STEPHEN: Ray. Ray. Not they. Ray. Ray went on vacation last Wednesday.

ANGEL: By *him*self?

STEPHEN: *(Mimicking her)* Yeah, by *his*self.

ANGEL: What do you call that?

STEPHEN: I don't call it nothin. Ya gotta attach a label to it, call it what they call it.

ANGEL: Well, what do they call it?

STEPHEN: They call it a legal separation. I call it a royal screwing of my ole lady. He left her with maybe five bucks to her name and the lousy house that was hers to start with. That's some profit for eighteen months hard labor.

ANGEL: *(A beat, trying to lighten the load)* Well, ya could always look at it that people aren't s'posed to get paid for hard labor.

STEPHEN: You think that's funny? I'll tell ya a secret: that ain't funny.

ANGEL: *(A beat)* Sometimes I think my mom and me oughta get a legal separation.

STEPHEN: Yeah, then you and the Crip could set up Home Sweet Home inside his color television.

ANGEL: Oh Stephen.

STEPHEN: Christ, look what's comin. Put on your ballerina formal, we're gonna have a concert.

*(Angel moves down toward Stephen's stool to get a look out. **CLARISSE** (pronounced clar-EESE) and **RICHARD ETHREDGE** enter. They are an attractive, informally well-dressed couple in their late thirties, early forties. Richard takes a deep whiff of the air in the diner as he steps through the door. Clarisse carries a violin case. Angel and Stephen's attention is drawn from the Ethredges to the violin case)*

RICHARD: *(To Angel)* Hi.

(Stephen flips up his newspaper before he has to find out whether the man will say hello to him too)

ANGEL: Good mornin.

(Clarisse moves toward the far booth)

RICHARD: Ah-ah—got to sit at the counter.

CLARISSE: Richard, I'd rather—

(Richard shakes his head, smiles, and points expansively to the counter. They sit in the middle of the line of stools. Clarisse places the violin on the counter with mechanical care)

RICHARD: What did I tell you. Just smell that.

ANGEL: Have you eaten here before or somethin?

RICHARD: Oh no. I grew up in New York. We had a lot of diners there. Spent a lot of my misspent youth hanging around diners.

(By the look of him, it seems unlikely that his youth was misspent for long if at all. There is about both of them the bearing of youthful success simply adjusted to. There does not seem to be anything intentionally pretentious about them)

ANGEL: What'll it be? Steak and eggs is our specialty.

RICHARD: *(To Clarisse)* Hon . . . ?

CLARISSE: Just coffee and a danish.

RICHARD: My wife would like a cup of black coffee, please, and a sweet roll toasted and buttered.

ANGEL: Uh-oh. *(Indicating the small collection of sweet rolls and donuts)* These are from yesterday still. They're pretty stale. Sweet roll man doesn't come on Sunday. How bout steak and eggs? That's our specialty anyway.

(Richard looks to Clarisse)

CLARISSE: Do you have half a grapefruit?

ANGEL: Sure!

CLARISSE: *(To Richard more than to Angel)* I'll have that, and an egg and a piece of toast.

RICHARD: All right, I think we're on our way. The grapefruit, one egg scrambled dry, a piece of toast on the light side, and coffee, black.

ANGEL: How bout you? Like to try the steak and eggs?

RICHARD: No, I don't believe so. Let me have two eggs scrambled dry, a couple of pieces of toast — closer to toasted than my wife's — a glass of orange juice, and black coffee.

ANGEL: Comin up. *(She turns to her work)*

RICHARD: Is there someplace I can pick up a Sunday paper?

ANGEL: Pass the paper, Stephen. *(Stephen ignores her)*

RICHARD: Oh no, I don't want to take his paper.

ANGEL: *Steph*en.

RICHARD: Isn't there a machine or —

ANGEL: *(Moving toward Stephen)* This is the customer paper. He works here.

(As a joke and afterthought, taking the paper from Stephen) He can't read anyway. He just looks at the pictures.

(The Ethredges smile politely. Lyle enters)

LYLE: All set for ya. Come to eight seventy-five.

(Lyle feeds Richard a dollar bill and a quarter change)

RICHARD: Ah—fine. Thanks very much.

LYLE: No trouble. Key's in the ignition. *(To Angel)* All right, kiddo, bring on my breakfast.

(Stephen goes behind the counter for some more coffee. His attitude intends to suggest to the Ethredges that he can go behind the counter and they can't)

STEPHEN: Christ, I gotta get outta here.

ANGEL: You oughta go home and get some sleep, Stephen.

STEPHEN: I ain't talkin about sleep. I'm talkin about gettin *outta* here.

LYLE: Made up your mind where ya wanna go, Red?

STEPHEN: How bout anywhere's more'n ten miles away from this hog trough.

ANGEL: How bout as far away as next door?

STEPHEN: Aw, shut up!

LYLE: Hey now, Redbird, that's no way to talk to a lady.

STEPHEN: *(Elaborately looking around)* Lady? I don't see no lady. *(Lighting on Clarisse)* Pardon me, ma'am, I did not see ya sittin there.

LYLE: What is it that you're insinuatin in my direction, Angel?

ANGEL: Stephen'll kill me.

LYLE: Stephen will not kill ya. Speak up.

ANGEL: I was just tellin Stephen that if he was sick of workin here that why didn't he ask you if ya could hire him on to help ya out with the station and the motel.

LYLE: Uh-huh. That's very int'restin, indeed.

ANGEL: Could ya do that, Lyle?

LYLE: Oh yes—uh-huh, could do that.

ANGEL: Ya could?

(Angel looks to Stephen, who picks and sucks his teeth, ignores them)

LYLE: I don't suppose that the Redhead has informed ya that not once but three times I have offered him in the last two months to come to work for me in the very capacity to which you allude.

STEPHEN: I'm gettin' *outta* here. How many times I gotta tell you guys that before it sinks into your thick skulls.

LYLE: Where are ya *goin* though, son?

STEPHEN: If it's any of your lousy business, a girl that I went to high school with's ole lady that moved to Baton Rouge said when they were in for a visit at Christmas that if I was ever leavin here and wanted to go to work for her that I should come on over to Baton Rouge and they'd put me to work in a *decent* job.

ANGEL: What girl's mom?

STEPHEN: Kay Williams'!

ANGEL: *(A beat)* She owns a restaurant, Stephen.

(Lyle laughs caustically)

STEPHEN: Nooooo . . .

ANGEL: What'd be the difference? I mean, what'd—

STEPHEN: *(Laughing sarcastically)* The difference'd be that this is a lousy hog trough and that's a *res*taurant—that's what'd be the difference. Ya wear a tuxedo there, for chrissake! The waitresses wear long skirts and ruffle blouses, not nurses' uniforms. And ya carry *food* out on a *tray*, ya don't sling hash across a grimy formica airstrip.

LYLE: Well why don't ya go on and *go*? What's holding ya back?

STEPHEN: If it's any of your lousy business, Lyle, I got somethin I gotta take care of first.

LYLE: Uh-huh, and what's that?—

STEPHEN: And I'll tell ya, when I got that somethin taken care of, you ain't gonna have to build no fire under my butt to get me outta here.

LYLE: What is it that ya have to take care of?

STEPHEN: No offense, Lyle, but that's none of your lousy business.

LYLE: If it's buyin your mamma that automobile . . . *(A beat)* Prez Potter and me go back a lotta way, son. He mentioned you was in to his lot the other afternoon.

(Stephen storms out of the diner. Lyle smiles with a certain pride of accomplishment and glances fleetingly at Angel)

ANGEL: I hope ya don't get indigestion from Stephen.

RICHARD: Oh no. Don't worry about it.

ANGEL: If ya wanna file a complaint or anything, I have forms Mr. Clark —

RICHARD: No, no, don't be silly.

ANGEL: Stephen don't mean nothin by all the noise he makes. He just needs to make a lotta noise.

LYLE: I just wish he'd put up or shut up. That's all I ask of him. A person oughta put up or shut up.

ANGEL: I wish that if he was gonna go, that he'd just get it over with and *go.*

(Stephen returns with a fresh newspaper)

STEPHEN: Hey, Lyle, coupla weirdos just pushed a VW van into the station. Look like just your type.

LYLE: If you was there, why didn't ya help 'em? You know how to pump gas.

STEPHEN: Like I said, they ain't my type. *(Lyle starts to get up)* Aw, sit there and eat your slop. They're comin in here. Yessiree-bob, they sure ain't *my* type. They might be yours but they sure ain't mine.

*(Stephen snort-laughs, flips up his paper. **TEDDY** and **CHERYL** enter. Teddy is 30–35, wears an army fatigue jacket and has long hair. Cheryl is no more than twenty. She wears a long dress and a light shawl. She is pretty in a straight-haired, un-washed, no-make-up way. She is bra-less, a fact which generates helpless interest in Stephen, an interest which he tries all too obviously to hide. Lyle, too, is drawn to her breasts, though less obviously and less frequently than Stephen. Teddy stops inside the door and looks across the diner)*

ANGEL: Good mornin.

(Teddy is silent a long moment. He turns to smile at Cheryl)

TEDDY: *(Affecting a stereotyped southwestern accent)* Mornin, neighbors.

*(Teddy holds another moment, then starts down the counter, past Lyle
and the Ethredges toward the far booth. As he passes Clarisse he suddenly stops and turns to her)*

Pardon me, ma'am, but . . .

*(Clarisse looks up at him. She obviously does not know him. Teddy holds
fleetingly on her and then averts his gaze . . .)*

'Scuse me.

*(. . . as if he's trying to suggest that he doesn't recognize her when in
fact he really wants to suggest that he does. Clarisse and Richard exchange
bewildered glances, and a strange dormant seed is planted in Richard's
mind)*

Well now . . . who runs that yere fillin station next door?

LYLE: Right here. Lyle Striker, owner proprietor, and janitor.

TEDDY: Well, sir, need a rebuilt generator for a VW van.

LYLE: Nothin open today. Sunday.

TEDDY: Sunday, is it?

LYLE: Ever'body sleepin it off or out prayin forgiveness for it.

TEDDY: Tell ya what I had in mind. Thought maybe in a town such
   as yours a man with a service station, and a good natured crippled man to boot, would be in a position to call up a parts store
   on a Sunday mornin and get a part anyhow.

LYLE: *(A beat)* S'pose I could.

TEDDY: We surely would appreciate it.

LYLE: Let's have a look at your van first and make sure —

TEDDY: *(Accentless)* Don't have to look at the van.

LYLE: Wouldn't want ya to spend —

TEDDY: *(Accentless)* Generator's gone, sir. If you'll be kind enough
   to get us a rebuilt, I'll install it myself.

LYLE: Well, that sounds like a tough offer to beat.

(He meets Teddy's eyes and then has to avert his gaze)

I'll just go on over to the station and see who I can rouse up.

TEDDY: Mighty accommodatin of ya.

LYLE: *(Rising)* Back in a jiffy, Angel. Don't auction off my eggs now.

(Lyle winks at Angel, then turns and exits with a glance at Cheryl's bosom and a small follow-up smile at her face)

ANGEL: *(As Lyle exits)* What do I hear for Mr. Lyle Striker's eggs?

(Teddy and Cheryl sit at the far booth. Cheryl is noticeably nervous and has been since they entered)

TEDDY: How are y'all this mornin?

ANGEL: Just fine. How're you folks?

TEDDY: Just fine. How you?

ANGEL: Fine.

TEDDY: That's fine. *(Slapping dust from his pants)* Y'all seem to have the dust market pretty well cornered out here. *(Looking to Stephen who is staring at him)* How you, kid?

STEPHEN: I'm okay, *dad.*

TEDDY: Gladda hear it. *(To himself)* Boy's got a sense of humor, gonna think about puttin him on TV. *(To the Ethredges)* And how bout you nice lookin folks? How you this mornin?

RICHARD: Excellent, thanks.

TEDDY: Excellent! *(To Cheryl)* Ever'body here's fine or okay or excellent. Whudduya thinka that?

CHERYL: *(Quickly, quietly)* Stop it.

TEDDY: The call has gone out for me to "stop it." All y'all in favor, kindly signify by raisin your hands.

CHERYL: *(To Angel)* Do you have some coffee?

TEDDY: *(To himself)* Looks like it's gonna be a close vote.

ANGEL: *(To Cheryl)* To go or to drink here?

CHERYL: Jesus — to drink here. Where are we gonna go?

ANGEL: Two?

CHERYL: *(To Teddy who stares at Stephen who stares right back)* Will you cut it out! Do you want coffee?

TEDDY: *(Turning away from Stephen)* Yeah.

CHERYL: Two.

ANGEL: Where you folks from?

TEDDY: Istanbul. *(A beat, then sings the rest)* Used to be Constantinople —

STEPHEN: You got California plates.

TEDDY: *(Squinting at Stephen, gaming)* Just who are you, mister?

(Stephen sucks his teeth)

ANGEL: Where ya headed?

TEDDY: *Mex*ico.

ANGEL: Oh, that's nice down there.

TEDDY: Get around a lot, do ya?

STEPHEN: Shee! She never been outta the state a New Mexico. She don't know.

ANGEL: I know more'n you think, Stephen. I seen books and I meet a lotta nice people've been there.

STEPHEN: Sure ya do.

ANGEL: *(Holding on Stephen a moment, then turning to Teddy and Cheryl)* You folks wanna order somethin to eat?

TEDDY: Don't mind if we do.

ANGEL: Steak and eggs is our specialty.

TEDDY: Steak and eggs it is then. And home fries ya sliced up with your own little fingers?

ANGEL: Stephen's fingers.

TEDDY: *(A beat, staring at Stephen)* Well, hell, I'll take a chance.

ANGEL: Ma'am?

CHERYL: Yeah — fine.

TEDDY: Now, over easy on them eggs, darlin, med-jum on that beef.

ANGEL: How bout you, ma'am?

CHERYL: Any way—it doesn't matter.

TEDDY: You surprise her, darlin.

(Angel retreats to her grill)

Where you nice looking folks from San Diego in that Cadillac car headin?

RICHARD: Do you know us? You know, I got the feeling when you came in—

TEDDY: *(Winking, whispering)* Saw the San Diego State Faculty sticker on the bumper.

RICHARD: Oh—that's my wife's.

TEDDY: Uh-huh. Thought for a second there she was my cousin Faye.

(Teddy and Clarisse stare at each other a moment)

Headin back to San Diego, are ya?

RICHARD: New Orleans.

TEDDY: New Orleans. *(Nodding at the violin case)* Packin a submachine gun?

RICHARD: Only a violin, I'm afraid.

TEDDY: Prefer a submachine gun, would ya?

RICHARD: *(Laughing)* I didn't mean I was literally afraid—

TEDDY: Yes, ma'am, I don't mind sayin that you tend to remind me a whole helluva lot of my cousin Fern.

(Again, Teddy's and Clarisse's eyes hold a moment)

That must be a mighty fine fiddle to get took to breakfast with ya.

RICHARD: It's a Guarnerius. *(Smiling)* Sometimes I think my wife has an added appendage.

TEDDY: Lady playin the hoe-down circuit, is she?

CLARISSE: No, I'm —

(Richard stops her from answering by touching her shoulder)

RICHARD: She's going to be with the New Orleans Philharmonic this summer.

TEDDY: Uncle Clyde Bob and Aunt Cissy must be mighty proud of you, Cousin Freda. *(To Richard)* And you just goin along to answer the tough questions for her? Just livin off the little woman's residuals, as it were.

RICHARD: Not quite.

TEDDY: Not quite. Doctor, lawyer, or Indian chief?

(Richard smiles indulgently)

Don't mean to be nosy.

RICHARD: No?

TEDDY: Just curious. Just makin a little roadside diner conversation. Pass the time. Hope ya don't mind.

RICHARD: As of yet I don't.

TEDDY: But at some future date you might. . . . Gonna jot that down here.

RICHARD: That accent you're affecting seems a form of condecension aimed at all of us.

TEDDY: Surely not. No law against havin fun, is there? Leastways, not yet.

(Teddy smiles broadly at Richard who smiles coolly back and goes on with his breakfast)

RICHARD: No. Not yet.

TEDDY: May I ask, what *do* you do?

RICHARD: I am in the *im*port business.

TEDDY: *Im*port. Well well. And just what do you im*port*?

RICHARD: *Tex*tiles.

TEDDY: *Tex*tiles. Had you figured for an osteopath. *(To himself)* Never have been able to figure out what folks got against osteopaths. *(To Cheryl)* Doctor here imports *tex*tiles. *(Cheryl nods uncomfortably. To himself)* Got me on a called third strike on that one, all right. Thought it was a fast ball comin at my head and then she suddenly dives down across the plate and I'm left alookin. Live and learn. *(Turns to Stephen)* And how bout my little buddy in the corner there? My, my, but I like your hairstyle. I'll bet that look'll be back before ya know it. Girls'll be climbin all over ya. Rolled up sleeves, the works. What do you do, buddy?

(Stephen stares at Teddy)

ANGEL: *(When Stephen does not answer)* He works the graveyard shift here.

TEDDY: The graveyard shift. That must be a mighty important position. Eh, buddy?

STEPHEN: Stinks.

TEDDY: *(Putting a hand to his ear)* Didn't quite catch that.

ANGEL: *(When Stephen doesn't repeat himself)* He said it stinks — workin the graveyard shift.

TEDDY: You his agent, honey? What's the boy's long suit?

ANGEL: What do you mean?

TEDDY: Well, I mean what's the boy *do* that's so im—pressive that an agent of your reputation took him on as a client?

ANGEL: I don't know. What's your long suit, Stephen?

(Stephen stares at her with fire in his eyes)

TEDDY: Lad doesn't talk much, does he?

ANGEL: You should hear him when no one's around.

TEDDY: When no one's around or just when someone like me's not around? *(A beat. To himself)* Like to listen in one a these days on a conversation between my little buddy there and my cousin with the fiddle.

CLARISSE: I wasn't aware I was under any obligation to carry on a conversation.

(Lyle enters)

LYLE: Well I don't mind confessin that our parts store fella wasn't tickled pink, but he'll have it up here inside fifteen minutes.

TEDDY: Obliged. Yessir, deeply o-bliged.

LYLE: Service is the name of the game.

TEDDY: I can believe it.

LYLE: Product lists at thirty-seven fifty, but he was in such an almighty hurry to get himself out on the lake before all the fish is gone, that I jewed him down to thirty-five.

TEDDY: Doggone if that ain't a bargain.

LYLE: Well I always say two and a half dollar is two and a half dollar.

TEDDY: I'll tell ya the truth, neighbor: I hope ya don't say it too often, you'd like to bore folks right outta their minds.

LYLE: *(Laughing)* Wouldn't be a bit surprised.

TEDDY: *(Laughing)* No sir, I wouldn't either. *(He stops laughing)* I surely wouldn't.

(Lyle stops laughing. Then Teddy lets out one more burst. Lyle laughs. Teddy stops. Lyle stops, returns uncertainly to his stool. Angel has served the Ethredges during the exchange between Teddy and Lyle. She goes after Lyle's breakfast)

RICHARD: It looks very good.

ANGEL: What? Oh—thank you.

RICHARD: Puts me right back in high school.

LYLE: How much ya short for the car, Redbird? *(Stephen ignores him)* Prez tells me ya got forty-five, but ya need another thirty.

STEPHEN: Prez is sure got hisself a big yap for a little ole wart of a guy, don't he?

LYLE: You wanna get outta here so bad, Red, you wanna go to Baton Rouge and wear a tuxedo, I'll lend ya the thirty dollar and you get your momma that automobile and get yourself outta here.

STEPHEN: *(Snorting)* Yeah, sure. At what kinda interest?

LYLE: No interest, son. Just a man to man loan. You just send me back the money when ya can.

STEPHEN: I like payin my own way. I don't like borrowin from nobody.

LYLE: Just pay me back when ya can. Ya forget for a year or so, what the heck. Next time ya remember, ya got the money, send it on back to me.

STEPHEN: I'll hang around a while longer, if ya don't mind, and loan it to myself.

LYLE: Up to you.

STEPHEN: That's just the way I see it too.

LYLE: Welp, I'll head on back to the station and wait for that generator.

(He gobbles a last bite and gets up to leave)

TEDDY: Much obliged. Say—how'd it come, neighbor, your infirmity there? Infantile paralysis as a child?

LYLE: Stroke.

TEDDY: Ah.

LYLE: Had a mild stroke back in forty-five.

TEDDY: Forty-five!—quite a year.

LYLE: Just after breakfast it was.

(Lyle heads for the door)

TEDDY: *(A beat)* Helluva way to start the day.

(A beat, Teddy stares at him, smiling)

LYLE: I better get movin here. *(He nods, smiles, exits)*

TEDDY: Nice old cripple, ain't he? *(To Stephen)* So you wanna get outta here, do ya, little buddy? Why don't ya come on down to Mexico with us.

STEPHEN: No thanks.

TEDDY: *(Referring to Stephen's pointed, lace-up, rather high-heeled shoes)* Ya got the shoes for it.

(Stephen sucks his teeth. Teddy, quietly, but making no effort to close out the others)

The ole man seems pretty anxious for you to leave town. Ya notice that, boy? I did. I noticed that. Whudduyou make a that?

(Stephen heads for the coffee)

Hey!—*(Stephen is brought up short, the others startled)*—you got a pass to go behind that counter?

(Stephen refills his paper cup. Teddy moves to Stephen's stool and sits on it)

The ole man called you Red, didn't he? Now that's curious. Why would somebody call somebody else Red if that somebody else had brown hair? That short for red neck, or what?

ANGEL: He had red hair when he was a child back in Pittsburgh . . . *(A beat)* . . . Pennsylvania.

TEDDY: Ah—the one in Pennsylvania, I see. But you call him Stephen.

ANGEL: I don't like to call him Red. I think it's silly to call someone with brown hair Red.

STEPHEN: Shut up, will ya!

TEDDY: Hey now, boy, don't talk thataway. I purely agree with our corpulent friend here, the agent. That is pretty silly, isn't it?

ANGEL: Not if he likes it though, I guess. I just call him Stephen.

TEDDY: Uh-huh.

ANGEL: His last name's Ryder.

STEPHEN: I told you to shut up!

TEDDY: And I told you . . .

(Exploding a laugh as the name catches up with him)

Red Ryder! Goddamn!

ANGEL: It's all right. We know each other.

(Stephen sits in a chair at one of the booths)

TEDDY: *(To Richard)* You remember Red Ryder, Doc?

RICHARD: Oh yes.

TEDDY: Boy, I do too. There was one straight shooter. Didn't dress like a fag and sing like Roy and Hoppy. And that Little Beaver—I tell you, there was a little redskin could handle a bow and arrow. What in the hell happened to those people, doc?

RICHARD: *(Off-hand)* Gone.

TEDDY: Gone, sir, or displaced? *(A beat)* I'll tell ya one thing for sure, Red—those boys had guts. You got guts, Red? How would you rate your own self on a gut scale?

(Stephen sucks his teeth. Suddenly Teddy crashes his hand down on the counter. Everyone starts. Teddy moves toward Stephen gunslinger fashion)

There ain't room enough in this yere town for you and me, Red Ryder. *(A beat)* So I'm leavin. *(Teddy laughs robustly at himself)* Just as soon as I get my hoss a new generator. *(A beat)* You're a real chickenshit, ain't ya, boy?

STEPHEN: Takes one to know one.

(Teddy laughs happily, he spots Stephen's tattoo)

TEDDY: What in the hell is that?

STEPHEN: *What—*

TEDDY: You got a tattoo on your arm that says "Born Dead."

STEPHEN: Noooo.

TEDDY: Yeah. Look. Boy, you're a walkin metaphor, ain't ya? You know what a metaphor is? *(Nothing from Stephen)* Huh?

STEPHEN: *(A beat)* Yeah.

TEDDY: Hogshit. What's a metaphor, boy?

STEPHEN: Well if you don't know, I'm sure as hell not gonna tell ya. *(Teddy laughs happily again)*

RICHARD: Do you mind? We're trying to finish our breakfast. *(A beat. Teddy stares at Richard)*

TEDDY: Just talkin to my friend here. We'll try to keep our voices down. Sorry.

(Richard turns uneasily back to his breakfast)

(To Stephen) When'd you get that tattoo?

STEPHEN: *(A beat)* You scare me.

(Teddy moves slowly to Stephen, stares into his face)

TEDDY: *(With quiet, deadly menace)* You bet your ass I scare you. Now, when'd you get that goddamn tattoo? *(A beat)*

STEPHEN: Coupla years ago.

TEDDY: Where?

STEPHEN: Carnival.

TEDDY: Why?

STEPHEN: Felt like it.

TEDDY: No. Why? What'd it mean? Why'd you pick that one?

STEPHEN: Didn't like the others.

TEDDY: Who you with?

(Teddy sits in the booth adjacent to Stephen's chair)

STEPHEN: No one.

TEDDY: Who ya with?

STEPHEN: No one.

(Teddy jerks Stephen's chair to him, jamming Stephen up against him)

TEDDY: Goddamn it, who were you with? *(A beat)*

STEPHEN: Davidson.

TEDDY: Big guy.

STEPHEN: Whudduya mean, *big* guy?

TEDDY: I mean Davidson was a big *guy*. Basketball, football player.

STEPHEN: He wasn't so big.

TEDDY: Had a girl with him. Good lookin.

STEPHEN: She was all right.

TEDDY: Yeah, I'll bet she was all right. You and Davidson and her. Her and Davidson and dot dot dot . . . *you.* Yeah. And what'd Davidson get tattooed on his arm?

STEPHEN: Nothin.

TEDDY: Bullshit. The girl's name.

STEPHEN: So big deal.

TEDDY: And then she said, What're you gonna get, Red Ryder? "R.R. loves L.B."?

ANGEL: Who's L.B.?

TEDDY: Little Beaver, darlin. And you said, no! — because you were plenty pissed; you said, I'm gettin . . . I'm gettin *that* one: "Born Dead." You should've said, I'm puttin your name on my arm too. You should've said, Goddamn it, I'm as good as Davidson any day, you just gimme the chance to show ya. And maybe . . . maybe if you'd said that to enough pretty little girls, and gotten enough of their names tattooed onto your body, you'd have started to believe you *were* as good as Davidson. *(A beat)* Even though you weren't. *(A beat)* Never could be. Sheeit! You disappoint me, Red Ryder. *(Silence. Teddy stares into Stephen's face)*

CLARISSE: Richard, I'm finished.

RICHARD: *(Rising)* Yes. *(To Angel)* What do I owe you?

(Angel, in pain at Stephen's humiliation, focuses slowly on Richard's bill)

TEDDY: *(Still holding on Stephen)* Hey, don't let me rush y'all out.

RICHARD: We're finished.

TEDDY: *(Backing off of Stephen, rising)* Aw, come on, have another cup of coffee. On me.

RICHARD: Some bicarbonate perhaps.

TEDDY: Come on, darlin, set Madame Professor and the doctor up with some more of your wonderful coffee.

(As a form of resistance, Angel keeps her head to figuring Richard's check)

Pour, darlin.

(She picks up the coffee. Richard puts his hands over their cups)

Hey . . . lemme take a look at that there Guarnerius violin before ya go.

CLARISSE: No, I'm sorry.

TEDDY: I ain't gonna hurt it. I just always wanted to have a in–person gander at one a them.

RICHARD: *(A beat)* Then you'll behave yourself and . . . ?

TEDDY: Word of honor.

(Richard stares at Teddy a moment, then averts his eyes and nods assent. Clarisse is not happy with Richard's decision. She challenges him with her eyes. Somewhat irascibly Richard nods at her. She lays the violin case down and opens it, but does not remove the violin. Teddy stares not at the violin but at her)

That musta cost a pretty penny.

RICHARD: I'm not through paying for it yet.

TEDDY: How much a mechanism like that cost, if ya don't mind my askin?

RICHARD: *(A beat)* Eleven thousand dollars.

TEDDY: *(Smiling all too broadly and without the accent)* You're kidding.

(Richard shakes his head)

CLARISSE: *(As angrily as she can be, given her fear of Teddy)* Why should he be kidding?

TEDDY: Playin the fiddle must be mighty important to you, cousin.

CLARISSE: Yes. It is.

TEDDY: Why don't you play us somethin on that there eleven thousand dollar fiddle.

(Richard and Clarisse look at each other. Richard shakes his head simply)

(Teddy, coldly) Why not?

CLARISSE: *(To Richard)* Can we please get out of here?

RICHARD: Yes. *(To Teddy)* We're in a big hurry. Maybe you'll catch her in concert one of these days.

TEDDY: Then again, maybe I'll catch her in something else this day.

RICHARD: I'm afraid I don't follow you.

TEDDY: I'd be afraid too, sir, indeed I would. *(To Clarisse, quickly)* Now why don't you make me a present of that there violin, cousin, and we'll call everything even. *(Richard laughs)* All right, you're right, that ain't fair. Make it the violin and a small monthly allowance—but that's all I could accept.

RICHARD: *(To Angel)* Miss—please!

TEDDY: I want that violin, cousin, and I swear to God you'd be wiser than you can imagine to give it to me.

(Richard moves to Clarisse, snaps the violin case shut and hands it to her)

RICHARD: You have a great deal of imagination, my friend.

TEDDY: An incredible faculty it is, sir.

CHERYL: Teddy.

(Cheryl's eyes are to the window. Teddy looks there)

TEDDY: Generator! Landsakes, man's in a hurry. Looks like the Pony Express man, Red, passin the mail and hightailin it off. *(To Richard and Clarisse)* Well, it appears you ain't gonna make me a present of that there Guarnerius violin, so if ya gotta go, they say, ya gotta go. You ever hear that one, Red?

(Richard turns to Angel. Clarisse moves to the door. Teddy stares at Clarisse who becomes uncomfortably conscious of his stare. Compulsively she snaps her eyes to his, but of course he does not look away . . . so she must)

ANGEL: That'll be two dollars and sixty cents with tax.

(Richard hands her three dollars)

RICHARD: Thank you, it was very good.

(He turns and opens the door for Clarisse)

ANGEL: Thank you.

(Richard nods bluntly toward her, passes his eyes across Teddy's, and exits behind Clarisse, who exits purposefully and head down, acknowledging no one. Angel calling after them)

Come see us again.

(Angel lifts a hand tentatively to wave, then drops it)

TEDDY: How's our steaks comin, darlin?

ANGEL: *(Turning quickly to the grill)* Almost done.

TEDDY: Good. Good. He give ya a nice tip?

ANGEL: Forty cents.

TEDDY: Hot dawggy. *(Fixed out the window)* What brought you out here from Pittsburgh, Pennsylvania, Red Ryder?

ANGEL: *(When Stephen does not answer)* His mother had emphysema.

(Teddy is noticeably distracted during the above and following lines, watching the Ethredges walk to their car. Cheryl is uneasily watching him watch them)

TEDDY: And the desert air cured her, did it?

(Angel glances at Stephen who stares straight ahead and smokes)

ANGEL: Uh-uh, she's still got it. *(Then as if she must fill space)* You should hear her cough sometime.

TEDDY: I'm sure that'd be a real treat. Say, darlin, what's the trade like in here of a Sunday mornin? Those steaks and eggs come flyin off the griddle?

ANGEL: Uh-uh. Sunday's our worst.

TEDDY: Come on.

ANGEL: Sometimes I read the whole Sunday paper Sunday mornin.

TEDDY: Don't say.

ANGEL: Things pick up at lunchtime for the enchilada special.

TEDDY: That's nice, ain't it? Not much fun for you and the Ryder when there's no business.

ANGEL: Oh, we talk till Stephen goes home.

TEDDY: *Just* talk?

(He turns suddenly from the window and moves from it)

Huh? Ya *just* talk? Tell the truth.

ANGEL: Sometimes we don't *even* talk.

TEDDY: Uh-huh.

ANGEL: Sometimes Stephen just goes home.

TEDDY: Does, does he?

ANGEL: Uh-huh.

(Angel brings their food to the table, glancing intuitively toward the window)

TEDDY: My my, that looks *good.* *(To Cheryl)* Dig in, honey. Just look at that grease. This where ya get your bear grease for your hair, Red?

ANGEL: Is it too greasy?

TEDDY: *(Ignoring her question, taking her hand)* Com'ere darlin. Now tell the honest to God truth. He ever give ya a little feel when the two of ya here all alone?

(Angel glances to Stephen and Teddy reaches up and honks one of her breasts) Mee-meep!

(Angel gets stuck between anger and amusement, then hustles back behind the counter. Teddy looks to Stephen who averts his eyes and storms back to his stool. Lyle and Richard enter)

LYLE: Got your generator but now these folks has lost their keys.

(Lyle and Richard begin to look around. Angel joins in. Teddy eats, Cheryl tries to)

I'll swear I left those keys in the ignition.

TEDDY: What do they look like?

RICHARD: Just a little flat piece with a ring and chain.

TEDDY: Little piece o *tex*tile?

RICHARD: Gold.

TEDDY: My my.

LYLE: Ya know, I thing I mighta left 'em on top of the premium pump.

(Lyle starts for the door. Richard stops him with a gesture)

RICHARD: I'll just go check on that. *(He exits)*

LYLE: *(To Teddy, when the door has closed)* Son . . . *(Teddy doesn't look up)* I thought I'd do ya a bit of a favor . . . so I went ahead and dismounted your air coolin shroud so's I could take off your old generator.

TEDDY: Uh-huh.

LYLE: Now, son, I like to think I'm a man that understands our young folks and I'm a man that minds his own business . . .

TEDDY: That's a fine approach to life, sir, a fine approach.

LYLE: . . . but you could surely find yourself in a passle of trouble if one of those Mexican border guards was to get the idea to search around and find what you got taped into that shroud.

(Teddy stares at Lyle a moment and then ducks his head back to his food. A beat)

And I'd surely hate to see ya compound your problems by takin that man's keys.

(Teddy glances up and holds on Lyle, forcing Lyle to avert his eyes, diverting the truth along with them)

I ain't makin any accusations, ya understand. I'm a man that minds my own business —

TEDDY: Seems to me you said that. *(To Cheryl)* Didn't he say that a while back?

CHERYL: *(Tensely trying to be cool)* Yes.

TEDDY: Goddamn if I didn't think as much. Ole man, you're repeatin yo'self. *(To himself)* 'Fraid for a second there I was goin crazy.

LYLE: Just gimme the keys if ya got 'em, son. I'll say I had 'em in my pocket the whole time and didn't know it. Then I'll go out there and put that new generator on and you can be on your way.

TEDDY: Damn, old crippled guy, if you haven't gone and compli- cated things. Didn't I tell you first thing that I'd put that gener- ator in.

LYLE: I just thought I'd do ya a bit of a favor.

TEDDY: Goddamn if you didn't say that before too.

LYLE: Ya got nothin to worry about. Like I said—

TEDDY: *(Rising suddenly)* Say it again, ole man, and I'll cut your tongue right out of your throat. *(A beat. He glances to the window)* Now here comes Gentleman Jim and Our Lady of the Violin. How you gonna feel if they found those keys?

LYLE: I'll apologize. I surely will.

TEDDY: All right then—let's just see what develops here.

(The Ethredges enter)

Found 'em, did ya?

RICHARD: No we didn't.

LYLE: *(Looking at Teddy who looks at him. A beat)* The boy's got 'em.

(Teddy rushes Stephen, grabs him off his stool, turns him upside down and begins to shake him. Stephen struggles, but Teddy is much the stronger)

TEDDY: All right, Red Ryder, cough up them keys. What's the Lone Ranger and Tonto gonna say when—

STEPHEN: You got 'em, you goddamn stupid son of a bitch!

(Teddy dumps Stephen, stares at him, evidently deeply hurt)

TEDDY: That's a vicious thing to say, boy. You're gonna make it rough for white and Indian couples all over the country with that kinda behavior.

RICHARD: You have my keys?

TEDDY: *(Moving to sit at the counter)* Well . . . now this is just specu- latin, ya understand, but let's speculate here a second—

RICHARD: *(Clipped)* Do you have my keys?—

TEDDY: Just a minute—I'm speculatin, goddamn it. Let's say for the sake of speculation that I do have your keys. Now I wonder—if I did have 'em—if you'd be willing to cough up a little ransom money to get 'em back. Just in the nature of speculation, of course.

LYLE: Give him the keys, son.

TEDDY: Whudduya say, Gentleman Jim?

RICHARD: If you do have my keys, I can assure you I'm not about to pay one red cent to get them back.

TEDDY: Then—just speculatin again—were I to be the possessor of your keys, I just don't think I'd give 'em back. No sir, I just don't think I would. *(To himself)* Couldn't. Impractical.

RICHARD: *(To Lyle)* Do you have a policeman in town?

LYLE: Sheriff.

RICHARD: Would you mind calling him. We'll let him see if he can find my keys.

TEDDY: Now—just speculatin again, if you'll beg my rapidly diminishin pardon here—I wouldn't do that. No sir, I just wouldn't.

RICHARD: *(To Lyle)* If you won't, kindly tell me the number and I will.

(Richard takes a step toward the phone. Teddy rises. Richard stops. They face each other)

LYLE: Son, my offer still stands.

TEDDY: And I appreciate your offer, ole man, but this here speculatin I'm doin is an offer of a different stripe.

LYLE: Then I'm gonna have to call Sheriff Garcia—

TEDDY: I pray to the very funny Lord that you don't attempt that, sir.

LYLE: Then give the man his keys back!

TEDDY: Darn it all, I can't do that.

(Lyle starts for the phone on the wall)

(Teddy drops all traces of the affected accent) Do not touch that phone! *(Lyle stops)* Now, when I say don't do something the way I just said it . . . don't do it. *(To Richard)* All right, let's cut the crap, friend. We're forty-five minutes from the Mexican border and permanently out of your lives. But we've got no money to pay for our breakfast, let alone a generator. We need money.

LYLE: Have the breakfast on me, son. Put their breakfast on my tab, Angel. Have the generator on me too. Let's just don't do anything you'll be sorry for. My offer still stands. You go calmly outta here and —

TEDDY: We accept breakfast and the generator with thanks but we've still got to have money. In the hand. Now I'm damn sure there's not enough money in this register of yours, ole man, to make cleanin them out worth my while, so if Gentleman Jim here doesn't come up with, say, three hundred dollars — cash! — I'm going to be very upset. What do you say, Jim?

(Teddy has slipped the keys from his jacket and approaches Richard, holding the keys out in his palm. Suddenly Richard leaps for the keys but Teddy, anticipating, secures them in a closed fist)

See that move, Red Ryder. Fastest fist in the west. Can I sign on as Little Beaver with moves like that?

(Richard breaks for the door. Teddy leaps between Richard and the door. Like a basketball player, Richard tries to fake one way and go the other around Teddy, but Teddy stays between him and the door. Richard loses his balance as Teddy moves at him and falls against the table with Teddy and Cheryl's dishes on it. Suddenly Angel breaks for the door, but Cheryl leaps up and blocks the way with what is, in fact, a nearly totally ineffectual stance against Angel's bulk should she decide to bust through)

CHERYL: Please don't do anything.

ANGEL: *(Screaming in Cheryl's face, close to tears)* They're nice people!

TEDDY: *(To Angel)* You just shift your tank in reverse and back over behind that counter —

(During Teddy's exchange with Angel, Richard has stepped close enough to Teddy to hit him. Rather than coldcocking him, however, Richard slaps him across the face. Teddy drops the keys and Richard grabs them. A beat)

Christ, Jim, what if I'd been wearing contact lenses?

RICHARD: We're walking out of here. We're going over to Mr. Striker's station and we're getting in our car. You have as long as it takes us to locate the sheriff and get him out here to get your car fixed and be gone.

(Richard puts an arm around Clarisse's shoulders and starts them for the door. Teddy pulls a small caliber revolver from his jacket)

TEDDY: Hold it!

CHERYL: Teddy!

(The Ethredges hold it)

RICHARD: Don't you dare point that thing at me.

TEDDY: Empty your pockets on that table.

RICHARD: I will not.

TEDDY: Friend, I don't need to shoot you, but if that's what it's going to take to make clear who's controlling this, then that's the way it's going to have to be.

RICHARD: That's the way it's going to have to be then.

(Teddy fires the gun at Richard and, simultaneously, the stage goes black)

ACT II

~

Some minutes later. Richard is the center of attention, seated at one of the tables, a first aid kit set out before him, Lyle putting the finishing touches on a wrapping of gauze and two-inch tape. Clarisse sits beside Richard. Teddy is eating the last of Cheryl's breakfast, having finished his own. His revolver sits on the table close to him.

TEDDY: How ya feeling, Gentleman Jim?

> *(Richard does not respond. Teddy turns to Stephen on his stool at the counter)*

> No more'n a flesh wound, Red. He'll be ready to ride by sun up. *(To Angel)* Darlin, them's was mighty fine vittles.

LYLE: I think the bleeding's stopped.

TEDDY: Didn't I just get through telling Red Ryder it weren't nothing more'n a flesh wound?

LYLE: How do ya feel?

RICHARD: I'm all right.

TEDDY: *(To himself)* Christ, I'm bein ostracized.

> *(Lyle moves away from Richard and gets caught on Cheryl's breasts as he rolls his sleeves back down and fastens them)*

CLARISSE: Can I do something?

RICHARD: No, really, I'm fine. Just shaken.

CLARISSE: Please let me do something.

RICHARD: There's nothing for you to do.

TEDDY: Red, ya know who I wished coulda been here to see the looks on ever'body's face when I put the hot lead to Jim? Cisco and Pancho. There was a couple boys could really appreciate a good facial expression.

(Teddy stares at Stephen, at his ineffectual toughness atop his stool, turns angrily away, seems to get lost in himself somewhere)

Goddamn, where did all those people get to so fast? *(A beat)* Where the hell's goddamn Tim Holt, Jim? Johnny Mack and the Durango Kid? *(A beat)* Lash LaRue. *(A beat)* Jesus Christ, somebody pulled a fast one. *(Teddy holds in himself)*

CHERYL: *(Agitatedly, impulsively)* Will you stop staring at my breasts, please!

(Lyle and Stephen's eyes dart away)

TEDDY: *(Fixing on Lyle)* Who's starin at your breasts, darlin?

LYLE: Not me.

TEDDY: Not you, old man?

LYLE: Not me.

TEDDY: Stuff like that don't interest you no more, do it?

LYLE: Well now, I wouldn't say that.

TEDDY: *(Utterly unamused)* No. I wouldn't either.

(Teddy turns on Stephen. The menacing quality of the first act seems suddenly colored now—and becomes more intense as the second act goes by—some internal well spring set rumbling by his searching after those missing heroes)

STEPHEN: Who says I'm lookin at 'em?

TEDDY: I say, boy. *(A beat)* But then she's got 'em right out there for you to look at, don't she? She don't want you to look at her bosom, she oughta cover the thing up. Ain't that right?

(Stephen barely nods. Teddy stares into him)

CHERYL: Could we please get out of here!

(Teddy holds on Stephen, his breath coming a little bit fast)

Teddy . . .

TEDDY: Yeah. Why don't you and Mr. Striker go on over to the gay-rage and put our new generator in. Mr. Striker, you go on now, but I surely hope, sir, that you won't attempt nothin bay-roque. *(Handing her the gun)* I'd hate for my little gal to have to decide if she'd use that thing. Put the gun in your shawl, sweetheart.

LYLE: You have my word. I just want to see you out of here and us no worse off than we are now.

(Teddy snaps his eyes to Lyle, stares at him hard)

TEDDY: That's a good old man. *(A beat)* Goddamn but you're good, ain'cha? *(A beat)* Yeah. You're a . . . good . . . ole . . . man. Ain-'cha? *(A beat)* You keep your eyes off my little gal's breasts. You understand me?

(Lyle nods with as much dignity as possible)

(To Cheryl) Bring back a coupla rolls of friction tape.

CHERYL: *(Quietly)* Teddy, I'm scared.

TEDDY: Run along, darlin.

(Teddy will not look at her. He remains fixed on Lyle. A beat)

CHERYL: Go ahead, Mr. Striker, I'll follow you.

(Lyle looks around, as if checking to see somehow that everyone is all right, then he exits, followed by Cheryl)

TEDDY: *(To Stephen)* Shame on you, boy. *(A beat)* What's goin on in your mind, boy?—way back there in the corners where you never been before? Don't let it touch ya, boy, ya hear me? Ya do and it's just liable to eat you whole.

(Stephen is unsure how to respond to what seems an almost intimate tone. He meets Teddy's eyes a moment, then drops his eyes into Teddy's fatigue jacket. Teddy continues to stare at him, to stay tight to him. Stephen glances back up at Teddy's eyes)

Go ahead, boy. Ask me somethin. *(A beat)*

STEPHEN: Were you in the war?

TEDDY: Yeah. You?

STEPHEN: Uh-uh.

TEDDY: Unfit . . . or pull a lucky number?

STEPHEN: Three-twenty-four.

TEDDY: That's too bad, ain't it? Ya mighta got yourself shot to shit and mailed home in a plastic garbage bag and buried down the road here. Ever'body woulda come to the funeral. You'da *been* somebody then, Red.

STEPHEN: Boy I went to high school with got killed in the war.

TEDDY: Uh-huh.

(A beat. Stephen can't remember the boy's name. He finally turns to Angel)

ANGEL: Billy Simon.

STEPHEN: Billy Simon.

TEDDY: Yeah — you'da been somebody, Red. I knew a lotta good ole boys who became somebody by gettin their good old asses shot off. I can't remember their names either. *(Teddy stares at Stephen, then turns abruptly away)* I wanted to go away once too. Figured one place was as bad as another. Went to college. Ya know what I remember? How to do the tired swimmer's carry — which ain't much use, say, here in the desert — and the succession of Tudor-Stuart kings and queens — which ain't *no* use even if ya happen to be close to water. *(He turns back to Stephen)* Yeah . . . you might as well stay here, boy. Maybe someday they'll make ya head of the parkin lot.

(Teddy points to his coffee mug. Angel brings the pot)

ANGEL: How old is she?

TEDDY: Cheryl? Eighteen, nineteen, twenty — don't rightly know, darlin. Why? She too old for me, ya think?

ANGEL: Where'd ya met each other?

TEDDY: Sock hop. Yes'm, we bopped our little be-hinds off that first glorious night. The Kalin Twins. Chuck Berry . . . How come they call ya Angel, dumplin?

ANGEL: My momma and daddy just named me it.

TEDDY: Angel, huh? Ya musta meant a lot to 'em. Then anyway. When did the bulk start to come up on ya?

ANGEL: *(A beat)* Ya mean when did I start to get fat?

TEDDY: That's right, darlin.

ANGEL: When I was little.

TEDDY: Glands, was it?

ANGEL: Uh-huh.

TEDDY: How come ya wear that weddin ring on your right hand? You married to Mrs. Christ's boy?

ANGEL: My daddy gave it to me.

TEDDY: How is your daddy these days?

ANGEL: *(A beat)* I don't know. He went away a long time ago.

TEDDY: Cause a you?

ANGEL: *(A beat)* Cause of my momma and my gra'ma, I think. *(A beat)*

TEDDY: You think anybody's ever gonna marry you, Angel?

ANGEL: *(A beat)* I don't know.

TEDDY: *(A beat, without malice)* No. Nobody ever is.

(Angel jolts away from him)

RICHARD: What the hell's the matter with you, man?

TEDDY: Generally, Jim, or in particular?

RICHARD: What's the matter with *all* of you?

TEDDY: Ah! All of us. You mean us here disaffected youth of the United States of America?

RICHARD: *Yes!*

TEDDY: We disaffected, Jim.

RICHARD: What happened to all of that Love and Peace garbage?

TEDDY: Ah! That was another group, sir. That was these other fellas. No—us, we're not in favor of Love and Peace. *(A beat)* How bout you, Jim? You filled with Love and Peace, are ya?

RICHARD: Not right now.

TEDDY: *(To Angel)* How bout you, dumplin? You filled with Love and Peace?

ANGEL: I think so. I mean . . . I think so.

TEDDY: Like the way ya said that twice thataway, darlin. Whudduyou love, lamb chop?

ANGEL: My momma . . .

TEDDY: Uh-huh.

ANGEL: . . . and my gra'ma.

TEDDY: How bout old Red Ryder here. You love old Red, don't ya, sweet gut?

ANGEL: *(A beat)* I like Stephen a lot.

TEDDY: Oh, I think ya love old Red, that's what I think. But he don't love ya back, do he? He don't *ever* stare at your bosom, do he? Lemme intercede in your behalf, darlin, and ask the boy a coupla questions. *(Angel cannot respond)* Now, Red, how come ya don't love sweet gut here? Not good enough for ya? Sharp dresser like you. Man with all the answers. How come?

STEPHEN: None of your goddamn business.

(Teddy leaps at Stephen and backhands him across the head, knocking him off his stool)

TEDDY: Don't you ever look at my woman's breasts again, boy, or I'll hurt you real bad! *(A beat. He stares furiously at Stephen)* Now you get in the middle of that room.

(Stephen gets up and moves to the middle of the room, trying somehow to affect a toughness even as he complies without question. Teddy goes right after him)

My God, the unspeakable audacity of a punk like you wearin a tattoo like that. The real Red Ryder would've hung 'em up if anyone were to tell him he was associated with pigshit like that.

And I'll tell you somethin else: You *never* would've found the real Red Ryder sittin around a dump like this starin at some tourist lady's tits. I swear to goddamn Christ I'm tempted to take those eyes out of your head and cut that tattoo off your arm. *(A beat)* Now I wanna see you ride the range. You just start ridin the range around this room till I tell you to stop.

STEPHEN: Whudduya mean, ride the range?

TEDDY: I mean like when you were a kid, you little pissant. Ride the goddamn range like you did when you were a kid playin Cowboys and Niggers, or Wetbacks, or whatever you shitheads played out here. Now *ride!*

(Extremely self-consciously, Stephen begins to ride the range)

Slap leather! You're Red Ryder and you're chasin a black hat across the desert out there. Go get him!

(Stephen slaps leather and rides the range a little harder)

Sound effects!

(Stephen adds weak sound effects—clicks and calls to his horse)

What was goddamn Red Ryder's horse's name, Jim?

RICHARD: I don't remember.

TEDDY: Thunder or Midnight, I think. *(To Stephen)* Your horse is Thunder or Midnight—pick one. That giddyap shit's no good no more.

(Stephen clicks and calls to his horse, calling him Midnight)

Stop! . . . Okay now ride up to the counter and dismount and tie your horse up. *(Stephen does)* Bad. Very bad. Okay, now, ya go into this here cafe here, see, and sweet cheeks is your only beloved—cause you're Red Ryder and you only got one truly beloved. I mean, as far as I can see, you just don't mess around on the side. But, unlike the homosexual fruit Lone Ranger, you do got yourself this one fine gal here. A great time it was, Jim, when we didn't know enough to wonder at all those vir-ile lads runnin around in weird couples. It's no wonder our generation despises women. All right now, sweet nubs, you come on down here and when Red comes in off the range, you say, Red honey, welcome home! Got that?

(A beat. Slowly Angel moves to her position, nods assent)

Okay, Red, get back there and come *gallopin* up this time, tie up ole Thunder or Midnight, and swagger into the cafe.

(Stephen rides up again, dismounts, and ties up his horse. He starts toward the counter)

Swagger!

(Stephen does something of a swagger)

ANGEL: Red honey, wel—

TEDDY: Not yet, for chrissake. Let him get in the door . . . smack some dust from his britches.

(Stephen smacks some dust, his eyes on the floor. Angel looks to Teddy for a signal. He gives it)

ANGEL: Red honey, welcome home.

(Stephen stands, his eyes on the floor)

TEDDY: Kiss her, Red, for chrissake. Where're your manners, ya schmuck? Pucker up, dumplin.

(Stephen leans across the counter. Angel presents her face forward, but he kisses her on the cheek)

Shit—cut! . . . Okay, Red, get over there. Sweet cheeks, back off. Our Lady of the Violin, com'ere, I got somethin for you to do.

(Clarisse looks to Richard)

Don't look at him like he's gonna give ya permission. This ain't the school dance, honey. If I call cutsees then we got cutsees. Now get behind the counter and when I ride up, you say, Red honey, welcome home! . . . Move!

(Clarisse doesn't move. Teddy walks toward them, then suddenly snatches up the violin case)

CLARISSE: Don't. Be careful. Please.

(Teddy oh so carefully opens the case and then suddenly, carelessly whips out the violin)

All right.

(Clarisse moves behind the counter)

RICHARD: Don't kiss her!

(A beat; Teddy holds on Richard as if he adores the idiocy of what Richard chose to say, sharing his reaction with Stephen, then turning to Clarisse)

TEDDY: At two minutes to curtain the female star is taken suddenly by a mysterious illness and you, the prop girl, are thrust into the part. Don't blow it. *(To Stephen and Angel)* Now, Red, nubs, watch this, cause this is the way I want it.

(Carrying the violin under his arm, Teddy slaps leather around the diner, whipping his horse on, calling to it. He gallops up to the counter, leaps off his horse, throws the reins over the rail and grandly ties them, swaggers into the cafe and slaps some dust from his britches)

CLARISSE: *(In a monotone)* Red honey, welcome home.

(Teddy leans across the counter but Clarisse turns her head away. Teddy grabs her through her pullover by the brassiere, twists the brassiere, and yanks her toward him. Richard comes for Teddy. Teddy raises the violin over his head as if he would smash it on the counter. Richard stops, slowly sits. Teddy stares at him a moment, then still holding the violin over his head, he leans in to kiss Clarisse. She turns her face away. He lowers the violin to her turned cheek and turns her mouth to his. He kisses her, taking his time. He breaks)

TEDDY: Thanks, Jim, take her away.

CLARISSE: Give me my violin.

TEDDY: Only if you promise to play us some background music.

CLARISSE: All right. Give it to me.

(Teddy points to a tray on the counter with a fork on it)

TEDDY: On those. *(Demonstrating)* First a little range-ridin music, then somethin soft and romantic. Play nice and when today's shootin schedule's finished—no pun intended, Jim—you'll get your instrument back. All right, Red, show me somethin, boy.

STEPHEN: *(A beat)* I don't wanna kiss her.

TEDDY: What's the matter, boy—you queer?

STEPHEN: I just don't wanna kiss her.

TEDDY: Cause she's fat?

STEPHEN: I just don't wanna.

TEDDY: Don't you know what it'd mean to her if you—

STEPHEN: I don't wanna.

TEDDY: Shut up! Don't you understand, boy, that you've got to learn to see yourself in relation to other people's needs. You think I enjoy this work?

STEPHEN: I just don't wanna kiss her.

TEDDY: Jesus Christ, I say something of consequence to you, and you give me back "I don't wanna" for the fourth time. I think you're queer, boy, that's what I think.

STEPHEN: I don't care what you think.

(Teddy suddenly tightens his arm around Stephen's neck)

TEDDY: Please care what I think . . . okay? *(A beat, Stephen nods)* Now you either do this scene the way I wrote it or I'm gonna make ya kiss me. Ya wanna kiss me.

STEPHEN: *(Straining in the headlock)* Uh-uh.

TEDDY: Then play the scene the way I wrote it. There can only be one writer on these films, otherwise the thematic core of the thing gets screwed up. Surely a man's made as many movin pictures as you knows that. *(A beat)* The orchestra's tunin up. Okay . . . *hit it.*

(Teddy sets the action and "music" going. Stephen plays the scene as Teddy called it, though with a marked lessening of intensity from Teddy's playing of it. Clarisse accompanies him on fork and tray. Stephen swaggers up to the counter. Teddy signals Clarisse to cut the music)

ANGEL: Red honey, welcome home!

TEDDY: Good. Now music!

(Clarisse slows her rhythm as Stephen leans across the counter to kiss Angel, who at the moment of contact turns away. Clarisse, disgusted as much with her own participation as anything, moves down the counter)

TEDDY: *(To Stephen)* Boy, I don't care *how* big you are over at Metro, this is the last picture *I'm* gonna use you in.

(Teddy turns, somewhat disturbed. A beat)

(To Angel) Sweet cheeks, what can I say?

ANGEL: Nothin.

TEDDY: You want this boy to make love to you?

ANGEL: No.

TEDDY: Sure you do. *(To Stephen)* You ever been to bed with a woman, Red? *(Nothing from Stephen)* I'm talkin to you, boy.

STEPHEN: Yeah.

TEDDY: Bullshit. Well, this girl wants you to make love to her and, by jingo, she's gonna have her way. *(Slapping the counter)* Right here.

ANGEL: No!

TEDDY: Our Lady, you'll accompany the action of course. Now here's the way we're gonna play it. Red, you'll say to nubs here that you're goin away and she'll ask ya, Why ya goin away, Red Ryder? — and you'll say, I don't know, cause you're Red Ryder and you don't know a goddamn thing unless someone tells ya — and that's a great way to be, wouldn't you say, Jim? Memmer how it used to be? Oh yeah, none a this horseshit you're into, boy, about re-sponsibility and ex-i-tential choice. All's the old Ryder knew is he got sealed orders to go away, so he was goin; and so you'll say, I don't know why I'm goin away; and she'll say, Is it because of me?; and you'll say, I don't know if it's because of you — because no one told ya whether that's it or not; and she'll say, I have to know why; and all's you'll be able to say is, I don't know. Say it!

STEPHEN: I don't know.

TEDDY: *(Showing him how)* I don't know.

STEPHEN: I don't know.

TEDDY: And then, sweet cheeks, you'll say, When you comin back, Red Ryder, and whudduyou say, Red?

STEPHEN: I don't know.

TEDDY: *(A beat)* Uh-uh, no, that's wrong. Because at this juncture, some unknown but officious individual steps to your ear and whispers: Never. You ain't never comin back, Red Ryder. And you say to your little dumplin here: I ain't never comin back. And nubs here's eyes fill up and she says, Make love to me, Ryder, before ya go; and you, bless ya, Red, you say, We ain't married, Missy Nubs, it wouldn't be right. I couldn't! I mustn't! Goddamn it! *(Turning on Richard)* You a Dodger fan, Jim?

RICHARD: *(Startled)* No.

TEDDY: *(To Stephen)* Baseball! Game grown men used to play when Jim and me was boys and you weren't the only Red Ryder around. Who'd ya root for, Jamie?

RICHARD: *(Unsettled)* Yankees.

TEDDY: *(Laughing distantly)* You shitbrick. Yeah—we ain't gonna forget Roger Maris' flattop overnight, are we? Ya stick with 'em when you moved west, Jimmy? I'll tell ya what happened to me: When they moved the Duker outta Brooklyn and into that friggin L.A. Coliseum, they ruined the career of the only man I ever loved. I'm talkin to you, Jimble. You speak to that!

RICHARD: I . . . lost interest when they traded Maris, and Mantle retired.

TEDDY: The Micker, Jesus. Yeah—yeah, maybe that was the end of it. And that goddamn Yogi Berra. Jesus, I hated that little bastard. What'd they used to call him?

RICHARD: Mr. Clutch.

TEDDY: Mr. Clutch, my ass.

RICHARD: The Dodgers were losers. You belong together.

TEDDY: Don't you ever imply in my presence that the Duke was a loser. *(Laughing distantly)* Ah, the Duker. Edward Donald Snider, friends, the Duke of Flatbush, pokin 'em into Bedford Avenue.

(A beat, turning on Stephen) Oh there was another time, boy, I know it . . .

(Caught somewhere deep inside himself, Teddy stops, retreats)

Yeah. But that was yesteryear and this is today, and there ain't nothin today to say that a coupla nice kids can't throw each other a nice fuck on a countertop in a diner in New Mexico if they want to. So . . . Mr. Red Ryder and Miss Angel Sweet Nubs, front and center, please, and dis-robe.

RICHARD: *(Rising)* Edwin! It's *Edwin,* not Edward! Edwin Donald Snider! Now stop degrading them! We are living in the present and if you —

TEDDY: *Do you* think this woman is impressed by all of this gratuitous bravado? *(To Clarisse)* Are you? . . . Are you impressed? *(To Richard)* Don't you understand there have been landmark discoveries in the fields of apology and psychology suggesting that there is more to manliness and husbandry than pretending willingness to do battle with men you cannot compete with. *(Teddy stares at Richard. A beat)* Hey, Red, how bout Our Lady of the Violin? Like to make love to her?

CLARISSE: Don't touch me!

TEDDY: Whudduya say to that, Red? Your first sexual experience of a complete nature with a concert violinist who's not at all unattractive for a woman creeping death quick into middle age. Maybe she'll even put the fiddle down while y'all consummate. *(A beat)* Red boy, goddamn it, I'm talkin to you.

STEPHEN: I don't want to.

TEDDY: I swear to God, boy, I think you're queer as a three dollar bill.

STEPHEN: You're a queer!

TEDDY: *(Furiously)* Rise to the occasion, boy! Rise! Rise to it! *(A beat)* Now look at it this way, Red. On the one hand, you got sweet cheeks here, untouched by human hands — correct me if I'm wrong, cheeks . . . cheeks? — *(Quietly)* Yeah — untouched. And then on the other hand, you've got Our Lady of the Violin . . . who's been around.

CLARISSE: You are an obscenity.

TEDDY: And you, madame, hiding behind your instrument and your paucity of word and deed, are a deceitful woman. *(A beat. He stares into Clarisse)* Hey, Jim, the little woman ever treat you as good as she does this violin you're payin for?

CLARISSE: You stinking filth. You rotten, stinking filth.

RICHARD: Clarisse, stay out of this —

CLARISSE: You come in here and you treat us as though we were somehow truly without worth, as if we were truly no more than dirt. But no, it's not us, it's not us. It's *you* —

RICHARD: All right, Clarisse —

CLARISSE: I know you and I'm not impressed. I *know* you and I want you out of here —

RICHARD: *(With a small self-conscious laugh)* Sshhh, it's all right.

CLARISSE: It's not all right. Don't tell me it's all right —

RICHARD: Don't demean yourself by —

CLARISSE: Don't you talk to me about demeaning myself. This mass of filth walks into our lives and you let him humiliate you beyond all pretense —

RICHARD: He hasn't humiliated me, Clarisse —

CLARISSE: Who gives a good goddamn about . . . *Ed*ward *Sch*neider when the little dignity that remains to you is being reduced —

RICHARD: He hasn't done anything to me but put a hole in my arm!

CLARISSE: You'd let him have intercourse with me on the counter if he really wanted to, do you know that? —

RICHARD: Don't be ridiculous!

CLARISSE: What would you do?

RICHARD: I'd do something!

CLARISSE: You wouldn't stop him because you can't!

RICHARD: I'd stop him!

CLARISSE: *(To Teddy)* All right, filth, come on, let's see if he can—

RICHARD: Stop it! Do you understand me! You're making fools of us! You're embarrassing me!

CLARISSE: I am not your added appendage!

RICHARD: I told you to stay out of this! Now you sit down and you pull yourself together—

CLARISSE: Haven't I been here? I'm in trouble too, Richard, and I don't trust you anymore.

(Silence. They stare at each other, having gone too far and fixed on the wrong thing in the wrong place and time. They stare, the realization of their stupidity catching up with their rage at each other and this circumstance. Richard suddenly bolts away. Clarisse holds, frozen, for some seconds, then she takes several steps toward Richard but stops well short of him)

TEDDY: This one's dedicated to the Ethredges, y'all.

(He strikes one of the strings of the violin and runs his finger down it. A beat)

Hey!—what is this? I thought we came here to dance.

(He drops a quarter into the jukebox and arbitrarily punches three selections. Cheryl and Lyle enter)

Get the van fixed?

LYLE: All set.

(Lyle hands Teddy two rolls of friction tape)

TEDDY: This is the last dance then, gang. Time's gone and I'm gonna ride off into the sunrise.

(A slow ballad comes on)

Come on, Red, one last memory. You and nubs lead it off. Get out here, dumplin.

(Angel comes out from behind the counter. She has been crying since the Ethredges exploded at each other)

What're ya bawling about, cheeks? My God, darlin, be jubilant. Red! Get your ass over to her.

(Stephen takes Angel loosely by the wrists and begins to do a little two-step shuffle)

TEDDY: *(Accentless)* Mrs. Ethredge, I believe this is my dance.

(Clarisse holds, glances at Richard)

RICHARD: The man's waiting to dance with you.

(Teddy hands the violin to Richard)

TEDDY: You get the violin, Jim.

(Richard takes the violin, looks at it a moment, then dumps it on the table. Richard and Clarisse stare at each other a moment. Teddy pulls her onto the dance floor and takes her to him. She stares with simple defiance into his face)

I love your style.

(He picks her up off the ground and begins to dance her around. He gets a look at Angel and Stephen)

Jesus, Red, if you and sweet cheeks don't make a picture to warm the heart, I don't know what does.

(He lowers Clarisse to the tops of his boots)

Memmer, my darling, when we used to do it thisaway?

(He digs his fingers into her buttocks, pressing her to his groin with such force that his arms quiver slightly. She slowly exerts herself against his strength and slowly he allows her to break from him. She stares at him again with that simple look of defiance)

All right, Red, break! You and cheeks pick new partners.

(Angel and Stephen break but neither moves)

Pick a new partner, nubs. Move it, darlin. *(Angel turns slowly toward Lyle)*

ANGEL: Wanna dance, Lyle?

LYLE: 'Fraid I'm not much for dancin with this thing. *(Indicating his brace)*

TEDDY: Sure ya are. Why there's crippled folks in bowlin leagues.

LYLE: I wish you wouldn't ask me to do this.

TEDDY: I fail to see, sir, that you have the right to any dispensations the others don't. Do it.

(Lyle and Angel begin to dance after a fashion)

Red, what're you doin standin around with your thumb up your ass. You see Cheryl standin there like a goddamn wallflower.

STEPHEN: *(To Cheryl)* You wanna dance?

CHERYL: No.

STEPHEN: *(To Teddy)* She don't want to.

CHERYL: Teddy, the car's ready. It's enough.

TEDDY: I'll say when it's enough. Dance with goddamn Red Ryder.

CHERYL: I don't want to dance, Teddy. I wanna get out of here.

TEDDY: And I want you to dance with this boy.

CHERYL: I'm not one of them, damn it, I'm with you.

TEDDY: So what, darlin? Were you under the misapprehension that makes you privileged? . . . Well, it don't. Uh-uh. No—you functional too, darlin. *(A beat)* Nothin else really. *(A beat, quietly)* Now you dance.

(She shakes her head. Teddy, quietly but absolutely firmly)

You gotta dance, sweetheart.

(She moves toward Stephen. Teddy steps to her, holds out his hand slowly. She passes him the gun)

(To Stephen) You keep your eyes off her breasts, boy. Okay?

(Stephen and Cheryl begin to dance. Teddy heads for Richard)

RICHARD: Stay away from me!

TEDDY: You dance with her, you sorry son of a bitch. The committee put a lotta plannin into this social.

(Clarisse reaches for Richard. He throws her hand off and moves onto the dance floor. He stands with Clarisse but does not dance, her hand unheld against his palm where she put it)

All right, everybody dance!

(Teddy stamps his foot and claps with the music, his stamping and clapping becoming maniacal. Suddenly he leaps at Richard and Clarisse and spins them round and round, screaming at them)

DANCE! DANCE! GODDAMN IT, DANCE!

(He derives no satisfaction from this and now throws Richard to the floor and against Clarisse's cries of resistance he clamps her arms above her head and peels her pullover up over her head and yanks her brassiere up, exposing her breasts. He bears her blindly to Stephen)

THERE, BOY, TITS! TITS!

(And now across to Lyle who backs away as if bitten)

THERE, OLE MAN, TITS!

(Richard has risen and reached Teddy. As he grips Teddy's shoulder from the rear, Teddy rifles his elbow into Richard's stomach, turns and kicks Richard in the groin. Richard drops like a sack of cement. Teddy is panting. He looks about him a moment, then with an animal cry he tears the jukebox plug from its socket. The music winds to a stop, the lights go out on the machine. Clarisse moves down to Richard, touches him)

RICHARD: Don't touch me! Please . . . don't touch me.

(Teddy slams his fists down against the counter. A beat. He snaps up the two rolls of friction tape. He goes behind the counter and gets a large French knife and a small paring knife)

TEDDY: Okay, Red Ryder, start taping hands behind backs and feet and make them tight or I'll cut your pecker off, if you've got one.

(He throws a roll of tape to Stephen)

Start with sweet cheeks. If her hands are taped, she can't touch you with them. *(Stephen moves to Angel)* Get some food together, Cheryl. *(Cheryl does not move)* Punishin me, darlin?

(Teddy comes out from behind the counter with the knives)

Gentleman Jim next. *(To Clarisse)* Get the big offenders first, huh?

(Stephen is waiting for something to cut Angel's tape with. Teddy slides the paring knife over to him. Stephen picks it up, holds it, looks to Teddy)

One last gesture for the old west? *(A beat. Teddy snort-laughs at Stephen)* Get on with it, boy. *(Stephen gets on with it)*

LYLE: You don't have to tape me, son.

TEDDY: What in the hell's the matter with you, old man? Tape him up!

(Stephen moves on to Lyle. Teddy finishes taping Richard by drawing his taped legs up to his taped hands and taping those together)

Here's the final ignominy, Jim: to be trussed up like a butchered hog and left on display. *(To Lyle)* Somehow, you old buzzard, with your tit-sucking eyes and your ass-kissing demeanor, you make me just as sick as the rest of us do.

(Stephen does Lyle's feet, then Angel's. Teddy moves Clarisse to the opposite side of the diner, sits her down. He takes the two-inch adhesive tape that was used earlier to bind Richard's wound and tears off a strip)

Red Ryder — *(Stephen looks around and Teddy throws him the roll of adhesive tape)* — mouths.

(Teddy tapes Clarisse's hands behind her back. He comes around to tape her feet)

Yeah, Jim, the truth of the thing is that there do gotta be somethin beyond the Cadillac. Ya know what I mean, Jim? *(A beat. To Clarisse)* And beyond the violin. Don't there, darlin?

(Clarisse says nothing but, then, she doesn't have to)

Yeah . . . well, if I took that away from you . . . I'm sorry.

CLARISSE: Are you?

(They stare at each other for a long moment)

TEDDY: No. But I wish I were.

(Hurriedly he presses the adhesive tape to her mouth. Stephen has finished his work and is seated at the counter. Teddy turns to him)

I want one more thing from you, Red. I want you to take this knife . . .

(He slams the French knife into the countertop)

. . . and I want you to cut that tattoo out of your arm. Then I want you to hand it to me to take with me. *(He stares at Stephen. Silence)* Ah, Stephen. Ah, Stevie, you despicable chickenshit.

(Teddy looks with disgust at Stephen, then moves toward the roll of adhesive tape which Stephen left beside Angel. As he does, Stephen yanks the French knife out of the counter, screams his insides long and open, and rushes with deadly earnestness at Teddy's belly. Teddy catches Stephen's wrists, heaves him backward onto the floor, and draws and cocks the revolver. He presses the revolver's muzzle into Stephen's face)

CHERYL: Teddy!

TEDDY: Red honey, welcome home.

(Teddy straddles Stephen, presses the gun against Stephen's eye)

It's no good anymore, boy. It's too late. I thought if anyone understood that, you did. *(A long pause, then Teddy releases the revolver's hammer)* But your sentence ain't to die, Red Ryder. It's to live, looking back on that inept charge across this room as the high spot of your life's prime . . . . Now roll over and put your hands behind your back.

(Stephen rolls over and Teddy tapes him)

Clean out Gentleman Jim's pockets, Cheryl.

CHERYL: Teddy, we're in so much trouble.

TEDDY: Well, you can stay if you want. Take your chances. It doesn't make any difference to me. *(To Lyle)* Think you can save her, ole man? Huh? What kinda game plan you give her for her salvation? *(To Cheryl)* Some choice you got, sweetheart.

(Cheryl looks from Lyle to Teddy, holds on Teddy a moment then goes listlessly to Richard and begins to go through his pockets)

How long's it been since you had a woman, old man? *(Lyle doesn't answer)* How bout that, sweetheart? Here ya got Mr. Striker who can't remember the last time he had a woman and Red here who ain't never had one and sweet nubs who ain't never really been kissed. My God, love, you could become a regular welfare organization around here. Except that would be just one more roll of blubber for you, wouldn't it, nubs? — This tight little girl with her fine, pointed breasts comin between you and Mr. Striker. *(A beat. He turns on Lyle)* Ah, Mr. Striker. *(He turns to Cheryl. A beat)* Get some food together.

(Teddy sits at the counter and strips Richard's wallet. Cheryl gets together several small boxes of Wheaties and other cereal, some sandwich meat and a loaf of bread)

Breakfast of Champions. That where it all started to go bad, ya think, Jim? The Reverend Bob Richards pole-vaulting into our churches and hearts for . . . *Wheaties!* Gonna have this bronzed and send it back to you and Red. *(To Cheryl)* You ready, sweetheart?

CHERYL: *(A beat)* I'm not going with you, Teddy.

(Teddy looks at her for several seconds, then goes for his fatigue jacket. That on, he tears the receiver out of the phone, gathers up his food, looks to Clarisse a moment, and then moves down to Stephen)

TEDDY: When you comin back, Red Ryder? *(Nothing from Stephen)* Tell me one last time, boy . . . tell me!

STEPHEN: Never.

(Teddy slaps a piece of tape across Stephen's mouth, dumps the revolver into the bread sack and exits without a look at anyone. Silence. Cheryl seems frozen for some seconds, then she moves to the edge of the counter. She is not quite able to make her decision. She comes tentatively out from behind the counter. She stares across the others, fixes on Lyle, takes several steps toward him. Then she hears someone coming and retreats behind the counter, pressing herself to the wall. Clark enters at his own busy pace)

CLARK: What in *the* hell!

(After a cursory glance around he makes for the cash register, much surprised to find the money still in the register)

What in the name of sweet Jesus! *(Taking Cheryl in)* What the hell're you doin?

(Cheryl does not move. Clark whips back into the room, grabs up one of the knives and goes to Stephen. He yanks the tape off Stephen's mouth)

STEPHEN: Ouch! Christ!

CLARK: What the hell happened?

STEPHEN: What the hell's it look like?

CLARK: *(Freeing Stephen's hands and feet)* Don't smart mouth me, Red. It looks like someone held ya up and didn't take nothin is what it looks like. *(Moving to Angel, indicating Cheryl)* Who's she? *(Compulsively babbling on)* They didn't take *noth*in?

ANGEL: Just some bread and sandwich meat and some cereal —

CLARK: How much?

ANGEL: He shot that man.

CLARK: Huh! *(Clark hurries to Richard, begins to free him)* How bad he get ya, neighbor?

ANGEL: Ya gotta take the tape off his mouth before he can talk.

(Clark glances irritably at Angel, then carefully removes the tape from Richard's mouth, as if he might be wounded there)

CLARK: Easy does it here . . .

RICHARD: Call the sheriff. I'm all right. Call the sheriff and don't let that girl out of here.

CLARK: *(Starting for the phone)* She ain't goin nowhere —

(He sees that the receiver has been ripped out) S'ome bitch! *(He turns to Lyle whom Stephen has freed)* Get over to your station and get ahold of the highway police and that goddamn Garcia.

LYLE: *(Indicating Cheryl)* What about her?

RICHARD: *(Infuriated)* What do you mean, what about her? She's going to be prosecuted, that's what about her!

LYLE: I got the license number, Tommy. He's headin for Mexico and he's got a loada dope.

CLARK: Time's short then. Move on, Lyle. He get across that border and the goddamn Mex's'll set him up in a hotel somewheres. Vamanos. Chop chop!

LYLE: Tommy, about this girl here —

RICHARD: Hold it! He's taking a load of dope *into* Mexico? You don't take dope *into* Mexico. You take it *out*. He's heading back to California. *(To Cheryl)* Is that right?

(Cheryl does not move. Richard drags her out from behind the counter and screams in her face) Is that right?

(Cheryl looks to Lyle)

LYLE: Ya better tell him, miss.

CHERYL: *(A beat)* Yes.

RICHARD: San Diego? *(A beat. Cheryl nods)*

LYLE: I'll tell 'em.

(Lyle hustles off while Richard is thrusting Cheryl onto a stool. Richard turns after him too late)

RICHARD: Hold it! Hold it . . . ! *(Turning to Clark)* I don't trust that man.

CLARK: Say now, neighbor, Lyle Striker's as trustworthy a man as ever's been my pleasure to know.

RICHARD: Really?

CLARK: Don't you worry yourself none — we'll get this fella.

RICHARD: I'm not worried.

CLARK: *(To Stephen)* Three men here and one fella did this?

ANGEL: He had a gun.

CLARK: *(Ignoring her)* And what'd you do, Redbird? Just sit there on your butt and drink coffee and grease up the customer newspaper?

STEPHEN: *(Powerfully)* Up your hole, Clark, with a ten-foot pole.

ANGEL: Stephen tried to do something. He —

CLARK: All right, boy, that's all for you. You're as of here and now fired. *(Turning to Angel)* You sure that's all he took?

RICHARD: He took some money from me. About a hundred and seventy dollars.

CLARK: *(Turning back to Stephen, ignoring Richard)* To tell ya the honest-to-God truth, boy, after that bypass open, I wanted to shut down at night, but cause a your momma, I kept you on and I stayed open, to the detriment of my nearly major source of income.

STEPHEN: You're a goddamn charity organization, Clark, no question about it.

CLARK: Boy, somebody oughta wash your mouth out with lye soap.

STEPHEN: *(Stepping up to Clark, face to face)* Yeah, and I suppose you're the one's gonna try it.

RICHARD: Why don't you both *shut up!*

CLARK: Say now, neighbor—

RICHARD: Shut up!

CLARISSE: Richard . . .

RICHARD: And why don't you shut up too!

(Richard stares hatefully at her and suddenly leaps at her violin, takes it up like a bat and flies across the room, evidently intent on smashing it against the opposite table. Stephen throws himself toward Richard, meets him, and the two of them become a piece of still statuary holding a violin above their heads and staring into each other's eyes. They hold unmoved for several seconds before Stephen says)

STEPHEN: I . . . *(A beat)* . . . I'm . . .

(—and slowly takes the violin from Richard's hands, holds it gently, and returns it to its case. Lyle enters)

LYLE: Got the highway police out after him. I told 'em ya had to be in New Orleans and they said you'd have to come on down to the station and sign some papers first. I told 'em you was shot a little. They'll have a doctor there.

RICHARD: Very philanthropic. *(Indicating Cheryl)* What did they say to do with her?

(Lyle says nothing, he obviously said nothing to the state police about her. Richard laughs a sardonic and incredulous laugh)

Surely you're not serious.

(He stares at Lyle, the laugh dead on his face. He turns to Clark)

Can you take this girl and lead us to the police.

CLARK: S'pose so.

RICHARD: Oh, I wouldn't want to put you *out*. Any of you! I'd hate to insist on any adherence to the *law*.

CLARK: Don't worry none about adherence to the law. We adhere plenty.

RICHARD: All right then, let's *go*. Clarisse.

CLARK: *(To Angel)* You get on that chile sauce. I be back to check the books in a while.

STEPHEN: Hey! *(Everyone holds. To Clarisse)* Take me as far as Baton Rouge.

RICHARD: I wouldn't take you as far as the front door.

STEPHEN: *(To Clarisse)* Will ya?

RICHARD: *(Laughing sourly)* What are you asking her for?

CLARISSE: You don't have your clothing, your—

STEPHEN: I'm ready to go just like I am. Gimme my pay, Clark.

CLARK: What's your momma gonna say, boy?

(There is a sting in that, but Stephen moves to Lyle, digs out a small roll of bills)

STEPHEN: Here's forty bucks. You lend me thirty-five and you buy that car at Potter's for me. You wanna do that for me still?

LYLE: *(A beat; he glances at Angel)* Sure, Red.

STEPHEN: Just tell her I'm goin to Baton Rouge and when I get settled in I'll write.

LYLE: Son, shouldn't you check in with Miz Williams first?

STEPHEN: *(Ignoring Lyle, to Clarisse)* You gonna gimme a hitch?

RICHARD: No, I'm sorry.

CLARISSE: We'll take you. *(She turns to Richard)* We'll take him as far as Baton Rouge.

RICHARD: I'm not at all sure I'm going on to New Orleans.

CLARISSE: *(A beat)* Then I'll take him. *(A beat)* I'd like you to come with me . . .but if you can't . . . *(A beat, she shrugs, not offensively, only simply)* All right?

RICHARD: Look—let's go down to the police station.

(Clarisse nods to Stephen as Richard moves to the door. They exit)

STEPHEN: *(To Clark)* Gimme my pay.

(Clark carefully peels off Stephen's salary. Stephen snaps it from him)

All right—now the next time you talk to old man Foster, you tell him for me that he can take this whole entire diner and ram it up his rosy red rectum. You tell him that for me, will ya?

CLARK: I'll be sure to tell him, Red.

STEPHEN: Yeah, you tell him that and I'll appreciate it. And then you tell him when he's got that digested real good in his intestines that he should ram you right up there after it.

(Stephen, a smile almost attacking his mouth, heads behind the counter to get his stuff together. Clark fires daggers after him, then grabs Cheryl. He looks to Lyle, as if Lyle and he are somehow in it together against Stephen, is about to say something, doesn't, and throws off at Angel)

CLARK: I be back.

(He exits, pushing Cheryl ahead of him. Stephen comes out from behind the counter with his carton of Raleighs and a Playboy magazine. He goes to his stool, smiling at Lyle and Angel as if he has just conquered the world. He stuffs his pockets with his pack of cigarettes and his matches, snaps up a lightweight flannel shirt, and heads for the door)

ANGEL: Stephen!—

(Stephen stops between Lyle and Angel. A beat)

—you take care of yourself now. Okay?

(Stephen doesn't know what to do, though he knows he must do something)

STEPHEN: Don't worry about ole Number One here.

(A beat. Then he walks self-consciously over to her and in lieu of kissing her or hugging her, he kind of mushes her with both hands on the shoulder and tells her)

You just worry about your own self.

(A beat. Then he crosses to Lyle, stops, gives Lyle a little elbow in the chest and says)

So long, suckers. *(And exits)*

ANGEL: G'bye.

(Lyle looks at her but she can't look at him. He starts toward her. As he gets close, Angel moves away from him and back behind the counter. Silence)

LYLE: It's good. He'll be better off.

ANGEL: *(Nodding vigorously)* Oh—I agree.

LYLE: Yep, got himself a real good future in stock if he can get goin with Mizzes Williams.

ANGEL: I'll bet it's a real nice place she's got.

LYLE: Oh yeah—no doubt about that. Ya don't have a restaurant in Baton Rouge where the help wears tuxedos less'n you're runnin a high class establishment.

ANGEL: I'll say. *(Silence)*

LYLE: Welp, guess I better get to cleanin some rooms. *(A beat)* Comin over for TV tonight? Sunday. Got "Bonanza."

ANGEL: Oh, gee, I don't think so, Lyle. I think . . . my mom and me, we had a extra special good one this mornin. Maybe I oughta just go on home and spend the evenin with her and gra'ma.

LYLE: Sure. Sure. No need to explain. *(A beat)* Maybe tomorrow night. *(Angel smiles thinly)* You know you're welcome anytime, kid. Any-time.

ANGEL: Car just pulled into the station, Lyle.

LYLE: Hmm?

ANGEL: A car.

LYLE: Ah.

ANGEL: For gas, it looks like.

LYLE: *(A beat)* Welp . . . see ya at lunch, kid.

(Angel cannot meet his eyes. He stares at her head)

(Quietly, almost inaudibly) Okay, okay . . . I'm comin . . .

(He exits. Angel looks into space, then around the diner. A beat. She moves to Stephen's area, looks at it. She stabs up the remnant of his stale donut in her hand. She looks at it, then tears off a small piece of it and puts it in her mouth. She lifts her head, staring toward the windows, chewing. The lights fade)

THE HEART OUTRIGHT

A Play in Two Acts

For Gilbert Parker

OUT OF AFRICA

~

IN AFRICA I HEARD THE VOICE of Stephen Ryder again after a decade of silence. I'd known since he walked out of that diner that Sunday in 1969, leaving Angel behind with her partially eaten donut in her mouth, that I'd write about him and Angel again. I even knew sometime in the years between that they met in a bus terminal and that they hadn't seen each other or spoke to each other since that Sunday and that it was the occasion of Stephen's mother's funeral. But it was not until I was in Kenya and had been there for some days in that vast silence among all those animals that Stephen began speaking to me about the movies, and what has become *The Heart Outright* really began to happen in the mysterious way that my plays do: exploding suddenly in a moment in which my imagination begins to expand exponentially to accommodate whoever arrives to take up residence in it, usually for years on end, growing and changing, seducing and taunting me like the work itself.

Once upon a time there was an awful movie made of *When You Comin Back, Red Ryder?*, in which people who knew nothing about what really happened to the people in that play forced me into supplying them an ending to that Sunday which was preposterous (Stephen killed Teddy and left town with Angel). If you were one of the eleven people nationwide who saw that movie, know this: It didn't happen that way.

The continuing story of Stephen and Angel is a story about what happens when we yearn to speak and don't have the right voice and yearn to touch but fear we have the hands of lepers. Their story is also about forgiveness and redemption — as it occurs to me everything I'm writing now is. Why, I'm not sure, except that the older

I get the more there is to regret and the greater the need seems to be to come to terms with my humanness. Yet no matter what the pain, no matter how great the regrets and the self-recrimination, I think Yeats's advice to "never give the heart outright" is just plain crazy. Nothing else seems to make much sense at all.

Life after that Sunday in that diner for Stephen Ryder and Angel Childress happened this way. I know.

CHARACTERS

~

STEPHEN RYDER

DICK TURPIN

ANGEL CHILDRESS

RAYMOND FOWLER

THE DIRTY PICTURE MAN

~

The lobby of an old but beautifully restored movie theater, 1976. The popcorn is popping as the audience enters. There's a small but immaculate refreshment stand/ticket counter; a bakery box of cookies and a tray sit on the counter top. The poster window has a rolled-up poster pinned at the top. The display case has cookies in it and a variety of herb teas. There's a pitcher of what appears to be fresh lemonade on top of the soda dispenser.

As the lights come up, **STEPHEN RYDER,** *26, is sweeping dirt toward a dustpan across the floor, his sweeping brisk and meticulous. He has a pony tail, wears black pants and a black shirt, a black concha belt and black boots. He has a prosthetic hand, but works so well with it we might not notice it. Beneath the controlled exterior is a man trying desperately to keep from coming apart.*

He glances at us. Continues sweeping. Glances at us again, takes his watch from his pocket, sets it on the soda dispenser — as if allotting himself only a predetermined amount of time for this. He takes a deep breath — he distrusts us — and though he doesn't seem able or willing to make much eye contact right off, he begins to talk to us, occasionally stopping to clean.

STEPHEN: Right after I dropped outta high school, I worked in this
    diner back home. Fergit I said "home." Where I lived from the
    time I was nine till I made my gitaway at nineteen. Little boil

of a town in southern New Mexico left naked one day when the freeway went around 'er. Foster's Diner—"Steak 'n eggs, our specialty!" Shoot, steak 'n eggs was ever'body's specialty. What I hated more 'n anything then was the what-ya-call your basic custodial work—the scrapin off and cleanin out and sweepin up of a place meant nothin to me, the disposition and disposal of the garbage of other folks' passin through. Strangers—whether I knew 'em or not.

But now I find somethin downright satisfyin bout presentin a spankin clean environment to the folks come to my movie house here for relief and entertainment. There's even a certain art to the way a feller can work with the grain a the wood and the imperfections in the way the original carpenter laid this lumber in 1934.

Lookit here right here, ya see how the grain turns against itself. Ya see? So in order not to lose particles a dust you've swept to this juncture you got to curve your pile this way, then around—follow me here now—and back on course. Come on, little dusties—there ya go—right to your dustpan. Course I could sweep on into the dustpan before I hit that obstruction, that's what some of yawl are thinkin, right?—but then some a the challenge and therefore some a the enjoyment of the sweepin goes out the winder.

(He sweeps the dirt into the dustpan, takes the dustpan to a waste can, dumps it in, carefully tapping the dustpan to remove any lingering particles)

Myself, I like the long sweep of a thousand short strokes. Most of all, though, I like representin somethin other 'n folks' expectations.

(He means us and he stares at us so there's no mistaking that. Something in his eyes, though, gives the impression he's dubious about convincing us he's other than what he appears to be. He heads for the closet, indicates we should come along. He opens the immaculately arranged closet . . .)

How d'ya like this here closet?

(. . . puts the dustpan and broom away and gets Windex and paper towels and starts on the poster window)

Well. When I took over this buildin, it was a pornographic movie house. The winders was painted black, the facade out there was yellow, the floor—this tongue and groove walnut floor without a nail in 'er—was covered with green linoleum. There was no refreshment booth; the men's toilet made the latrines in the army smell like a tulip hothouse.

Hey, wait'll ya see what I've done to the lavatories. And none a that toilet tissue that feels like sandpaper on your nether parts. Yore best quality two-ply tissue in assorted colors. Scented.

How I came to be in the movie house business is when I got outta Nam—lost my hand there, might as well git that said—and they finally booted me outta the rehab hospital in Houston cuz they said I was unrehabilitatable, for some reason I started for that place that wasn't my home in southern New Mexico. Why? You tell me, you're discernin people, you know the minds of us little folks. Nothin back there in New Mexico 'cept the memory of a thousand humiliations, ten thousand stupidities. This hits me here in Austin where I stop at a truck stop out there on the Interstate—steak 'n eggs their speciality, too. So I checked in with the VA and next thing I know I got me a job sweepin up for a Mr. Alfred Goetz that owned a brand new quadriplex—the Video Quad—bout a mile from the University a Texas campus. Now I wasn't at that time wha'cha call real gung-ho bout very awful much. I mean, I'd clean up with the same sorta attitude that most folks—not you folks, I'm sure—but that most folks go bout mosta what they do—which is to say mainly that if ya do it about halfway that's about all anybody expects of anybody anyways anymore.

What I found though was I found that halfway was your basic major pleasant surprise to Mr. Alfred Goetz, cuz I learnt real quick-like that the other folks he had workin at the Quad—the box office manager, Mumbles Rossolini, and the two candy counter girls, Tactless Rita and JuJuBee Apodaca, and the projectionist, Bad Splice Cornelius—that they did things considerably less 'n halfway.

And their main interest as far as efficiency and the treatment a the public was concerned was gittin paid ever' Friday so's they could git broke by ever' Monday.

Give ya an idea what I mean: Four movies, s'posed to start, say, at seven, seven-ten, seven-twenty, seven-thirty—ya follow me? In my first six months there, how many times any one a the four ever started when they was s'posed to was . . . none. No times whatsoever. It was sorta like when folks got around to gittin there and Mumbles felt like tellin Bad Splice to bop on up to the booth they'd start one or another of the movies, usually with the wrong lens on or the pi'ture outta frame, or both. And Tactless Rita and JuJuBee Apodaca didn't give a fiddler's hoot that about maybe halfa your popcorn was unpopped kernels or if the carbonated water and the syrup were mixin in the proper proportions in your soda pop.

And me, hey, I couldn't care less that there was graffiti all over the bathroom walls and boogers stuck up over the urinals in the john where guys picked their noses and wiped the treasure up on the plaster, or that there was a two-inch build-up of sticky stuff on the floor a each a them four theaters.

Was Big Steve Ryder gonna scrape boogers off walls or git in the auditorium there with paint thinner and clean those floors ever' coupla days? Shoot, what the heck for? Nobody cared. Not Mr. Alfred Goetz, who was workin on his hunnerd 'n twelve handicap out at the golf club ever'day; not us that was employed there—shoot, we all saw this as jist a temporary stoppin off place on our way to the presidency of Exxon or some such; and most of all who didn't care was the payin customers that was used to livin in a world where nobody expected nothin to be no better 'n half-assed in the first place. Pardon my language but, doggone it, that's the way I feel.

Well, I woke up one mornin and it wasn't like I had me a vision or nothin—I don't want ya dismissin me as some visionary lunatic; I'm sure you'll figure plenty a other ways to dismiss me, ya gotta mind to—but I looked at myself in the mirror as I found I had to on occasion and I says outloud, I mean I said it right outloud even though I was all by myself in the bathroom. I said, "You suck eggs." And, ya know, it jist felt good, felt right. "You suck eggs. And if ya don't stop, I jist really don't want ya to go on livin." Now, this isn't a new notion, my not wantin to go on livin—I wished for the guts to kill myself or git myself killed before, but what was dif'rent was admittin what the crux a the reason I was wantin to be dead was all about: It wasn't ever'body else I wanted to escape, not the population a the world in general that I'd figured for years was conspirin against me directly, Stephen Ryder—uh-uh, no. I wanted to escape no one or nothin on earth as much as I wanted to escape my own self. Boy howdy, ya think that didn't spin my head round on its stand.

So whudduya do when enlightenment hits? Shoot—join a church—right? And I know, ever'body's rediscoverin religion, but what can I tell ya? I was raised a Lutheran, ya know, but my mom, she wasn't no good at it, my ole man wasn't no good at it, my stepfather, he wasn't no good at it (or nothin else, for that matter), so why would I be any good at it? I wouldn't. Wasn't. But I found myself cravin to have faith and in a particular brand—not an old one with centuries a fairy tales and killin and lunacy to recommend it;

somethin . . . I wanted somethin that'd growed outta my lifetime, that was tryin to deal with what I was and wasn't.

Shoot, you woulda thought I *was* the president a Exxon out to purchase a automobile the way I shopped around. Until I come to the Church a the Causative Yeast. Yeah, go on, git it outta your systems. Yuck-yuck-yuck. They believe ever'thin's gotta rise upward, through fervent faith in the meaningfulness of human effort. Okay, okay, so the real name a the church was the Church a the Twenty-third Century; but the folks, ya see, they had a sense a humor about theirselves and I was in need of a few yucks about then, I'll tell ya. What struck me bout this church is it was made up a all sortsa folks—plumbers, bank tellers, a sanitation truck driver—garbage collector in the old days—coupla lawyers, coupla doctors, buncha teachers from the university and the public schools—and the idea, ya know, was to connect with a higher way of life through dedication to doin wha'cha do as good as ya can. They believed that if ya work as good as ya can at your vocation—whether it was collectin garbage or performin brain surgery—it'd make a difference in the resta your life and in the lives a those folks that your life touched up against. Well, I tell ya, at first it didn't strike me as exactly your basic revolutionary idea, but in this day an age it shore sounded like pie in the sky to me. Doin wha'cha do as good as ya can! What the heck *for?* I'll tell you what for: Cuz I hadda care about somethin or go outta my mind!

I had to git on to *believin* in somethin.

So I did. So I accepted the Church a the Twenty-third Century as my savior and dedicated every fiber of my bein to bein a janitor. I took a knife to the boogers on the walls over the urinals and soap and a sponge to the graffiti and I took paint thinner to the floors of each a them four theaters. And, whudduya know, folks quit stickin to the floors; and to compete with the smell a the thinner, I'd mop at night with soap and water touched with a half a bottle a Aqua Velva. No lie.

And whudduya know, my change in attitude . . . my change in attitude didn't mean doodly-squat to anyone else. Thought I was gonna say lotsa things changed, didn't ya? Uh-uh, no, no, sir: Mumbles and the gang still didn't give a flyin flip. And the folks, the patrons, they still paid outrageous prices for this trash and still threw ever'thin on the floor and rattled their candy wrappers and talked to each other in loud voices, and figured that a lack a punctuality and bein over-charged and sittin in slop was the best a person could hope for, or maybe . . . maybe all they deserved. I mean, hey, maybe the vast majority a the movie-goin public, they had about as much respect for theirselves as I did—previously—for mine.

And then Mr. Alfred Goetz found out what I was doin. At first he was suspicious—who wouldn't be? "Vat gives," he wants to know. "I'm s'posed to clean this place up," I tell him, "so I'm cleanin it." He says, "But you, you're really cleanink it"—he had a sorta wha'cha I guess call your basic Jewish accent—I'm not makin fun a him, that's jist the way he sounded.

And so Mr. Alfred Goetz, he kept your basic close eye on me for pret'near a year. And I went to the church a the Causative Yeast and got fired up ever' Sunday and, believe it or not—and I find it a little difficult m'self—I kept on cleanin better 'n better even though nobody else was workin any different and nobody seemed to appreciate in the least what I was doin. And what else happened is I started in to enjoy the cleanin—never mind that it was the sorta work that any . . . well, that any twenty-six year old, one-handed, half-wit high school drop-out could do.

Well, one night, it was about two A.M. usually when I finished up now—I like cleanin at night 'steada the mornin cuz I didn't like the sticky stuff to harden into Super Glue overnight—he says to me, Mr. Alfred Goetz, when I'm headin out the door, he says, "How come you are vorkink so hard?" "Cuz," I tell him, "it's . . . it's my religion." And he nods at me, like maybe he actually believes what I'm telling him and I start maybe at that moment to really believe it myself so I nod at him and he keeps on noddin and I'm noddin and he's noddin and all of a sudden I'm thinkin: What's goin on here, somethin's goin on—and he says, "You know how much money I'm losink in this place every month?" I say I don't got any idea. Losin money?—I figured he was haulin a suitcase full down to First National ever' week. "Two thousand a month," he says, "I'm losink. Ven I open, I'm needink a tax shelter." He could see by my face I didn't know what the hell he was talkin about. "Never mind," he says—"Now I vould like to be makink some money. My vife may need a surgery, I'm havink two children in the college, I vant to stop losink and start makink." Why was he tellin me? At two A.M.? Quick as I am, I figure there's gotta be a reason, so I say to him . . . Get this, this is unbelievable—I say to him, "I understand, Mr. Goetz." I'm in Siberia, right, but some impulse makes me say: "Can the others,

Mr. Goetz, fire 'em, lemme hire my own help, and I'll turn it around for ya." And he says—to me, to Stephen Ryder that's never been in charge a nothin in his life—he says: "I was hopink you vould say dat, my boy." *(A beat)* And so I became manager a the Video Quad. Steve Ryder. Head Honcho.

I fired Mumbles, Bad Splice, JuJuBee and Tactless Rita. And to take all their places I hired my wife, Lin. Well, not to take all their places. What we did was Lin worked the box office and I took tickets and ran the projection booth and kept on with the custodial work. And we quit sellin food. You heard me. We put up signs explainin to folks that the stuff we sold was over-priced and that what they oughta do is go to the K Mart and buy their own stuff before they came. Mr. Alfred Goetz jist about had a conniption fit, I'm tellin ya— that's the only place he was pullin in any net profit—but I *promised* him word'd git around and folks'd start comin in wagon loads cuz we was runnin an honest and clean game. A class operation. We did this ad campaign: "You don't get ripped off at the Quad—and you don't stick to the floor!" And, hey, we started the movies on time—I mean we started 'em on *time*. And guess what happened? Business went through the roof! Mr. Alfred Goetz startin makin a bundle! His wife had that operation jist in the nicka time! Multiple movie houses all over Texas were callin me to be your basic coupla-hundred-bucks-a-day consultant!

Uh-uh. No-siree-bob. We went right on losin money. More, a course, cuz we weren't chargin folks out the wazoo for colas and popcorn and that other glop, and Mr. Alfred Goetz, ya know, I think he was startin in to hate my lousy guts. But he didn't fire me and, miracle a miracles, I didn't quit.

Took me awhile to figure out what I figured the problem to be. And the way I figured it out is I started watchin the movies. It wasn't too tough then. It ain't just that the general public don't care. It's also the movies themselves. They stink. Okay, okay, maybe they don't all stink, jist mostly, and then a lot of 'em that don't stink don't not stink neither.

And, ya know, the big thing that I figured made most of 'em not any good is that they have ruined sex. Now hear me out. Started in about 1969 when jist about ever' movie that they made hadda have some woman's naked bosoms up there on the screen. I mean, there's no movies for kids anymore. I mean, ever' once in a while there's a PG with jist a lotta cussin and maybe jist a touch a what they call your "brief nudity." It's like a movie ain't worth makin, it don't have any value, unless there's naked lady bosoms in it. But naked lady bosoms, ya see, don't necessarily make a movie good, and there's so many naked-lady-bosom movies around by now, people don't jist go to the movies anymore to see naked lady bosoms. You don't gotta pay four bucks to see a pair on screen. Walk down a street in any town in summer and look for ladies in your tank top T-shirt affair. Go to the topless bars. Go to a nudist beach. Join a motor-cycle club. Git married.

Ya ever wonder how come it's always ladies' private parts? Why's it always naked ladies and the guy gits outta bed in his jockeys or with a towel wrapped around him? How many guys you know really honest-to-Christ sleep in towels? I started to realize it's all really pretty goddamn degradin to women, but course what do I know about who's in charge out there in Hollywood. Five'll git ya ten, though, who's runnin them studios is jist a buncha horny guys with-out any respect for ladies.

Pardon me for philosophizin. Never mind my naked-lady-bosom theory. Mr. Alfred Goetz, he's gittin desperate. So he figures now, he figures if four movies ain't makin money, buy a fifth. Sure. So he buys the town's porno house—this one—and asks guess who to go into partners with him. Well, needless to say, I'm flabbergasted and deeply touched. Till I figure out *why* he wants me to go into partners with him. You think Mr. Alfred Goetz was gonna put his name on a porno house? Are you crazy! "I hef a vife and children," he tells me, who it seems to have slipped his mind is also married and has children. But never mind that—he offers me half the profits to front the business and manage it and quote "to get rid of vut is in my stomach dat *you* are givink me."

My first thought was *what* profits—if the Quad was any indica-tion what we had in store for us. My second thought was that I couldn't possibly git involved in pornography. What about my repu-tation? *What* reputation? Nobody here held me in any esteem; and if anybody back home got wind of it, who'd be surprised? See what come of that little slug, Steve Ryder? Tsk-tsk—much shakin of heads. The only person I didn't wanna embarrass was my mom, but I figured I could keep it from her, and if I couldn't, I'd quit as soon as she found out.

(He seasons the popcorn—garlic salt, cayenne)

Now my wife Lin, though, she wasn't all that thrilled about the thought a me watchin a lotta graphic sex, but I told her American men only find sex attractive when they think it ain't available and that I was for sure positive after a week or so of gittin to look at all I wanted, I'd git bored.

Then too, we were drivin a '52 Plymouth with Hi-Drive that only worked in second gear and had bald tires we couldn't afford to change and our kids rode in that car—because it was the only one we had—and Lin had two outfits—one for church and one for work—and poverty ain't got nothin to recommend it 'cept the anger you're allowed to feel for bein trapped in it.

So Lin stayed at the Quad and I went into the porno game.

I noticed right off, a course, that only men came and that they sneaked in sorta. I mean there are a lotta ways they came to the window—which used to be outside there, so they hadda stand on the street where anybody goin by could recognize 'em. Most of 'em tried to come to the window like they'd made a mistake or they weren't really plannin to come in but somehow they were *ejected* into the buildin. Gee, how'd I git in here? Oh well, shoot, I'm here, might as well see what's playin.

(He pulls the pin and the porno one-sheet rolls down. He pins it at the bottom and closes the glass)

One a the first things I noticed about the porno movies is that they weren't much different from the Hollywood movies in that women really got the short end of it—no pun intended, because the truth is there ain't no short ends in these movies—whoever makes 'em is real careful bout that. But most of 'em are movies bout more than one guy fillin the three major openings in the female body, and bout half the time it ain't done with any great tenderness, I'll tell ya. That first week I learned a lot about how *not* to make love to a woman, although the women in these movies certainly pretend to be enjoyin gettin the stuffin poked out of 'em.

The main feelin I had at the end a my first month in the business is that the men who came were embarrassed to be there and I was embarrassed to be showin 'em what they were embarrassed to be seein. That meant everyone in the building was embarrassed. Except Mr. Alfred Goetz, who wouldn't even come *into* the buildin.

But somethin in me liked watchin those movies, liked watchin all those guys do those women, or one guy gettin done by several women, makin him feel like as how he was really somethin important; somethin in me I'm sure ain't all that healthy liked that, and I started wonderin if that made me all that much dif'rent from mosta those men sittin out there in the dark, that somethin in us that feels the need to degrade women. And I started in to thinkin maybe one a the reasons ever'body was embarrassed to come on in here was because a the way women were bein treated up there on that big screen, and so I decided to only book films that I previewed first and that *seemed,* at least, to be about . . . to be about love.

And I talked Mr. Alfred Goetz into lettin me do some renovatin and pickin up a coupla antiques and gittin 'em refinished. I reminded him that a lotta your houses of ill repute go to great lengths to make your customer feel to home, not like he's some kinda slimewad that all ya want is to git him in here and snake his money. Got the box office inside here now so the customer doesn't hafta stand out there in line on the street where ever'body goin by can look at him and call him a pervert. And I started makin chocolate chip and oatmeal cookies and nutritious sandwiches and fresh lemonade and herb tea. Hey, laugh all ya want. My customers appreciate it and that's what counts.

And here's a little sidelight for ya: Lin and me weren't doin all that great in the sex life department. So one night she come to pick me up after she got off at the Quad and I was previewin a new picture and I asked her to siddown for a minute, it was almost over. And the next thing ya know we were on the very clean floor makin love. We've sorta made it a practice now that Friday nights she comes on in and we watch the preview together. And end up on the very clean floor.

Well, never mind that. Box office, you're wantin to know what was happenin at the box office? What was happenin at the box office was this: Business picked up. Didn't boom right off, but picked up. The place was supportin itself and Mr. Alfred Goetz actually sent me down to the Big "O" Tire Store and told me to charge four new retreads for my Plymouth. But no, business didn't boom . . . it didn't boom till the Church of the Twenty-third Century got into it.

Now the Church of the Twenty-third Century had been real supportive from the minute I took over the Video Quad. I mean those fifty families saw ever'thing I put in those four theaters. They knew

I was a walkin, breathin example of ever'thin we all stood for: that I was doin the most best that I was absolutely capable of and anybody with a pair a eyeballs could see it. But a course, needless to say, their patronage didn't mean a whole lot in the long run; their moral support did.

Well, sir, when I went into the porno business I kept it kinda quiet. Kinda quiet? I kept it absolutely and totally quiet. But when I started in to change how the porno business does business, the local newspaper wanted to do a feature on me. Well, I only been mentioned in the newspaper once before in m'life and that was none too terrific—got held hostage back at the end of the sixties in that diner where I worked out home—but that's another story. Sure, I said to this reporter. Sure, why not, be good for business, let folks know I'm tryin to dignify somethin ain't usually viewed as havin any dignity. Well, this article come out with a big ole photo of me out front here and this King Kong-size headline: THE DIRTY PICTURE MAN—and the next Sunday Lin and me's confronted by the whole church, to which I'd given a lotta credit in the article for helpin gimme the push to try to do what I do the best I can.

(Pickin out one of the laughers in the audience)
What's so damn funny about that, mister? What's so damn funny?

I didn't think it was funny because now the big boys—and lemme emphasize that it was the boys, the men, not the women—the big boys in the church are tellin me—politely, mind ya, all of it couched in various forms of righteous flim-flam and church pride—cause the last thing any of 'em wanna do is insinuate they got anything against me doin what I believe in—but the bottom line they're handin me is they're embarrassed by what I'm doin and by my connection to them. I told 'em I'd resign from the church, that I didn't wanna embarrass them. No! No! We don't want ya to do that! Cries comin from all parts a the church. All right, I said, thank you for your support, I won't quit the church, I love the church, I love comin here ever' Sunday and sittin down with you folks. Much relief among the assembled good people in that good and proper place. But, I says, I won't, I will not give up what I'm doin out there in that other world neither, cuz yawl gave me the strength to go to it and, folks, I ain't got nothin else.

So I quit the church. *So I quit the damn church. So I quit the goddamn church!* Not officially, no letter to the board. I jist quit attendin. . . . And nobody called or come by to find out why we weren't attendin anymore. Ah but, shoot, it don't matter what they thinka me anymore 'n matters what you thinka me. I dress for me, I work for me, and it jist don't matter a tinker's damn what you or them . . .

(A beat. He's a man alone, cut off. He goes behind the counter, opens the bakery box and angrily puts the cookies on a tray and into the case)

Anyhow, word about what happened got around and actually helped business, I think. Yes, I do. Coupla fellas kinda whispered to me over the concession counter there, said to me, "Hey, Mr. Ryder, they can't do that to you; no sir, I'm gonna come *twice* this week."

My church now, I guess you could say, my friends, are the repeaters, the men who come to see my movies and eat my popcorn and cookies and drink my lemonade and herb tea ever' time I change the program. The repeaters, some of 'em, they've even takin to speakin to me — you bet they do — no names yet and no conversation's gonna satisfy the soul's ultimate longin, but we speak, damn it, and that's somethin. It's somethin. And, shoot, I don't know what my soul's ultimate longin'd be anyhow, even if someone got around to askin.

Lord, things can all go to hell in such a little minute. Seems like ever' time ya think ya got a handle on your life, some coupla cogs gotta catch and jam and chew up half the wheels and wires allowin the mechanism to function, and ya start in to hate and ya git so fulla pus and venom ya just wanna . . . ya wanna hurt someone. I miss that church, those gatherins, those sermons, that — what was the phrase this one fella used — that "unanimity of purpose."

Been thinkin a lot lately about the butts in and the boogers over the urinals in the men's room. Maybe even some of you fellas prob'ly noticed that wherever ya go — it ain't just places populated by guys like me — doesn't matter how fancy a place it is, ya find butts *in* and boogers *over* the urinals in the men's room. What is it, ya figure, about men, about the way in our secret insides we really see ourselves? Is it we need help — men? Is it that we don't know it, or that we jist can't admit it to anyone, mostly includin our own selves, and so we . . . so we flick our butts in urinals and urinate on what's jist been there in our mouths and stick our fingers up our noses while we're standin facin a wall with our apparatus clutched in our fists and then wipe what's up there on a wall for the next fella that wants to do

the same thing to see 'n to know, maybe, that there's other men in
the world feelin the same things about theirselves he is?

Or do we do it so someone'll have to clean it up, so some man,
or better yet, some woman'll have to degrade themself by pickin those
butts outta there and scrapin those crustations off the wall? Lord
God—men! We're s'posed to head families, lead nations and churches,
be heroes to children and wives and girlfriends. Be other 'n what
we, most of us, are.

Boys like me grew up thinkin we were gonna be big men, but
there was Nam and women's lib and all those assassinations and,
Lord, so much awful stuff the last coupla decades that maybe we're
just feelin powerless against the world. Maybe I do know why they
don't show men's private parts in all those naked-lady-bosom movies:
In their hearts, the what ya call your unconscious mind, the fellas
makin them films don't know they're showin us what we won't
admit: that somewheres back there in our brains, we don't believe
we *have* private parts no more.

(A beat. Stares at us, seems to return to us from a great distance)

Aw shoot—look, I'm sorry if I got carried away there . . . Lord, lookit
the time, ten A.M., I gotta open the box office. Lookit there, see,
there's a couple fellas loiterin across the street there, pretendin to
winder shop till they can slip on in here for relief from out there.

(He goes to the "door")

Fellas! Hey—mornin! Come on over! I'm open!

*(He puts his coffee mug away, makes sure everything's in readiness, comes
back at us)*

Tell ya what. It scares the unholy hell outta me but I told my wife
Lin I'm gonna do somethin one a these days right soon as I git m'self
worked up to it. Some afternoon I'm gonna pretend the film breaks
and while we're waitin for it to get spliced, I'm gonna offer ever'-
body fresh lemonade or an herb tea on the house and I'm gonna find
the courage to visit with them about what they think it's all about—
them, me—bring up the whole subject of butts in the urinals and
crustations on the walls and what's wrong with us fellas that maybe
just oughtn'ta be left here in mystery and anger and silence in the
darkness a that room. Maybe if I try to be honest, so will they. Lin
says I'm crazy, I'll never ask and even if I do, they'll never answer.

But who knows—I figure I gotta try.

Hey, nice to see ya again, good buddies! You're lookin good! What'll it be—the usual?

(He goes behind the counter, reaches for a popcorn box, but looks once more at us)

Film'll be startin in coupla ten minutes here, any of yawl care to join us.

(BLACKOUT)

TERMINAL

~

Four years later—1980.

A small town bus station in southern New Mexico. Soft drink machine; glass case with sandwiches, gum, candy bars; a jukebox. Door to "Rest Rooms." An exit behind the counter leads to the freight and baggage hold. There's a front door and a door to the buses. A large funeral arrangement stands on one of the benches. A valpack of moderate quality sits on the floor beside the flowers with a bookbag. It's nine-forty-four in the evening. On the phone behind the counter and, at the same time punching out a ticket, is **DICK TURPIN, 33.** *He has an old, weathered newspaper article in hand.*

DICK: How do I know it's him? How do I know it's him? I did a blood test on him, whudduya think? Who's been carryin a newspaper article round with his pi'ture on it for practically half his life? He hasn't been here for near eleven years, and now I got him right here! . . . Hold it, hold it, make sure I don't do what to him? . . . I ain't gonna bother the only hero this stinkin little sinkhole's ever had, Aunt Float. I'm gonna read him the article I saved and then I'm gonna git him to sign it, Aunt Float. You had any sense, you'd git your flabby ole butt down here and

say how-do. . . . Oh! Oh, you don't care to say how-do to a real
live American hero — cuz you meet so many heroes sittin on your
porch with your head up your ass, right, so what's another one
to you? Aunt Float, you say that one more time and I'm gonna
come home and rip your saggy ole titties off your ribs!

*(STEPHEN RYDER, 30, clean shaven, his hair styled, dressed in boots
and a western suit, enters from the "Rest Rooms." Dick whispers into
the phone)*

I ain't gonna bother him, I promise, I promise! 'Kay, bye.

*(He fires a couple of quick little kisses into the phone and hangs up, to
focus on the very distant and distracted Stephen. He holds the ticket out
to him)*

There ya go, bud. *(He whistles. When Stephen doesn't respond)*

Yo, buddy boy . . . !

STEPHEN: *(Taking the ticket)* Thank you.

DICK: That bus is runnin bout an hour late — guess we got ourselves
a wait.

(Stephen nods, wanders over to the jukebox, begins to peruse the selections)

Well, I'll be darn — nooo. Say, ain't you Steve Ryder?

(Stephen doesn't appear to hear)

Yo, bud . . . !

(Stephen turns)

You got trouble in your elementary canal ya don't hear a hunnerd percent?

STEPHEN: No, sorry.

DICK: You wouldn't happen to be Steve Ryder what rescued all them
folks over to the diner here coupla eleven years ago? *(A beat)*

STEPHEN: Yeah, I'm Steve Ryder.

DICK: No. Steve?

STEPHEN: Yeah.

DICK: Well, I'll be darned. I don't believe it! It's me — Dick!

STEPHEN: Well, Dick . . . !

DICK: Dickie!

STEPHEN: Well, I'll be darned.

DICK: Turpin.

STEPHEN: Well, I'll be — Dickie Turpin, how are ya, fella?

DICK: Oh great — ya don't remember me.

STEPHEN: No, I don't guess I do.

DICK: You're kiddin. Tenth grade geometry.

STEPHEN: Don't believe I took geometry, Dick.

DICK: Course — algebra!

STEPHEN: Dick Turpin, sure — Miss Sandoval's algebra class.

DICK: Who? No!

STEPHEN: Believe I had Miss Sandoval for algebra.

DICK: Like hell ya did. No — think!

STEPHEN: Listen, Dick, I'm tryin bout as hard as I can to be accommodatin here. I don't remember ya, I'm sorry.

DICK: Aw, sure, Steve. Oh, hey, your mommy died.

STEPHEN: Yeah, she did.

DICK: Yeah, darn sweet lady, your mommy. Waited on me I bet a hunnerd times there in the little Post Office over to the Piggly Wiggly. I bet me 'n Aunt Float was her best customers on your commemorative stamps. 'Member Aunt Float? Hey, we'd sure like to show ya our collection sometime ya got a minute.

STEPHEN: I'd like that, Dickie.

DICK: And I bet your momma was one a the fastest checkers in the whole Southwest. When she was checkin folks out on that Express Lane, *that* was an Express Lane. Ya *would?*

STEPHEN: Would what?

DICK: Like to see our stamp collection?

STEPHEN: Oh . . .

DICK: 'Cause I can have Aunt Float bring it over in three minutes.

STEPHEN: . . . hey, I wouldn't wanna put her to any bother now, Dickie.

DICK: Are you kiddin? Show the only hero this stinkin little sink-hole ever had your stamp collection a bother? Git serious, son.

(As he dials . . .)

STEPHEN: Listen, Dickie, do me a favor, would ya?

DICK: You bet, name it. Doin you a favor'd be my honor, Steve.

STEPHEN: Let's not talk a lot about that diner business, whudduya say?

DICK: Oh, sure, Steve, hey, I understand. Be lunatics climbin all over ya for pi'tures, autographs.

(The line's busy at Aunt Float's)

Git off the phone, nipplenose! . . . Been a long time, Steverino.

STEPHEN: Yes it has, Dick.

DICK: Since that Sunday, bud. Course I didn't exactly see ya that Sunday. I mean I tried to—don't think I didn't—but them high rankin law enforcement officials had ya how they say *in communicado* and then you were gone 'fore nightfall.

STEPHEN: Listen, Dickie, I hope ya won't think me impolite but I got me a book I gotta finish readin before Monday mornin, so . . .

(He has the book out—Herzog, by Saul Bellows—and indicates he'd like to sit and read. Dick dials again)

DICK: *Herzog,* oh that's a fine book, helluva fine book, yeah.

(Into phone) Aunt Float, listen up now, dumbo. A certain party what's got a bus to catch in bout an hour wants to see our com-memorative stamp collection.

STEPHEN: Excuse me, Dick . . .

DICK: . . . I didn't twist nobody's arm.

STEPHEN: . . . but I really don't think . . .

DICK: He wants to see 'em, shitface, and you're gonna bring 'em down or I'm gonna . . .

(Dick has waved Stephen off and disappeared into the freight hold, from where we hear only his voice . . .)

Aw, please, Float, c'mon, please. . . . You stink, Aunt Float, you stink, I hate your lousy, rotten Nazi guts!

(Off-stage, he slams the receiver down on the cradle three or four times. A beat. Then he appears smiling from the freight hold)

She'd love to bring 'em on down but she's crochetin a canoe or something—I don't know, she thinks I'm botherin ya. She's old, ya know, had diarrhea for about thirty years, she doesn't really give a damn about anything 'cept takin about forty dumps a day.

STEPHEN: Fact is, Dick, I'm really not all that keen on lookin at stamps today—ya know, with buryin my mom 'n all.

DICK: Oh hell, hey, I understand—I got dead people clutterin up my family all over the place, even bout half the ones are supposed to be alive.

(Stephen tries to disappear into his book as Dick accidentally on purpose flips the yellowed newspaper article out of his shirt pocket and onto the floor where he "discovers" it. He "reads" most of the article from memory)

What the hell's that? Well, whudduya know—lookit here what I found. "*Las Cruces Sun-News,* June 16, 1969. A former Vietnam veteran, Theodore Franklin, what wounded one man and held the man's wife, a concert violinist, and three local citizens hostage for more than three hours yesterday over to Foster's Diner, was shot to death following a high speed chase on the Interstate just north of Hatch."

(Stephen becomes helplessly mesmerized)

DICK: So on and so forth—who else was there, what sorta awful things the fella was doin to folks, how he was scarin the crap outta everybody and then . . . here we go: "Miss Angel Childress reported that Franklin left after young Ryder attempted to free the hostages by rushing the terrorist with a butcher knife, nearly losing his own life for his heroics. 'The man threw Stephen to the floor,' a badly shaken Miss Childress reported, 'and stuck his gun right in Stephen's mouth. But something in Stephen's heroic act made the man quit, made him leave, and let us be. I think he'da killed us all if not for Stephen.' "

(A beat. Stephen far away)

I'da give bout sixty bucks to've been out there with ya that Sunday, buddy. You 'n me. I was still liftin then. Kicked some ole boy's tail down to the Mambo Club just the night before. You 'n me are legends in this county, son. Monument downtown prob'ly when we go out the shoot, fists on hips like this — lookee here — flexin our lats. Huh, whudduya think?

STEPHEN: Yeah, we'da been a pair, Dickie. 'Nother set a good lats woulda been a big help that day.

DICK: You still liftin, guy?

STEPHEN: No. Matter of fact, I never did lift, Dickie.

DICK: What? C'mon, you used to come on down with me coupla times a week, work out on the Universal.

STEPHEN: No, fact is I never lifted, Dickie.

DICK: *The hell you didn't!* See, when folks said to me how amazin it was how ya whupped that demented fool when ever'body was sayin how fatigued ya most prob'ly was from stuffin your wienie in poontang the night before, I said ya crushed that ole boy's nads like pecans cuz you was down to the gymnasium with *me* workin out on the Universal.

STEPHEN: *(At the sandwich/candy case)* You recommend any a these sandwiches, Dick?

DICK: Stevie, in good conscience I sure can't. Tell ya sompin, buddy, listen to me, hey: You're lucky your mommy went fast. Mine, she hung on like snot to a lamp post.

STEPHEN: Who said mine went fast?

DICK: Heard she did — heart attack — bang! — right out the ole shoot.

STEPHEN: No.

DICK: Oh. Heard she did — bang and out the ole . . . you feel like talkin? Find lotta folks gits relief sharin their troubles with ole Dick. I mean, I know you don't never hardly ever get your basic hero spillin their innermost guts, but the way I figure it, most of ya'd prob'ly'd *like* to. *(When Stephen doesn't answer)* You care to comment on that, Steve?

STEPHEN: Gee, that's a nice offer, Dickie, it sure is, but what I think I'll do is I think I'll just slip on into the men's room here and see if I can't git my thoughts together and then come on out and have me one a these ham and Americans on a roll here.

(Stephen tries to hand Dick money. Phone rings)

DICK: Are you kidding — that samidge is on the house, Steve.

(Answering phone as Stephen goes into "Rest Rooms")

Hold, please!

(Dick hurries to the "Rest Rooms" door, calls after Stephen)

Steve, it ain't nothin I said, is it?

STEPHEN: No, no it's nothin you said, Dickie.

DICK: Okay, thanks!

(He selects a sandwich for Stephen on the way back to the phone)

DICK: Y'ello — Terminal, Dick Turpin, Night Manager on the horn — kin I help ya? . . . Hold on, I'll check 'er out for ya. Hang tough — right back, buddy.

*(He arranges the sandwich ever so nicely on his hat for Stephen and disappears into the freight hold . . . as **ANGEL CHILDRESS**, 32, runs in. She's somewhat overweight and looks just slightly thrown together. Sensing she's missed who she's looking for, she looks out the back door and around the terminal, almost on the edge of panic)*

ANGEL: Oh, shoot! Dang!

(She's about to leave when she sees Stephen's valpack, checks the name tag on it and takes a hasty look in her compact mirror as Stephen comes out of the bathroom and looks out the back door)

Hi.

STEPHEN: How're you, ma'am?

ANGEL: "Ma'am"? Gee, God, has it been that long?

(The voice hits him smartly)

STEPHEN: Oh my God, it's "This Is Your Life," Steve Ryder.

ANGEL: . . . Stephen Ryder.

(He turns to her)

ANGEL: I got to your ma's house and they said you'd left for the terminal, and I went chargin out and forgot all I hadda do was pile in my damn car and bust on over here. Lord, I'm sorry bout your momma. You okay?

STEPHEN: Oh yeah. So you forgot your car?

ANGEL: Can you believe that?

STEPHEN: Yeah.

ANGEL: I was afraid I'd miss ya. I ran all the way.

STEPHEN: I can tell.

ANGEL: Listen, I was gonna be at the funeral, but I had a sudden emergency. And then I got a speedin ticket; but course if I hadn't a been speedin I probably woulda . . . boy, I oughta shut up, I don't know what I'm sayin.

(A beat. They stare at each other)

STEPHEN: Ya look good.

ANGEL: "Fit." I look "fit" — that's the polite way of sayin I look just the same. *You* look good. Look at you. You changed your hair. You don't have the ducktail and all that Brylcream anymore.

STEPHEN: Yeah, I've made a serious commitment to the dry look these days. *(A beat)*

ANGEL: So this is what Stephen Ryder looks like at thirty years old.

STEPHEN: Yeah.

ANGEL: My my.

(She starts for him, her arms coming up to embrace him . . . but though he starts instinctively to raise his arms, he ends up offering his hand and out of the confusion they laugh and manage to shake hands. The closeness, still, is too much for him and . . .)

STEPHEN: Ya know, I got me a bus to catch here, coupla minutes now.

ANGEL: Oh sure, hey, I understand.

STEPHEN: I mean, not that there's a whole lotta preparation necessary to gettin on a bus.

ANGEL: Yeah.

STEPHEN: How bout a sandwich—I was just gonna have me a ham and American on a roll here.

ANGEL: No, no, nothing for me, please.

STEPHEN: Like some chewin gum? They got Big Red.

ANGEL: No, nothin for me, really.

(Dick returns to the phone)

DICK: Ain't got 'er yet, buddy . . . you bet—'n you have a good night too now, ya hear.

(He hangs up, puts his hat on in order to properly serve Angel)

May I be of service, ma'am?

ANGEL: Oh no, I'm with him.

(Dick is not pleased to hear that)

STEPHEN: *(To Angel)* Well, siddown.

ANGEL: Are you sure?

STEPHEN: Well, sure I'm sure.

(They sit on separate benches)

DICK: You want some mayo, Steve, she'd go right good with that ham and American?

STEPHEN: No thanks, Dickie—this'll do 'er just fine, thanks.

DICK: How bout some Arby's barbecue sauce—I got a little squeezer pack a that too.

STEPHEN: No thanks, Dickie.

DICK: Okay.

ANGEL: Well, it surely appears you're doin right well for yourself, cowboy. We hear tell you went into the motion pi'ture business coupla six years ago.

STEPHEN: There's my mom, tellin folks things that's just accurate enough not to be downright lies. Makes it sound like I'm out to Hollywood drivin me a big ole Mercedes down to Sardi's ever' noontime. I went into the motion pi'ture *house* business bout six years ago.

ANGEL: Well, that's still pretty awfully impressive, I'd say. Course, you used to swear that when you got shed a that short order job in that diner, you were never workin for anybody but Number One again.

STEPHEN: Yeah.

ANGEL: So, tell me, you still takin ever'body's money at bowlin alleys all over creation?

STEPHEN: Haven't rolled a frame since I left here.

ANGEL: No! Stephen, you were so good, though.

DICK: *"Good?"* You were primo, son! Hey, I was there the night you bowled that turkey gizzard from Chamberino. Won eight bucks on ya. Huh—yeah, you 'member me now, don'cha? Guy my size wore a John Deere hat round backwards like this, bill turned up. Sure—that was *me*.

STEPHEN: Well I'll be—sure, I remember you real well now, Dickie, I do.

DICK: *(Knowing a lie when he hears one)* Yeah. . . . I gotta label me some freight. You gimme a holler anyone comes in, that wouldn't be askin too much of a hotshot Hollywood pro-ducer.

STEPHEN: Be glad to do that for ya, Dickie.

DICK: Uh-huh. Ever' damn Hollywood producer we had in here thinks he's King Shit a the highways. *(To Angel)* I been carryin this newspaper article about him for eleven damn years. You think I was doin that for my health or what?

(Mouthing to Stephen behind Angel's back)

Get her outta here so we can talk!

(Dick exits into the freight hold)

ANGEL: Lord a'mighty—Dickie Turpin?

STEPHEN: Who is that guy?

ANGEL: Oh, you musta heard the story. When he was in eighth grade, his daddy busted him up one day and he stole a neighbor's pick-'em-up truck and went highballin down the old highway toward El Paso—

DICK: *(Entering)* Don't you be talkin bout me now! Don't you do that! . . . Okay?

STEPHEN: Sure, Dickie.

ANGEL: We won't.

DICK: Okay. Cuz I can hear back here if I wanna. I got a secret intercom system.

(He does something "secret" to the phone and exits)

ANGEL: What's that article's he's been carryin around for eleven years? Not somethin about—

STEPHEN: Nothin, I don't know, forget it.

ANGEL: I was just wonderin if it had somethin to do with us out at that diner that—

STEPHEN: I said forget it!

ANGEL: Sure, Stephen.

STEPHEN: Appreciate it, thank you.

ANGEL: See, I'm already gettin on your nerves. Should I shut up? I should shut up. Should I? Please say no—I got about a million questions.

STEPHEN: But then that'll be all, right—after the first million?

ANGEL: Promise.

STEPHEN: Shoot.

ANGEL: So ya give up bowlin. Whudduya do for fun? Go to those charity golf tournaments and attend world film premieres?

STEPHEN: Oh yeah, yeah I can hardly get to work or any of my classes cuz a all those golf tournaments and premieres.

ANGEL: Classes? College, ya mean? You're goin to college?

STEPHEN: My business partner hassled me into startin night classes out at the university bout four years ago. He's payin for it, I figured what the hell. 'Nother fifteen, twenty years I'll have my degree.

ANGEL: So, what're ya takin, business administration?

STEPHEN: I think that's what Mr. Alfred Goetz had in mind, but somehow I took me a wrong fork in the registration line and started takin courses in comparative religion and phee-losophy and contemporary lit'rature.

ANGEL: La de da! Ya like it?

STEPHEN: Oh. I love it! All that existentialist dread and angst. I love bein confused and depressed all the time.

ANGEL: So why d'ya keep doin it?

STEPHEN: After four years of it I'm sorta like a junkie, can't seem to kick the cravin.

ANGEL: Well, I'm sure impressed.

STEPHEN: Well, I hope so.

ANGEL: So, hey, ya still smokin Raleigh cigarettes?

STEPHEN: Na, as a matter of fact, give 'em up the day I started out to the college. Figured if I was gonna be confused and depressed the resta my life, I oughta at least drag it out as long as possible.

ANGEL: Oh, Stephen, that's so good. I'll bet you feel a million times better.

STEPHEN: Actually I don't. I miss 'em bout every thirty minutes ever' day since I give 'em up.

ANGEL: Well, I'll bet your food tastes a lot better.

STEPHEN: Nope.

ANGEL: You used to collect the coupons, remember?

STEPHEN: Yeah . . . I remember.

ANGEL: And I used to fantasize—delude myself—that you were savin 'em up to git me somethin. Boy, was I smitten with you back then. My my.

STEPHEN: *(Crowded, frightened)* Yo, Dick, what's the story on that bus—ya got an update on 'er?

DICK: *(Entering)* 'Fraid not, Steve. But you can bet she's streakin through the night fast as the constitution of the land allows.

ANGEL: Stephen, hey, I'm sorry . . . I was just thinkin back about a million years ago—I wouldn't want ya thinkin I was—

*(A large man in his early fifties peeks around the front door, smiling with false conviviality. This is **RAYMOND FOWLER,** Stephen's stepfather)*

RAY: Hey, I bet you thought you was gonna get away.

(He enters)

You didn't sign this. I thought ya told me ya signed it, real estate feller comes fer it and it ain't signed. You musta fergot so I brung it on down.

ANGEL: Hi, Mr. Fowler, how're you?

RAY: Hey.

ANGEL: I used to work out at the Foster's.

RAY: Oh yeah—you're the little girl used to work out at the Foster's.

STEPHEN: Gee, how'd you know that, Ray?

RAY: Hey, I know who she is! How's things out at the diner, April?

ANGEL: I really don't know, Mr. Fowler—it's been gone bout as long as I have.

RAY: That was a damn fine diner. Steak and eggs! Don't git over here that much anymore.

(Ray starts toward Stephen. Sensing trouble, Angel instinctively tries to stop it)

ANGEL: So, how's the house paintin business, Mr. Fowler?

RAY: House paintin business? I don't paint houses no more.

ANGEL: Oh.

RAY: I'm president of the Deming Chamber of Commerce . . .

ANGEL: Oh.

RAY: . . . and I sell Ford automobiles.

ANGEL: Oh well, I didn't know — I'm not all that familiar with what's goin on over in Deming. I sure do like those Ford Broncos yawl sell, though.

RAY: Well, you come on over to Deming, I'll practically give ya one.

ANGEL: Oh no, I like what I'm drivin just fine, thanks, but the next time —

RAY: *(Dismissing her)* Well, that's fine. Good to see ya.

(Moving to Stephen) Got a writin implement right here, Stevie.

STEPHEN: I said I'd think about signin it, Ray.

RAY: But I can't sell it if ya don't sign it.

STEPHEN: I don't know yet if I want my momma's house sold.

RAY: You want it to sit here vacant? I ain't commutin from Deming to live in it, son, and I don't need me a second home in this little dustbowl of a town. I want me a second home, I git me one in Honolulu or Miami Beach. Sign right here, Stevie, and Century 21'll have a check in the mail to ya 'fore the month's out.

STEPHEN: I may wanna turn the house into a museum, Ray.

RAY: Say agin.

ANGEL: He said he may want to turn his mom's house into a museum.

RAY: Museum? What kinda museum?

STEPHEN: To my mom.

RAY: A museum to Ceil Ryder? You gonna make a bundle sellin tickets to that. What the hell kinda museum ya got in mind, boy?

STEPHEN: A museum to just a regular mom and person and wife that had this habit a givin everything to men that weren't worth the cost of their feedin. Men like my daddy and you . . . and me.

RAY: *(To Angel)* Would you go powder your pretty little nose, April.

(Angel moves a short distance away)

RAY: You're signin this paper and I'm sellin that house. You're not screwin me outta my community property. You think I don't got my share comin cuz your momma 'n me separated, but we never divorced, we never divvied up our holdins, and I got half the proceeds from that house comin to me, that's the law in this here state.

STEPHEN: It was her house, Raymond, you never put a dime into it. She owned it when you married her.

RAY: You're signin this, son.

(Ray grabs Stephen's good arm, leads him firmly to the counter, slaps the contract down)

STEPHEN: Raymond, get your hands off me.

DICK: Take him, Steve, crush his nads!

RAY: Sign the paper, son.

STEPHEN: Ray, I said I'm not—

(Dick suddenly shoves Ray away from Stephen)

DICK: Hey! Git your hands offa him!

RAY: Who you think you're shovin, boy?

STEPHEN: Dickie, I can handle this.

DICK: Who do think *you're* shovin, pisswad?

STEPHEN: Just lemme know when you're finished, fellas.

RAY: Whu'chu call me, boy?

DICK: Pisswad, pisswad, I called ya a pisswad. Now you git outta here 'fore I stick my fist up your ass 'n take your tonsils out.

RAY: I think I got me a rubber glove out in the truck we done used on that mama cow this mornin, Dickie, lemme run git 'er.

(Stephen steps between the two men . . .)

STEPHEN: Excuse me, gentlemen. *(. . . takes the contract from Ray's hand, slaps it on the counter and signs it . . .)*

DICK: What're ya doin, Steve? Don't sign that!

(. . . folds it, slaps it in Ray's hand. Ray pockets it without looking at it)

RAY: I'm real sorry bout your momma, Stevie.

(He tips his hat to Angel) April, nice to see ya again, darlin. *(And to Dick)* Nutbag.

(Ray exits. A beat)

DICK: Pisswad. . . . Thought you'd crush his nads, Steve. Huh?

(But Angel gets Dick's attention behind Stephen's back, indicates he shouldn't do this . . .)

Aw, shoot, he's your stepdaddy, ain't he? Can't do a Jose Greco all over your stepdaddy's face, can ya? Shore — that explains it — Well, I got freight to label, so don't be whisperin about me — cuz I can't be checkin up on ya ever' two minutes.

STEPHEN: Look, what about that bus?

DICK: What about it? It's comin. When it gits here, it's here. 'Kay, buddy?

(Dick goes . . . Angel stares at Stephen)

ANGEL: Boy, Ray sure was in a good —

STEPHEN: Don't say anything.

ANGEL: I just mean he seemed —

STEPHEN: You don't understand what's goin on, so I'd appreciate if you didn't say anything.

ANGEL: You want me to go?

STEPHEN: Up to you.

ANGEL: I bet you'd prefer to be alone.

STEPHEN: I said it's up to you.

(She debates, reaches tentatively for her purse)

Siddown.

(She sits. A beat)

I hear you moved to Santa Fe.

ANGEL: Santa Fe? I moved to Albuquerque. Who told you Santa Fe?

STEPHEN: Hell, I don't know. Gonna get me a pop — ya want one?

ANGEL: They got a TAB?

STEPHEN: How about a Diet Dr. Pepper?

ANGEL: I been meanin to try me one a them — why not? You been askin someone where I was livin or what?

STEPHEN: Someone just volunteered it up. "You remember Angel Childress," like as maybe I'da forgot ya. "She's up to Santa Fe now," the person says, "workin for the governor."

ANGEL: The governor? I swear! Folks sure do get other folks' lives fouled up, boy.

STEPHEN: Ain't that the God's truth.

ANGEL: Prob'ly who said it, I bet, was Melodie Sanchez.

STEPHEN: Who?

ANGEL: Stephen Ryder! Only the gal that worked with your mom at the Piggly Wiggly that you was so sweet on all that time I was waitin like a dumb hippo for ya to get me somethin with your Raleigh coupons.

STEPHEN: The checker next to my mom?

ANGEL: "Why, Angel honey, you could get yourself double the number of Oreo Cream Sandwiches for what you're payin for that eensy l'il bag a Pepperidge Farm Mint Milanos."

STEPHEN: Melodie thought I was a contagious disease. She had the good sense not to get close enough to prong me with a fork.

(Distantly to himself)

Melodie. . . . So, whudduya do up in Albuquerque?

ANGEL: What? Oh—I'm an LPN.

STEPHEN: I think I ingested some a that on a sugar cube over in Nam one night.

ANGEL: You did not! Did you take LSD, Stephen Ryder?

STEPHEN: What's an LPN, girl?

ANGEL: A Licensed Practical Nurse.

STEPHEN: No kiddin . . . ?

ANGEL: What'd you think I'd be—a short order cook the resta my life?

STEPHEN: Yeah.

ANGEL: *(Whispering)* Did you take LSD?

STEPHEN: No. So where ya work?

ANGEL: *(Whispering)* What a stupid thing to do! What was it like?

(Dick stares suspiciously at them)

STEPHEN: Incredible.

ANGEL: *(Whispering)* Really good, huh?

STEPHEN: No. Not good at all. . . . So ya work in a hospital?

ANGEL: I did. But now I do private, in-home contracting with geriatrics. Old people.

STEPHEN: Is that what that is—geriatrics—old people? I didn't know that cuz I just stepped off the boat from the Congo.

ANGEL: I figured ya prob'ly knew but I remember ya used to like to make me explain things to ya sometimes that I didn't know if they really needed explainin or you were just teasin me.

STEPHEN: Prob'ly bout eighty-five percent of the time I tried to make ya think I was teasin ya so ya wouldn't know I was some moron that needed mostly everything explained to him.

ANGEL: You weren't a moron, Stephen.

STEPHEN: Bein a nurse makes ya an expert on morons, does it?

ANGEL: Can I tell ya, Stephen—sometimes back then I sure thought you hated my lousy guts.

STEPHEN: Can I tell you that sometimes back then I thought if you asked me one more Childress-type question about my personal private life, I'd choke your eyeballs out, but I never hated your lousy guts.

ANGEL: Well, mosta the time you didn't even look at me when you talked to me. The only time I was sure you were talkin to me was if I was the only other person in the diner.

STEPHEN: That was prob'ly a dead giveaway, wasn't it—if there was nobody else in the place and I appeared to be talkin to somebody.

(Dick comes hurtling in)

DICK: Angel Childress!

ANGEL: You scared me!

DICK: You was out there that Sunday. You was the one ever'body said tried to gentle that feller down when none a the so-called *men* would stand up to him. Ain't that right?

ANGEL: No, that ain't right.

DICK: Yeah it is! I'm back there thinkin, now where'd I know that ole girl from. And then I 'member, and when I 'member I 'member what I heared bout you and them spaghetti dicks out there.

ANGEL: Well, I can't help what you "heared." You prob'ly got so much you-know-what in your ears, you couldn't hear an atom bomb go off in your nose.

DICK: What'd you say?

ANGEL: I said you're about as sensitive as a toilet seat. After what happened to you, the way folks sympathized with you, I'da figure you to be a little more understandin of what Stephen went through that Sunday. For your information, he charged the gentleman with a knife and just about got hisself killed for his troubles.

DICK: I know that! Don't you think I know that!

STEPHEN: Hey!

(Dick and Angel are stopped by the sharpness of his voice)

Do ya think, folks, just maybe it'd be possible to quit talkin bout that Sunday? Whudduya think?

DICK: I could, talk to her.

STEPHEN: Now, Dick, if you don't mind, would you excuse us here now, please.

DICK: You tellin me to leave, Ryder?

STEPHEN: No, Dick, no, I'm just askin ya to —

DICK: Hey, hey, hey! Cuz I'm the manager here, so I hope to God that's not what you're suggestin, Mr. Hostage Cock.

ANGEL: Dickie . . .

DICK: And she called me a terlot seat and said I got doody in m'ears.

STEPHEN: She didn't mean it, Dickie.

ANGEL: Dickie, it's just that day's hard to talk about. And you know what it's like to have a day of the week you'd like to put behind ya and keep there.

DICK: No, I don't know!

ANGEL: *(The peacemaker, walking Dick to the door)* Dickie, you may think it was romantic somehow to get held hostage, but trust me, there are better ways to spend a Sunday mornin. Now that bus's gonna be here any minute and you're gonna wanna have that freight labeled and ready to go, don'cha think?

DICK: *(Whispering)* Get her outta here!

(A beat . . . and Dick looks long and menacingly at Angel and goes off)

ANGEL: Damn crazies ever'where ya look! I'm so tired a bein scared all the time. Ya wanna try to be sympathetic, ya really do, but

ya might as well just go ahead and scream in their crazy faces
and let 'em slit your throat and get it over with.

STEPHEN: Take a hit on that Diet Dr Pepper.

ANGEL: Ya'd like to make it simple 'n say it's because of that awful
war or TV or fluorescent lights, but, Lord, it's prob'ly as many
things as there are folks sufferin, so what're ya s'posed to do about
it? Don't ask me, I don't know!

(She takes a hit on her Diet Dr. Pepper)

Lord, I hate food. I swear I wish I could get that disease, ya know,
where ya puke your guts out if ya touch food and ya weigh about
sixty-two pounds. Lemme give ya your fifty cents back.

STEPHEN: Hey, come on, that was worth fifty cents.

ANGEL: You're so calm—you on tranquilizers or somethin?

STEPHEN: Sleepy Time Herb Tea. *(A beat)*

Hey, so what was this sudden emergency made ya miss my
mom's funeral?

ANGEL: Oh nothin.

STEPHEN: What happened?

ANGEL: Nothin, really.

STEPHEN: Come on.

ANGEL: Are ya sure?

STEPHEN: Sure I'm sure.

ANGEL: Well, I was just gettin ready to leave for the drive down here
and this sweet ole poop I been with nearly a year had a massive
M.I.—heart attack. I accompanied him to the hospital—I didn't
want him to regain consciousness and see strangers all around—
his family doesn't care doodly-squat about him. But he didn't.
Regain consciousness. He just punched on out.

STEPHEN: I'm sorry.

ANGEL: Me too. But ya work with old people, one a the main things
they do, ya know, is they die.

STEPHEN: Yeah.

ANGEL: Hey, Stephen, I'm sorry, I knew I shouldn'ta said that.

STEPHEN: No, it's not that.

ANGEL: What is it?

STEPHEN: Nothin. *(A beat. Disturbed, he turns away)*

ANGEL: So how come ya didn't drive?

STEPHEN: What?

ANGEL: How come ya took the bus on over?

STEPHEN: Oh, car's in the shop.

ANGEL: So, what're ya drivin these days? Chevrolet Corvette Stingray convertible the color a money?

STEPHEN: Little German foreign job.

ANGEL: Ew, they're complicated.

STEPHEN: I think it's some kinda law that if ya only got one automobile and somebody in your family drops dead, the car's required to be in the shop that day.

ANGEL: So tell me, where ya livin—right there in Hollywood or what?

STEPHEN: Austin.

ANGEL: Austin—Texas?

STEPHEN: No—Nicaragua.

ANGEL: Sorry. Just surprised me that . . . gee, well, here ya are livin practically right next door.

STEPHEN: What can I say? I oughta join me one a them penitent churches so I can beat the hell outta myself once a week for not gettin in touch with ya.

ANGEL: Oh, no, I wasn't tryin . . . I wouldn't join one a them churches. My gra'ma was into that—ya won't like it. *(A beat)*

STEPHEN: How is your ole gra'ma?

ANGEL: Well, fact is she beat herself to death. No, I'm sorry, that was just a little joke, I . . . *(A beat)* She did die last summer.

STEPHEN: Oh, always kinda liked her.

ANGEL: Me too, but I'll tell ya, it was relief of Excedrin Headache Number Sixteen for my mom. She's been a new person since.

STEPHEN: She quit chewin tobacco?

ANGEL: She never chewed tobacco, Stephen Ryder. She can't help doin that — it's her bridgework.

STEPHEN: I think you been coverin for her all these years; I think she chews through bout a poucha Red Man ever' second to third day.

ANGEL: She has got a *boy*friend.

STEPHEN: Get out.

ANGEL: She does; and he takes her to a seafood restaurant in El *Paso*.

STEPHEN: I'll bet they catch 'em some fine seafood down in El Paso.

ANGEL: They fly it in, fresh, Stephen. Ever' day.

STEPHEN: That's what they tell the yokels like you from up here.

ANGEL: Uh-uh. It's fresh! . . . Amazin what freedom from obligation to another person can do for someone. Hear all your life that you're obliged to care for folks, care *about* 'em, then ya git shed of 'em or they die and . . .

STEPHEN: . . . ya hate your own rotten guts for bein relieved. How do ya handle livin with dyin? I mean whuddu you do for them old folks? Try to reaffirm their hope of heaven, or what?

ANGEL: I'm afraid I'm not real big on the hope of heaven anymore, Stephen. I just try to let 'em know I care and let 'em know that it's not a crime to be old and loaded down with a buncha parts don't function no more like they're s'posed to. Try 'n make 'em feel loved.

STEPHEN: Yeah, but whudduya put your faith in?

ANGEL: Folks. People, I reckon.

STEPHEN: Are you goddamn nuts! Puttin your faith in other human beins don't get it! Don't kid yourself, girl! We're in this alone. I give it a shot. Drilled me one big dry hole.

ANGEL: What happened, Stephen?

STEPHEN: What happened is what I said: Folks' resolve's got limits! And I ain't wastin no more time puttin my faith in somethin's got human limits.

ANGEL: Love isn't without limits, Stephen, or without end neither.

STEPHEN: Tell that to my mom or to Jesus Christ. They give their hearts outright. Here, take it all, take ever'thin, I'll git more, give ya that too ya need it. But the thing is, them of us that are specialists in the takin, there ain't no way you can *ever* give us enough, we're just gonna keep chewin it up, emptyin out the ole receptacle, wailin for more.

ANGEL: Stephen, you're not like that.

STEPHEN: Whuddu you know about me? Don't you be givin me nothin; don't give me nothin cuz I got nothin to give back!

ANGEL: I didn't ask for nothin.

STEPHEN: No?

ANGEL: No!

STEPHEN: You don't want anything from me?

ANGEL: No!

STEPHEN: Then what're you doin here? No, course not, you never ask for nothin! Cause you can't let anybody give anything to you! That'd scare the crap outta you! You can only give it! Well, give it to somebody else! Don't ya have some worthy soul to give it to? Huh? Sure! Huh—ya got a fella?

ANGEL: What?

STEPHEN: You heard me! Fella, fella, don't ya have a fella?

ANGEL: Well, you know, I date around but nothin serious.

STEPHEN: You oughta get serious with one of 'em. These are your child-bearin years.

ANGEL: I know that, Stephen—God, ya don't hafta tell me that; I am a nurse, for Godsakes, ya know. Just how am I supposed to get serious with some gink you're not serious with? — Why would you say somethin mean like that?

STEPHEN: Cuz I'm a mean S.O.B., okay! Sorry. . . . Hey, you're a nice person, I'm sure ya must go out with some nice fellas.

ANGEL: Sure, Stephen, I'm quite often escorted around town by exactly the type a fella all your magazines and TV shows hold out as the ideal man for the young American career girl. *(A beat)* What about you, cowboy? I'll bet you got lotsa girls, if I know you.

STEPHEN: One.

ANGEL: Just one? Come on now. Serious?

STEPHEN: Yeah.

ANGEL: A steady, huh? Well, the truth is, ya know, Stephen, I really kinda do too, really, Stephen. Dr. Michael Siegel. He's a "fit" young man like me and whenever we get the ole biological urge, ya know, and don't wanna indulge in self-abuse, one of us picks up the ole el telephono and phones the other one up and we stuff ourselves fulla junk food and then stuff ourselves fulla each other. God, I wish there could be another opposite sex that didn't hafta be men! . . . I really oughta get outta here. I mean, this hasn't turned out anything like what I hoped it'd be . . . but the thing is, Stephen, I been waitin for eleven years to say some things to you and I'm afraid if I don't say 'em today, I'll never get 'em said, and I need you to talk back. Now, whudduyou say?

STEPHEN: Well, I reckon you'll just have to start and see if I respond.

ANGEL: You think a lot about that boy that captured us?

STEPHEN: He wasn't no boy, Angel.

ANGEL: That man then. Huh — ya think about him?

STEPHEN: Was a time. You?

ANGEL: Me? Oh no, I rarely think about the gentleman. Just had to go to a head shrinker for two years to get some room in my head to think about anything else.

STEPHEN: Na — hey, don't do that — you handled the whole thing better'n anybody.

ANGEL: Why do you think that, Stephen?

STEPHEN: Tryin so hard to keep him from doin anymore damage 'n he'd already done, you were the best of us.

ANGEL: You really think that, Stephen.

STEPHEN: Wasn't easy for me to accept for a long time, but yeah, I do.

ANGEL: Why wasn't it easy for ya to accept?

STEPHEN: Who knows — I don't know.

ANGEL: Coulda it been all that macho garbage, Stephen? Lord, aren't you tired of all that macho awfulness? Even eighty-year-old men that I gotta wipe their rear ends for 'em, they still gotta keep pretendin that they're real men, that they're on this earth to preserve and protect my virginity when's all they really want, Stephen, is to git through life without bein made to look like some weakling fool that some other fool man humiliated in a bar or out on some football court . . . or in some diner some Sunday mornin. *(A beat)*

STEPHEN: Gonna git me another cola here. You want one?

ANGEL: Why ya gotta keep ever'thin inside, Stephen? Why can't ya ever just say what you're thinkin?

STEPHEN: I told ya I give it a shot.

ANGEL: You know what it feels like — to never just be able to speak the truth with somebody?

STEPHEN: I spoke the truth with some good church folks some years back they nailed me good and permanent.

ANGEL: What'd they do to ya?

STEPHEN: You got one nickel?

ANGEL: Oh sure — I usually got about forty dollars in change in my purse.

STEPHEN: Tell me bout goin to the head shrinker. *(A beat)*

ANGEL: Well, I couldn't stop havin nightmares bout it — humiliatin ever'body like he did. And then I'd wake up screamin when he had you on the floor, that gun in your mouth after you come at him with that knife. Destroyin my mom's beauty rest, ya know, so she made me go. I got about twenty dimes but not one nickel.

STEPHEN: Gimme a dime. What'd he say — the shrink?

ANGEL: Well, Stephen . . . he said my problem is I was a little bit in love with that man and I felt sorry for him and I was punishin myself for not hatin him like I thought I was s'posed to by relivin what happened.

STEPHEN: How come ya felt sorry for him?

ANGEL: I guess all that stuff at the inquest and in the papers after the highway police had killed him — I wished I didn't hafta know all that. I mean, he had children.

STEPHEN: Abandoned 'em. He didn't give a hoot about those babies.

ANGEL: Oh, Stephen, I just know he did. And he was a war hero.

STEPHEN: He wasn't no war hero.

ANGEL: They said he was a captain in one a the most decorated divisions —

STEPHEN: That don't mean *he* was decorated.

ANGEL: But he was a captain though, in one of the —

STEPHEN: But *he* wasn't decorated.

ANGEL: How d'*you* know, Stephen Ryder? You're just jealous! *(Short beat)* I didn't mean that.

(Stephen grabs his bags and heads for the door)

Don't go, Stephen! Please don't go!

(He hurls the bag down, turns on her)

STEPHEN: I checked the son of a bitch out, okay? When I went into the service a my country, I asked around, till I found out.

ANGEL: What'd ya find out?

STEPHEN: Hey, I wouldn't wanna destroy no great romance 'tween folks!

ANGEL: I didn't wanna feel what I did, Stephen!

STEPHEN: Yeah, well it seems he shorted his toaster one day, killed a water buffalo . . . along with the farmer that owned the buffalo, the farmer's wife and three kids. They psychoed him out. *(A beat)*

ANGEL: Was he a nice man before that? A good father and husband before he . . . shorted his toaster?

STEPHEN: Nobody said nothin one way or another where those notions were concerned, Angel . . . *(A beat)* . . . but I bet maybe he was prob'ly. *(A beat)*

ANGEL: We were all sure surprised when ya joined up—havin such a fine draft number 'n all.

STEPHEN: Didn't have much choice.

ANGEL: Cuz ya hadda find out about that fella?

STEPHEN: Hadda find out about young Steve Ryder.

ANGEL: Course. That was stupid of me. What'd ya find out?

STEPHEN: Found out men hate. And they fill their women up with it and together they poison their children. Lord God—men. Keep tellin myself we gotta quit hatin, we gotta give it up; but then I think, Gotta hate somebody, don'cha? And if not your own self, who? *(A beat)*

ANGEL: I wrote ya three letters when ya were over there but then I stopped cuz I guessed ya didn't git 'em.

STEPHEN: Lotta times the mail didn't reach us at the front.

ANGEL: We heard ya were decorated and got a promotion right out there up at the front. Staff Sgt. Stephen Ryder, huh—just like in those John Wayne films.

STEPHEN: Oh yeah, great deal a similarity.

ANGEL: Ever'body was sure proud of ya. Especially your mom. You were a good son, Stephen.

STEPHEN: Whu'chu tryin to pull now?

ANGEL: Whudduya mean?

STEPHEN: Don't be sailin that "good son" bullroar at me. You're sayin that cuz ya know she died alone.

ANGEL: I didn't know that.

STEPHEN: Don'cha think I know what they were all sayin behind my back today: Ten years he ain't been home to see his momma—woman ever'body in this town knows is second cousin to a saint and hadda die alone.

ANGEL: But it was so sudden, Stephen.

STEPHEN: She been gittin eaten from the inside out for mosta two years and you know it! Your mom's terminal, ya come on back a coupla times a month ya only live a day's drive away. I let her die alone, fulla my lies.

ANGEL: No, ya didn't.

STEPHEN: Stop whitewashin me! You were always tryin to clean me up! I got your damn letters over there—I burned 'em! What'd you hafta show up here for? I'm practically out the door, never see this town again the resta my life, and you gotta come puffin in the door! Why?

ANGEL: I guess for me, to say some things I gotta say, Stephen.

STEPHEN: Well, you got somethin to say, say it, get it said and then leave me alone!

ANGEL: All right, Stephen . . .

STEPHEN: Yeah . . . ?

ANGEL: All right: I did fall in love with that man that Sunday mornin. I fell in love with him cuz that man was so strong he changed our lives, Stephen, in just those coupla hours. And I wanted you to be stronger than him. See, my doctor, he said I was so afraid you were the very thing I most didn't want ya to be—just a boy fulla hollow promises and empty dreams—that I wanted ya tested. I told my doctor he was crazy, that that was a mean, terrible thing for him to say; but ya know the most terrible part of it? He was right: I did want ya tested, so I said things that Sunday that made that man pick on ya, that made ya have to try to prove yourself . . . and thank God—or whoever—ya did, ya proved yourself. And I guess what I've been wantin to say all these years is I sorta disbelieved in ya and I'm sorry for doubtin what was in you was really there. *(A beat)* Well, Stephen, it was nice to see you again.

(She embraces him as he stands immobile. She starts for the door, stops)

Ya know, Stephen, even if you're right about people like your mom and there's no end to their willin'ness to give, well nobody's forcin 'em to do it, Stephen. Maybe they do it cause that's what they need to do. Maybe they have just as much right to be what they need to be as you do.

(She turns to go and Dick enters)

DICK: Hold it, Miss Angel Childress! I know what you're thinkin and you're wrong—I said, hold it! Cuz I pay rent, you guys! Don't be thinkin I don't hold up my end. I ain't some damn charity case livin there. I wasn't contributin, my Aunt Float'd be starvin in rags. People in this town respect the way I look after that old mutt. Are you listenin to me?

(Dick grabs Steven's arm and Stephen grabs him back hard; they're locked together a moment, an explosion waiting to happen . . . but Stephen gently presses Dick's arm to his chest and lets him go)

Hell, where'd my damn manners got to? A celebrity that a boy was near to best friends with comes in to avail hisself of a boy's transportation system and the boy don't offer him the hospitality a the house. Take a pulla Dickel, Steverino?

STEPHEN: I don't drink.

DICK: Come on now, bubba, whu'chu tryin to pull—I know you, boy.

STEPHEN: No, you don't know me, Dickie. Not then, not now. Neither of ya knew me. Not then, not now.

(Raymond enters, whacking Angel on the butt in the doorway. He's had a few drinks since we saw him last)

RAY: 'Scuse me, April. *(Spotting the whiskey)* Well well well, what does we have here? Consumin an alcoholic beverage in a public, unlicensed facility. As a member of the county's sheriff's posse, boys, I could make me coupla citizen's arrests here.

DICK: Fella come in here with the bottle a whiskey, Mr. Fowler—I told him there's no drinkin in here, but you know these former heroes here think they—

RAY: Former what?

DICK: Heroes. They think they own the damn world—

RAY: Hero? What hero you talkin about?

(Dick indicates Stephen)

Little Stevie? Where'd you get a notion like that?

DICK: He saved them folks over to the diner bout eleven years ago. I got the article right here if ya wanna—

RAY: Well, I'll agree this country could do with a coupla heroes just now, but Lord help us if we gotta stoop down as far as little Stevie Ryder.

(Stephen goes through the "Rest Rooms" door)

Where you goin?

(Callin through the door)

Good 'n decent woman like your momma havin to put up with a slug like you that wasn't even at her side when she went to her reward—that'd make a decent son get down on his knees and weep for forgiveness.

ANGEL: Why ya doin this, Mr. Fowler?

RAY: Cuz he's bout the farthest thing in the history a the planet from heroism; cuz he's trash.

ANGEL: No sir, he is not. He was a boy in pain—without a daddy, without any man to look up to, who went out and proved himself.

RAY: Sheeit.

ANGEL: You think that was easy, livin in this man's world and not havin one ya could respect enough to drop your drawers and pee on.

RAY: You mind your manners, girl.

ANGEL: You got nothin I need, Mr. Fowler, so you'll get my respect when you earn it, and in the meantime you can just kiss my boheinie.

RAY: Well, darlin, why don't you just slip on into the lavatory there, drop your drawers, and bend over. I'll lather up m'lips and be right with ya.

(At the "Rest Rooms" door)

Got a piece a paper here for ya to sign, Stevie.

ANGEL: You leave him alone! He already signed it!

RAY: Yes indeedy-do, he sure did. Signed it clear as day: Dick M. Nixon. *(A beat)* I'm not a man to be trifled with, Stevie.

DICK: Then don't let him trifle with ya, Mr. Fowler. Come on, let's see ya make him not trifle with ya—

(Stephen storms out of the "Rest Rooms")

STEPHEN: Raymond, you should get down on your knees and thank God every day of your life that my momma gave you food 'n shelter.

RAY: Amen.

STEPHEN: Don't try to take half her house.

RAY: I need the money, Stevie. The el dinero—follow me?

STEPHEN: I can't let you drink my mom's remains away, Raymond.

RAY: I don't think you're listenin to me, boy!

STEPHEN: Raymond, could I speak to you privately?

RAY: You bet.

(Ray winks reassuringly at Angel and steps aside with Stephen)

Well?

STEPHEN: My mom died 'n I just buried her.

RAY: Well, I'm with ya so far.

STEPHEN: I never liked you, Raymond, you weren't a nice man, and you keep on comin at me here tonight, I'll kill ya.

RAY: *(For the "witnesses")* What—you'll do what was that?

STEPHEN: I'll kill ya. I'll end your life.

DICK: Do it, Steve.

RAY: Well, ya know I believe that's some kinda threat.

DICK: Self-defense, buddy, I'm your witness—kill him.

RAY: Boy, you been watchin "Hawaii Five-Oh" too long—

STEPHEN: Raymond! For once in your life, have the grace to keep your mouth shut. You keep on comin at me with this big-man stuff, I'll take the heel of my hand here and faster 'n your eye can follow, I'll drive your nose up into your brain.

RAY: Don't gimme that Vietnam vet karate bullshit!

STEPHEN: I'll do it and I'll plead insanity—cuz ya see, I was psychoed outta the army, it's all down in pen and ink—I'm nuts, I'm not responsible for my actions—ain't a court in the land'll put me away. I'm goin home—this ain't my home—I'm goin there and I'm gonna see me a lawyer; he tells me I gotta sell my mom's house and share the proceeds with you, I'll do it. But not you and every other half-wit redneck in this town with knives and bazookas is gonna make me sign some paper I ain't required to sign. Now get the hell outta here.

RAY: You're goddamn nuts.

STEPHEN: That's what I'm tellin ya.

(Ray appears ready to back off, but then suddenly grabs Stephen, hurls him across the room, and slams him up against the soda machine. He continues to bang him rhythmically during the following as punctuation)

RAY: Now lemme tell you what's gonna happen here, Stevie.

DICK: Don't let him do that to ya, Steve!

RAY: I'm givin you this contract and I'm sendin ya packin. I suggest you satisfy yourself that ya got no recourse by showin it to your lawyer and respondin to me within one week's time. Ya don't, I'll have a duplicate made up, forge your signature, sell the house anyway, and keep ever'thin.

DICK: Self-defense, buddy.

RAY: Sure, come on, Stevie, kill me. Let's see that right hand drive my nose up into my brain faster 'n my eye can follow. C'mon!

(Ray swings Stephen around and turns him loose. A beat . . . and Stephen falls into Ray's arms, clutching Ray—not threateningly but out of some desperation, and a sob escapes him)

STEPHEN: Aw, Raymond. . . . Ray . . . Ray . . . !

RAY: Whu'chu doin? Come on now. Don't be hangin on me here.

(Embarrassed, confused, Ray wears Stephen on himself, and as Stephen continues to cling to him, Ray has to finally peel himself free and prop Stephen up against the counter. He slips the contract into Stephen's jacket, smoothes the jacket in some effort to touch his stepson gently, and picks up the bottle of Dickel)

I'll just take this off your hands, nutbag. . . . I run into any American heroes along the road, I'll be sure to send 'em on over. Yawl take good care.

(He exits. Outside, he hesitates a moment as if he would do something else . . . but can't, doesn't know what or how . . . and disappears)

DICK: How could ya let him do that to ya? . . . I'm talkin to you, Ryder! You . . . you *cried!* How come you didn't do what ya said, what you shoulda, what ya had a right to?

STEPHEN: Gotta respect somebody.

DICK: What? What'd he say?

ANGEL: He said ya gotta respect somebody.

DICK: But not Mr. Fowler. Him! He was the hero. *(To Stephen)* You! You were the goddamn hero! You were the friggin hero! I respected you!

ANGEL: No, Stephen's just a man, Dickie, like you, tryin to make his way.

(Dick blows. He leaps at Angel)

DICK: You shut the hell up!

STEPHEN: Dickie . . . !

(Now he swings around on Stephen)

All right, come on, Ryder, you 'n me, son.

(Stephen gets one of the benches between him and Dick)

STEPHEN: No, now, Dickie, let's not now.

DICK: Let's do.

(Dick pursues Stephen around the bench during the following, throwing several wide and furious punches . . .)

You can't come back here once ever' eleven years like some Hollywood hotshot and cry when I been carryin your article in my wallet half m'stinkin life! Come on, big man!

STEPHEN: Shoot, you used to lift, Dickie—you'd bust me in little pieces.

DICK: You lifted too!

STEPHEN: No, I never did, Dickie.

ANGEL: Stephen bowled, Dickie.

(Dick goes at Angel)

DICK: I know he bowled—

STEPHEN: Dickie!

DICK: *(Turning back on Stephen)* —don'cha think I know that! But he lifted on the sly.

STEPHEN: I didn't mean to offend you in any way, Dickie.

(Dick seems to settle, to resign and calm during the following . . .)

DICK: Okay. But you two comes in here and treats me just like ya used to. Well, it ain't eleven years ago, you ain't no hotshots got locked up with some crazy pendejo made ya famous. I'm somebody too!

(Dick reaches for Stephen. Stephen reaches comfortingly for him in return . . .)

STEPHEN: Course ya are—

(. . . but Dick knees Stephen in the stomach and hurls him against the counter. Angel belts Dick from behind with her purse with all her might)

ANGEL: You cut this out! You just stop this! We're not doing this again!

(Dick rams his head into her stomach, knocking her across the room. He starts after her, but Stephen jumps him. Dick throws Stephen over the bench onto the floor, leaps the bench himself, lands on Stephen, and begins to choke him)

STEPHEN: Don't make me hurt you, Dickie!

DICK: Hurt me! Go ahead! Stomp me! You can't! Cuz you're nothin! You're all lies! You're not even here!

(And now we see that Stephen might have been able to do to Raymond Fowler what he said he could, because in a fluid series of hand-to-hand combat moves, punctuated by a blow to Dick's face with his prosthetic hand, Dick is on his back, his mouth bloodied, and Stephen stands over him in a fighting stance. It's during this that Angel sees the prosthetic hand for the first time. Dick sits up, dazed, wiping blood from his mouth)

DICK: I knew you'd been liftin, you lyin son of a bee!

(Dick wraps his arms around Stephen's legs, hugs them to his face as Stephen takes his handkerchief and wipes Dick's mouth)

That's the hardest punch I ever took, Steve. God, that was a helluva fine punch.

(And now, clutching Stephen's hand to his face . . . he realizes it's not real)

You got you a fake hand. Where'd you get you that fake hand? You lucky son of a bee!

(Dick fondles the hand until Stephen pulls him up and he remembers his duties)

Oh God, I got freight to label—you gimme a holler that bus comes in—gonna be here most any minute.

STEPHEN: I'll give ya a holler soon's she rolls in, Dickie.

DICK: I'll hear it prob'ly—always do—but you holler anyways so's I know you're my buddy that's lookin out for me.

STEPHEN: I will, Dickie.

(Dick goes. A beat)

You all right?

ANGEL: How come I didn't notice it all this time?

STEPHEN: Learned to hide it.

ANGEL: What happened?

STEPHEN: Just a deal that come down in Nam.

ANGEL: Oh.

STEPHEN: Shoot, he got me right in the nose, got it to ticklin. Lord, I hate when ya wanna sneeze and your sneezer don't wanna coop— *(He sneezes)* Ew-wee, that feels grand.

ANGEL: Oh Lord, I just find out a person's got a fake hand, you won't believe what I thought of when you sneezed.

STEPHEN: What's that?

ANGEL: When we were kids, junior high maybe, what Dick Turpin used to do that made ever'body almost barf.

STEPHEN: What was that?

ANGEL: The ole cole slaw sneeze. 'Member? At lunch, like you'd be sittin there across from him and ya wouldn't see him get some slaw between his thumb and index finger, ya know, and then he'd go ah-ah-ah-choo, and let the slaw hang down from his nose.

STEPHEN: Cole slaw! Lord, I never saw that!

ANGEL: Oh, you missed a great moment in local etiquette, I'm tellin ya! *(A beat)* When he was in the eighth grade, his daddy busted him up one day; he stole a pick-'em-up truck and went through a school zone doin about eighty-five. He killed three children. He was so funny and handsome, we thought he'd grow up to be an airline pilot. . . Seems like it was just a coupla weeks, months at the most, we were all of us just funny little kids, fulla the hope of heaven and faith in our own dreams. *(A beat)*

STEPHEN: You're really somethin, ya know that? How can ya do it—give so much to other folks?

ANGEL: I don't.

STEPHEN: Oh yes ya do.

ANGEL: Well, if I do, Stephen, I do it outta fear.

STEPHEN: No, love! That's the difference between us. You give outta love.

ANGEL: You got me mixed up with somebody else, Stephen. I'm afraid for my own self, dyin, that I won't have anyone. Come to me that lotta times I don't care at all, that all I'm doin is I'm accumulatin this vast debt that'll be owed me when I'm old and alone.

STEPHEN: Don't you say that! You just gotta find ya some terrific fella. Ya lookin? Ya can't be hidin out in old folks' homes bein shy. Now, you listen to me. I got me a coupla three friends with a veteran's organization in Albuquerque—I'm gonna give 'em a call and ask 'em if they know some terrific fellas you could get acquainted—

ANGEL: I don't want your charity, for Godsake!

STEPHEN: Then ya gotta ask for what ya want for yourself then! You can't be thinkin bout the other fella all the time. All them folks ya think you're accumulatin that debt with for your old age, they're all gonna be dead; there ain't gonna be one of 'em around to collect from! Ask for your own self one time!

(We hear the bus outside as Angel stares intently at Stephen and he realizes what she's about to ask for "one time")

Yo—Dick! Bus!

(Stephen goes for his bags as Dick enters wheeling freight)

DICK: I heard it, buddy, but thank ya for tellin me.

(Dick goes through and out to the bus. Stephen starts for the door)

ANGEL: Stephen . . . !

(He stops)

My mom and her boyfriend, they went up to Ruidoso for the weekend. . . . Stay the night with me.

STEPHEN: Don't ask me to do that.

ANGEL: You said to ask for myself one time. All right, I'm askin. It's one thing to fear dyin alone in my old age or to see thirty-five comin on and the enda my child-bearin years, but it's somethin else to think I might never lay down with you inside a me.

STEPHEN: Oh, girl, I can't.

ANGEL: You find me repulsive.

STEPHEN: Oh no.

ANGEL: Then stay with me, damn you!

STEPHEN: I can't!

ANGEL: Ya gotta!

STEPHEN: I'm married! *(A beat)* I been married ten years. I got two little girls. *(A beat)*

ANGEL: I didn't know.

STEPHEN: My mom didn't either.

DICK: *(Passing through)* Be a minute here, Steve—little problem with the on-board outhouse.

ANGEL: What's her name—your wife?

STEPHEN: Lin.

ANGEL: Oh. Lynn. That's nice. For Lynette, I bet. No, I bet it's prob'ly Linda.

STEPHEN: No. Just Lin.

ANGEL: Oh, Lynn—sure, it could just be Lynn—don't know why I thought Lynn'd be short for . . .

STEPHEN: It's L-I-N. She's Vietnamese. She worked in the hospital where they took me when I was wounded. I brought her home with me. Her husband'd been killed; they had two little girls.

ANGEL: They're her babies.

STEPHEN: Ours now.

(Dick crosses through with freight again and out)

ANGEL: I'll bet it's a fine marriage.

STEPHEN: No, not particularly. Thing is, ya see, I don't know who it was married her—*that* Stephen Ryder. Don't understand all that much about this one now either, I don't guess, but I know I can't leave her—leastwise not till my two little girls are grown. Bout the only things I've managed not to contaminate in my life—those two little folks.

ANGEL: You never contaminated me, Stephen. That year of seein you ever' mornin in that diner—mean as you could be—those coupla cupsa coffee while we switched shifts—those were the happiest minutes of my life to that time . . . and, I reckon, since. I have remembered you only with love. I loved you, Stephen.

STEPHEN: Ya couldn't.

ANGEL: Oh, but I did. I reckon I still do. Whoever ya are or become flows directly to me. It's like that with some folks.

STEPHEN: Listen to me, girl: If ya knew the truth about me, ya'd hate me.

ANGEL: You stop that, Stephen! You shut that up! You hafta forgive yourself for whatever you imagine you've done; forgive yourself even what ya actually did do.

STEPHEN: Girl, you don't know me!

ANGEL: Then help me get free of ya! What don't I know that I gotta know to hate ya!

STEPHEN: Ya wanna know what ya gotta know?

ANGEL: Yeah, please!

STEPHEN: Okay! Ya know what I do for a livin? I run every pornographic movie theater in Austin, Texas. My little German foreign car is a seven-year-old Volkswagen. And the only reason I was decorated in Nam is they gave me a Purple Heart for blowin my own hand off. I was afraid to die but I had no reason to live. I wanted to kill myself but I didn't have the guts to get it done. So I blew my hand off. Got me psychoed out, got me a medal, let me keep right on lyin, keep right on pretendin I was somethin I wasn't. Ya understand? That Sunday in the diner, I wasn't tryin to kill that fella with that knife to save alla yawl; I was tryin to get him to kill *me* so's I wouldn't hafta be there anymore, so I wouldn't hafta live with the shame a bein shown to be just what I was and what you knew I was. You knew me, you knew all along, just like that fella did, what I was. A coward! I am a coward, I been a coward my whole life long.

ANGEL: Okay, Stephen, so am I supposed to hate ya cuz you're human, cuz there's a limit to what ya can endure? I forgive you for whatever you think ya did to me. I forgive you forever and all time, Stephen. Have mercy, Stephen, on your own good self. For the love a Jesus, the love a your two little babies, the love a anything, Stephen. But somethin. Please. *(A beat)*

STEPHEN: You do the same.

ANGEL: I'll try.

DICK: *(Entering)* Let's roll 'em, Stevo.

(Before Stephen can collect his bags . . .)

Steve, would you sign this here article I been carryin? Would that be possible, to have ya just scribble sompin here on the edge a the paper? Thanks.

(Stephen manages to take the pen Dick offers. He scribbles something on the article, using Dick's back for a desk, his eyes rising several times to Angel . . . and then disappears. The bus pulls away, Dick in the doorway waving it off. Then Dick looks at the inscription)

DICK: Know what he wrote? Huh? Whudduya think?

ANGEL: I don't know, Dickie. "Best wishes"?

DICK: Get serious. "To Dick. Thanks, Steve." *"Thanks,* Steve."

(He fixes Angel)

Ya know, always thought you 'n me oughter been better friends, Angel Childress.

ANGEL: When you had your accident, I thought I tried. . . . But I think I prob'ly didn't try hard enough.

DICK: You was always too busy goin to night clubs. Queen a the Mambo Club, you.

ANGEL: Dickie, in the twenty-two years I lived here regular, I never once went to the Mambo Club.

DICK: Bout time then, I figure.

ANGEL: What?

DICK: How bout tonight? You 'n me—Mambo Club.

ANGEL: Oh, Dickie, gee, that's awfully nice of you—

DICK: Don't say no, okay?

ANGEL: The thing is, I've really gotta be goin.

DICK: One lousy cocktail.

ANGEL: I really have to be goin.

DICK: Not a beer—a goddamn mixed drink! CC and ginger, Black Jack and Coke—name it!

ANGEL: I have to go, Dickie! *(A beat)* Please. *(A beat)*

DICK: You gimme a call next time you're down this parta the state.

ANGEL: Well, I just might do that, Dickie.

DICK: We'll go down to El Sombrero, eat some burritos, drink us some brew.

ANGEL: That sounds very nice, Dickie.

DICK: You gimme call, 'kay?

ANGEL: I sure will try.

DICK: 'Cept ya won't, will ya? *(A beat)*

ANGEL: No, I don't guess I will, Dickie. *(A beat)*

DICK: Be closin up in bout five minutes.

ANGEL: Oh, that's fine since I really hafta git goin anyway.

(Dick comes toward her. She freezes. He goes past to the jukebox and she continues toward the door)

DICK: *Hey* . . . ya know, I always play a song when I'm closin up. Like to hear it when I'm goin down the street, comin through the walls from inside where I do my life's work. *(Handing her a coin)* Here, you pick 'er tonight.

ANGEL: Oh no, I—

DICK: C'mon, pick the song, for chrissake—it don't mean we're engaged or nothin!

(Angel takes the coin)

Don't play no disco, okay? I mean, it's your choice, but *don't.*

(She puts the coin in, makes a selection)

Tell ya how good that boy was. He coulda been bowlin for big bucks on ABC television he hadn't hadda change his whole life to the service a others. "To Dick. *Thanks"* —

(A sweet western instrumental begins)

Oh, great, I hate that song, thanks a lot! Go on, just git outta here, will ya. *Hey, but call me though . . .* ya git a chance.

(As he disappears into the freight hold, we hear quietly one last time . . .)

"*Thanks,* Steve."

(Angel picks up her purse, picks up Stephen's uneaten sandwich, puts it in her purse, looks at the funeral arrangement, picks it up and heads for the door . . . as Stephen walks back in. A beat)

STEPHEN: Ya know, I don't recall that I ever once told her I loved her. Didn't know how. Needed help. My mom, though, she knew how to give it, but not how to get it. Must be a heckuva tough thing to learn to do, ask that somethin be given in return, ya ain't had much practice at it or ya ain't sure ya deserve it. *(A beat)*

ANGEL: Hey, ya know what I was thinkin? Huh?

(He shakes his head)

I was thinkin how I used to dream bout you 'n me dancin. At a real dance. Where they dressed up and there was a theme to the evenin and a lotta clever decorations and the boy gave a corsage. And I thought, I'm gonna take these flowers here and I'm gonna get me a *real* big safety pin and just pin this whole damn thing to my left boob and wear it till the last flower craps out.

(He takes several flowers from the funeral arrangement and holds them out to her. She takes them. Indicating the music . . .)

STEPHEN: This a two-step or a waltz?

ANGEL: Two-step.

STEPHEN: You're darn lucky, girl—that's the only dance I know how
to do.

*(He holds out his hand to her and she takes it. They freeze there a moment
before they come together formally . . . and that before she presses her head
to his shoulder and he presses his head to hers, holding her close, and
they dance, his eyes closed now and hers, as her face comes around the
last time into the light, open.*

*The lights fade, but for the illumination of the jukebox . . . and then that's
gone)*

THE MAJESTIC KID

To My Children
Debra, Rachel, and Jessica
and to
their Mother,
Stephanie,
my Wife

What is the use of being a little boy
if you are to grow up to be a man.
"IDENTITY OF A POEM"
GERTRUDE STEIN

MIDDLE AGE MAN
CONTEMPLATES MAJESTIC KID

~

THE MAJESTIC KID started developing in its current form in 1981 when Ronald Reagan started crowding my fantasies more than I thought I wanted him to. Here was this old cowboy and gridiron hero from my childhood and early adulthood (host of "Death Valley Days") who'd become President of the United States in a decidedly unheroic era, and I began to dwell on how much easier it had been to save the mythical old West and "win one for the Gipper" than it was going to be to save the real world and win one for the ole U.S. of A. In cynical middle age, I was certain that, though we'd finally elected someone out of the mythology of our dreams, he wasn't going to be any more successful than his very pedestrian predecessors, Carter, Ford, and Nixon, and that though we would always recall his mythical proportions, he would, inevitably, end up as a sizable joke.

I also began to realize that the people we refer to out here in New Mexico as the folks out East—basically anyone who lives east of Abilene, Texas, or west of Gallup, New Mexico—that those folks had pretty well finished decimating their parts of the country and were looking omnivorously our way. There was a great deal of speculation about what the folks out East were going to do with all their nuclear and toxic and household waste, the implicit answer being that they were going to ship it in this direction. There is a good bit of ill will developing between those westerners who'd like to make a buck off the easterners and those who want to preserve the sanctity of the land.

I was also haunted by a visit my wife and I made to the Indian city of Acoma, perched atop a mesa west of Albuquerque, at the end of the seventies. The memory of many pairs of tennis shoes on many Indian feet and the image of a Betty Crocker cake mix and a bottle of Gatorade in a resident's window remain vivid to this day. Couple those images with the resort hotel the Mescalero Apaches built and run in Ruidoso, New Mexico (which supposedly has gambling equipment stashed in the basement awaiting the day they convince the courts they're living on sovereign Apache land and have the right to run a gambling den), and I had some interesting paradoxes working about memory and fact, fantasy and reality, misconception and truth.

Then add to all of that the realization that I wasn't living in the sixties and early seventies anymore, when I was an assiduously cranky young writer and freewheeling bachelor, and I sat down to write a comedy about a young man trying to deal with the ideals of masculinity and preferred behavior he'd picked up from the era of the cowboy hero while at the same time trying to live a decent life in Mr. Reagan's solipsistic eighties.

The realization Aaron Weiss, The Majestic Kid, comes to — that he wants to live a "simpler, more graceful way of life" and to dedicate himself to a family — is a mirror of the decision I came to myself as a result of my marriage to my wife Stephanie in 1972 and the arrival in our life together of our children. I realized that I would not only die for my children, but that as a writer I wanted to live for them; that is, I wanted to find something positive to say about the very inhospitable and lunatical world we live in so that life might be more hospitable and less crazy for them.

The lives they live and the world they live it in will be as much a measure of my journey on earth as the written work I leave behind.

Nov. 1, 1988

CHARACTERS

~

WILLIAM S. HART FINLAY

AARON WEISS

AVA JEAN POLLARD

THE LAREDO KID

LISA BELMONDO

TWO GRIPS

Time: Not very long ago.

Place: Out West.

Setting: As the audience enters, an old cowboy movie is playing. There might, in fact, be three projection screens at the back of the set, on which we see appropriate slides throughout (only some of which are suggested in the script).

The playing area should be sparse. In the New York Production, Director Derek Wolshonak used to excellent effect only a road box and a number of small crates. The road box became everything from dining table to bed to hiding place, in addition to being a great place to store and dump unneeded props and costume pieces during quick scene transitions. Derek also made wonderful use of two grips, who helped move the road box and crates, delivered props, but also, along with the other actors not in a particular scene, sat at the edge of the stage throughout and did all necessary crowd, animal, and background sounds.

ACT I

~

*An old cowboy movie plays silently as the audience enters the theatre. Music accompanies the movie. **AARON** enters and watches the end of the movie, as the house lights fade and the play begins. (Slide: "The End")*

AARON: I came here, I think, "out West," because I imagined I could still somehow become who I've wanted to be since I was nine years old, could climb out of the Saturday matinee of my childhood and become at twenty-nine who I was then: The Majestic Kid. Who knew it was possible to help people without hurting other people; a hero who bloodlessly snuffed out injustice wherever it lurked; who could commit his very life, against whatever obstacles, to fulfilling precious ideals. And who inevitably, in the end, preserved and returned to its rightful owner the land . . . What a schmuck, to think I could be like the Laredo Kid—hero, mentor, in a way, father—who inspired and guided that Majestic Kid.

(Laredo Theme music starts)

Oh, second feature's about to start. I think it's a comedy.

*(Slide: "The Majestic Kid." Lights fade to black and in the dark we hear **JUDGE WILLIAM S. HART FINLAY**, a contemporary rancher and Magistrate's Judge, coming at us over a microphone. **AVA JEAN (AJ) POLLARD**, like Aaron, a lawyer sits to Aaron's left. **LISA BELMONDO** sits taking notes on stage right. Slide: "Somewhere in the West")*

BILLY: Thank you, Raymond, that was a salient point; normally I think you can't distinguish 'tween c'mere and sic'em, but that was well taken. Say, Raymond, as Magistrate's Judge a the district, lemme remind you, sir, that sex is a misdemeanor in these parts. The more ya miss, the meaner you're gonna get! *(Suddenly swinging on Lisa)* Don't you go puttin that in the minutes of the meetin now, Leesey!

(Billy enjoys his joke a great deal. AJ points at her watch)

All right, all right, 'fore we adjourn we got us a coupla legal eagles from up on the Apache reservation say they got somethin of importance to communicate to us. Boy here's a Mr. Aaron Weese —

AARON: Weiss.

BILLY: 'Scuse me — Aaron Weiss — that some kinda Italian name? — and his associate, Miss AJ Pollard. Which a yawl has the dubious honor of addressin this buncha rednecks?

(Aaron rises. Billy steps back to shake his hand)

Let's press along, Mr. Weese — mosta these folks is bout twenty minutes overdo for a wet one.

AJ: Take your time, babe.

AARON: *(Quietly, to Billy)* I don't appreciate you trying to embarrass us, Judge.

BILLY: Sonny boy, I was trying to embarrass you, I'd whip your undies down and tie your ding-dong in a knot.

(Billy takes his seat. Aaron turns to audience)

AARON: Good evening, ladies and gentlemen. AJ and I are grateful to you for allowing us to come before the Farm and Ranch Association. Growing up in Chicago, the view we had of the West was one in which life centered around love of and respect for the land, land I know many of your families have farmed and ranched for five generations. But before your land belonged to you it belonged to the Apache, the original settler, the so-called native American, our Indian brother.

(The first stirrings of wariness from Billy. Lisa raptly attentive, no longer taking notes)

BILLY: Excuse me. *(He picks up hat)*

AARON: To look at this valley today, there are no indications of the bloodshed, the greed and avarice, the myriad deceptions and patent illegalities perpetrated by the white man, by—let's be honest—

BILLY: What're you pullin, boy?

AARON: Excuse me, Judge.

AJ: Judge.

AARON: . . . by you and your forebears—to take from the Apache this valley, sacred to them out of a thousand years of myth and memory.

BILLY: Get to the point, Weese.

AARON: We have to restore the original spirit of this nation and live in true brotherhood while there's still time. And so we've come to propose to you a plan in which the valley is shared.

BILLY: Are you crazy? You siddown 'fore I knock you down!

(Aaron stands firm. Grips do agitated crowd noises)

AJ: *(At the audience)* Please, just hear us out! *(To Billy)* Judge, let him finish, please!

(Lisa whispers something to Billy, who then gestures the "crowd" to quiet down)

AARON: We don't want you to think we're threatening you, but if we cannot come to an equitable settlement of land usage, AJ and I have been retained by the Apache Tribal Council to prepare a suit . . .

BILLY: Suit!

AARON: . . . to be filed within six months . . .

BILLY: Boy, you're through. *(He takes the microphone from Aaron)* Night, night, yawl. I'll take care of it. Thanks for comin. See yawl next week.

AJ: Do you know what an imbecile you are, Judge Finlay?

BILLY: Ram it, sister. *(Microphone out)*

AARON: . . . reclaiming this valley
. . . as part . . . of the
Apache . . . nation.

AJ: *(Calling after the "crowd")*
Wait, please! We felt we
owed you the courtesy of
informing you of this
impending action face to
face. At least have the
good grace to . . .

BILLY: Boy, lemme give ya a friendly piece of advice. Listenin? You endeavor to take this valley from us and give it back to the Apache, I for one take no responsibility for what misfortune might befall you.

AJ: Is that a threat?

BILLY: I'm shore yawl both are familiar with this little bit of wisdom from one of the foundin fathers a this republic. Goes like this: "If ya do what ya should not, ya must bear what ya would not." Mr. B. Franklin. You hear me good, cuz I'm hell when I'm well . . . and I ain't never sick. And yessir, *that* is a threat. Leesey, let's go.

(Billy slaps Lisa on the behind as he exits. Lisa lingers a moment beside Aaron. She touches his cheek gently . . . and follows Billy off. Aaron and AJ look after her)

AJ: *(Meaning the touch)* What the hell was that about?

(Aaron shrugs, stares after Lisa. He has a pain in his stomach. AJ gets DiGel out of her briefcase and hands it to Aaron)

All right, we gave them a fair chance. Now we kick ass!

AARON: You kick ass, AJ. All these years talking ass kicking, it seems to me we've yet to discover a group of asses that'll hold still long enough to get really kicked. I'm going on sabbatical, AJ.

AJ: What are you talking about—sabbatical?

AARON: I'm calling time while I give some thought to how best to pass the final forty, fifty years of my life.

AJ: You're not serious.

AARON: Oh, but I am.

AJ: Buster, this might be the last stand. Some of us have got to stand firm.

AARON: Ya know what, AJ—I'll betcha throughout time, people like you and me have tried to convince each other that the last stand was imminent. Yet the world has continued on its dizzy path to this day and nothing has improved.

AJ: That's bullshit, Buster. If some of us don't plant our feet, we're gonna be swept away.

AARON: Maybe that would be best—start over with the paramecium, hope for a better break in the evolutionary cycle next time.

AJ: You're walking out on me, on everything we've committed ourselves to all these years?

AARON: I had this sudden flash out there in front of that lynch mob, AJ, that our commitment to popular causes is a kind of irresponsibility disguised as righteousness because we don't have the guts to live a simpler, more graceful way of life. Time, AJ. Time out.

AJ: I have never been so disappointed in another human being in my life. *(She goes . . .)*

SCENE 2

Aaron focuses on us.

AARON: The Majestic Kid . . . *(raspberry)*

(Sound: The Laredo Theme. The Laredo Kid appears, that black-clad hero of yesteryear, a little overweight and older but splendid nonetheless. Smoke surrounds him)

LAREDO: *(Sings)*

The Laredo Kid, you know
He rides a righteous trail
Bearin all he can
A other folks' travail
Reapin justice and redemption

All along the way
Leavin to the pure of heart
A sweeter, better day.

(Laredo, guitar over his back, comes toward Aaron)

Ride Laredo ride
Ride Laredo ride
Everything will be all right
With Laredo by your side.

(Laredo stands with hands poised over twin pearl-handled six-guns)

LAREDO: Hey, Kid . . . !

(From memory, Aaron goes for his finger but Laredo is much faster. Laredo holsters his guns with panache, pulls the mask across his nose and mouth down. [Unless he's working, he keeps the mask down])

AARON: Laredo!

LAREDO: Howdy, buckaroo!

AARON: What are you doing here?

LAREDO: Ya wished fer me, pard, so here I am.

AARON: But you're gonna hate me.

LAREDO: Hate ya?

AARON: I've grown so far away from the example you set.

LAREDO: Grown away from faith in justice and redemption, from love of the land? Ut—yore teasin yore Laredo, you l'il dickens, you. So, how d'ya like bein out here in the Old West, buckaroo?

AARON: So far it really sucks, Laredo.

LAREDO: The Old West?

AARON: I could sure use some help.

LAREDO: Well, you've come to the right feller. Got anything to eat on ya, pard—popcorn, piece a jerky?

(Aaron fishes a box of Junior Mints from his shirt)

Junior Mints—one a m'favorites. All right, buckaroo, let's git
started. Which a my pi'tures we in here?

*(Lisa enters, sweetly singing "Home On The Range," a rope and halter
over her shoulder. Laredo and Aaron watch her come. Slides: cowgirls)*

Oh—oh yeah, she looks perfect, pard—uh-huh.

AARON: Perfect for what?

LAREDO: The Majestic Kid to the rescue!

AARON: Rescue her from what, Laredo?

LAREDO: Bad fellers, outlaws, bandidos.

AARON: Doesn't seem to be any bad feller to rescue her *from*, though.

LAREDO: Always a bad feller, pard. Otherwise, there wouldn't be
no Laredo Kid, Conqueror of Injustice, Keeper of the American
Spirit.

*(Billy has crept in and toward Lisa stealthily. He is about to bounce.
Slides: Black-hatted "bad guys")*

Ut—what'd I tell ya.

SCENE 3

BILLY: *(Kissing Lisa, trying to capture her)* Giddy-giddy-gotcha!

LISA: Oh my God, you scared me!

BILLY: Godey-godey-gonna-gitcha, m'little bean burrito.

LAREDO: Come on now, lemme see whut you kin do.

AARON: Forget it, I'm on leave of absence from the rescue business,
Laredo.

BILLY: Now I'm gonna slather your toesers with molasses and suck
'em like lollipops.

LAREDO: Lord, pard, do sompin—he's gonna lick her!

(Aaron slaps Billy on the shoulder)

AARON: Excuse me, Judge.

BILLY: *(Turning)* Well well well, if it isn't the ole land grabber. I believe you assaulted me, counselor . . .

AARON: Really? Assault by shoulder tap—

BILLY: . . . so I got a right to defend myself.

(Billy suddenly belts Aaron in the stomach, then bolo punches him behind the ear. Aaron goes down. Lisa kicks Billy in the butt)

LISA: Billy—get outta here!

BILLY: *(To Aaron)* Whatever you do, counselor, don't get it in your head to mess with my Leesey cuz that . . . that would *really* chap my hind end.

LISA: Go on! Git! Scat!

BILLY: *(To Lisa)* I be seein you later, cuz I'm gonna bury my brownie in your fudge sauce tonight.

LISA: No, that part of it's over, Billy.

BILLY: Don't say that, Leesey. I beg ya. Now, I see ya later, okay? You bet.

(Aaron, gasping, tries to rise up, to strike back at Billy . . . but Billy moves just as Aaron manages a feeble, panting lunge and crashes back to a heap on the ground)

SCENE 4

Lisa, on her knees, beside Aaron. (Slides: Out West)

LISA: Ya hurt? Move your hand, lemme see.

LAREDO: Say, pard, the thing is they ain't s'posed to rescue *you*, but t'other way around.

AARON: I knew something was wrong.

LISA: Nasty hematoma behind your ear. Lemme press this here. *(She takes off her bandana, presses it behind his ear)*

AARON: Laredo, can I get away with this?

LAREDO: Well, shoot, she's the gal, it's her job to look after the hero when he gits bushwacked by some drifter.

AARON: That wasn't some drifter. That's William S. Hart Finlay. Largest landowner in the valley and trying to become the *only* landowner in the valley. He's also the Magistrate's Judge of this district.

LAREDO: Big landowner who's a judge, huh . . . ?

AARON: *(To Lisa)* Attend a lot of beatings, do ya?

LISA: Only when it's some pilgrim way out of his depth.

AARON: Why'd you touch my cheek the other night?

LISA: I had the feeling I knew you from another life.

AARON: Another life?

LISA: Samsara. Are you familiar with Samsara?

AARON: Actually, I think I had lunch there yesterday.

LAREDO: Sam Sara—I think I tangled with him in *Croak Creek Desperadoes.* Wasn't a judge, though.

LISA: Not a Hinduism fan, huh?

AARON: Are you serious—I went to all their home games this season. Sorry—Samsara:

LAREDO: *(To himself)* Big landowner judge . . .

AARON: . . . We live many lives; if you screw this one up, you can still salvage eternity through enlightenment, discipline, and a substantial daily ration of opium.

LISA: You into a lotta synthetic substances?

AARON: Oh, you know, I dabble in some dacron polyester, but I don't *have* to have it.

LISA: You're very funny.

AARON: Yet you don't laugh.

LISA: Oh, I can. Sometimes it just doesn't make it to the outside.

LAREDO: Ut! Got the movie we're in here. *Six-Gun Justice!* Lordy, pard, big trouble comin. But first, how bout a song?

AARON: *(As he and Lisa stare at each other)* Got a love song?

(Slides: Heroes with horses)

LAREDO: Love song—you bet. *(Singing)*

> Oh Lightnin, yore a mighty fine horse
> You run all day and never complain
> Good ole Lightnin . . .

AARON: So what are you, one of those psychic cowgirl healers?

LISA: Finishing my Masters degree in Range Management.

AARON: Uh-huh. Then what? Manage some range, I suppose. Got a ranch?

LISA: My mother's. She took off with husband number four bout two years ago; they got divorced but she stayed on in Houston; Judge Finlay's runnin the ranch for me till I finish school in June. Hope to take over then . . . if the land stays mine to work.

AARON: Listen, I'd like you to understand that Ava Jean and I are aren't—that *she* isn't trying to reclaim the valley for the Apaches to hurt you or Judge Finlay or anybody else here.

LAREDO: Apaches? Whut Apaches?

AARON: You believe me?

LAREDO: We're in the wrong movie here.

LISA: Yeah.

AARON: Why?

LISA: Like I said: I remember you from before.

LAREDO: Ask her which pi'ture she 'members ya from, pard—cuz I'm stumped.

LISA: Think I got the bleedin stopped. I gotta go shoe me a horse or my professor's gonna fry me. You wouldn't wanna go on a picnic one a these days, I don't guess.

(Laredo nudges Aaron—you bet)

AARON: I'd like that.

LISA: Great. Tomorrow. Three o'clock. I'll pick ya up.

(Offering her hand) Lisa Belmondo.

(Aaron takes her hand. The hands linger together a moment, then she takes off, Aaron staring after her)

AARON: Laredo, those women in your movies . . .

LAREDO: Gals, pard, we call 'em gals.

AARON: . . . those gals, they weren't simply beautiful and capable— they were so sensitive.

LAREDO: Ya got anything else to eat on ya, pard? I'm bout gutshrunk.

AARON: *(Giving him a box of Dots)* Yet, when you got to know the essential woman within, did you often find a more complicated person than you were currently equipped to deal with?

LAREDO: I jist rescued 'em, pard—all that other googaw wasn't none a my concern. Okey-dokey, let's practice yore quick draw.

(They square off, turn, step . . . Lisa goes to the "road box." She gets out a blanket and picnic basket and slams the lid just as Laredo draws, taking Aaron's attention away)

LISA: Hey!

LAREDO: Hey, Kid . . . !

SCENE 5

LISA: Let's go! Picnic!

LAREDO: Landogoshen, pard, don't never let a gal turn yore head from a feller with a gun.

AARON: Your neighbors are going to think you're keeping strange company, aren't they?

LISA: I find you right attractive. Figure I'm old enough to put a move on ya if I feel so disposed. *(They spread a blanket and take out food)*

LAREDO: Ya know what I think, pard? We're not in the wrong movie—we're in a different movie. *Carpetbaggers of Stoney Rock.* Judge in cahoots with a buncha eastern blue bellies. After the gal's land. Buncha redskins fried over all the buildin goin on on the buffalo grazin land the redskins sold fer a basket a junky wampum to this judge.

AARON: Indians.

LAREDO: That's whut I said—redskins—hunnerds of 'em!

LISA: Ya hungry?

LAREDO: Well, shoot, shore, I could maybe git jist a little sompin down.

(Laredo suddenly pulls his guns, points them at the ground)

Uh-oh—grizzly!

(Slides: Huge bear)

AARON: *(Terrified)* Bear—where? *(A beat)* In the desert?

LAREDO: Oh. Oh yeah.

(Obviously mistaken, Laredo covers the tracks with his foot and an "X" appears over the bear slide. Slide: Out West)

LISA: Always fascinated that lookin in this direction here you can see for maybe fifty miles nothin but earth, fertile and hospitable. Gives the illusion of bein uninhabited by humans—white or red. Seems to exist only to grow crops and livestock, to be revered, serve a simple good.

AARON: Really means a lot to you, doesn't it?

(Lisa sets out the food)

LISA: Doesn't seem much'd be important without it, I guess.

AARON: *(To Laredo)* I used to be you in a place like this.

LAREDO: In *Chicago*?

AARON: In my dreams. Hat at a fiercely jaunty tilt, capguns blazing, I used to ride down from a mesa to Ava Jean's rescue on my horse Spike.

LAREDO: Spike? Stinky name for a horse, pard.

(AJ throws herself to the ground, hands "bound" behind her back)

AJ: Buster, Buster, help, save me! *(Aaron and Laredo mount imaginary horses)*

AARON: The Majestic Kid to   LAREDO: The Laredo Kid to
    the rescue! Giddyap,   the rescue! Giddyap,
    Spike!   Lightnin!

(They gallop to AJ, dismount)

Don'cha worry none,   Don'cha worry none,
ma'am, ever'thing's gone   ma'am, every'thin's gone
be all right.   be all right.

AJ: *(Playing, of course, only to Aaron)* Who are you? You're not that mild-mannered Buster Weiss. Why you're . . .

AARON: Yes, ma'am, I shore am.   LAREDO: Yes, ma'am, I shore am.

(A beat. Aaron and Laredo look at each other, back at AJ)

AARON: Now you go nuts over me, Ava Jean.

AJ: How come I always gotta be the one that gets rescued? You be in trouble for a change.

AARON: Me?

LAREDO: Whut's she talkin bout?

(AJ pops up, walks away. A grip hands her a paperback and AJ plops down on top of the road box)

AJ: Yeah, well you can find somebody else then.

AARON: What? — Wait, Ava Jean, you can't . . . Whu'chu readin? *(She shows him)* Fanny Hill —

(Looking to Laredo) — that some kinda pioneer adventure?

LAREDO: I reckon it is. Boy howdy, you wasn't much good at bein me back then, was ya, buckaroo? All right, before we sing her a song . . .

(Through this next, Aaron is a word or two behind the master)

LAREDO: . . . tell her yore wounded from being bushwhacked by rustlers. She finds ya out on the north forty dyin.

AARON: . . . Pretend I'm wounded from bein bushwhacked by rustlers. You find me out on the north forty dyin.

AARON: *(To Laredo)* That's good!

AJ: That stinks.

AARON: What?

LAREDO: Huh?

AJ: Some outlaw got the drop on you . . .

AARON: Who did?

LAREDO: Whoa!

AJ: . . . and I have to pull a derringer on him to save your life.

AARON: No outlaw got the drop on *me.*

LAREDO: No outlaw got the drop on *me.*

AJ: You're not that fast, Buster. And if you keep pretendin ya are, you're gonna have a very difficult pubescence.

LAREDO: Difficult pu . . . ?

(AJ suddenly plants a big wet kiss on a surprised Aaron's mouth — his first kiss. She skips off)

Who was *that?*

(Whipping his guns out, starting off)

I'm gonna see if she's workin alone or in cahoots with them easterners.

LISA: Okay, let's eat.

LAREDO: Course, I s'pose it can wait till later.

(He holsters his gun and returns to the picnic)

Aw, lookee, pard, l'il gal burned the grits.

AARON: It's paté.

LAREDO: Huh?

AARON: Goose liver.

LAREDO: Burned goose liver—P.U. Always be polite to the gal, though.

AARON: Looks wonderful.

LAREDO: Shore does.

AARON: Whuddya got there? Cornish Game Hens?

LISA: Quail.

AARON: Quail?   LAREDO: Quail?

LISA: Shot 'em fresh this mornin.

LAREDO: She kills birdies?

LISA: My mother's third husband was a gourmet cook. He never did warm up to me, but now I can't seem to stop cookin.

LAREDO: Pard, I ain't eatin no goose's liver and no dead birdies. But I'm hongry.

(Aaron digs out a pack of M&Ms. Laredo settles down elsewhere, has an M&M or two and dozes off)

LISA: So this Ava Jean person—what's the story there?

AARON: We've known each other since we were six.

LISA: What happened?

AARON: I haven't grown up to be what she wanted me to be.

LISA: Boy, you sure work hard at bein unruffled, don'cha?

(A beat . . . and he decides to tell her)

AARON: OK. Six months ago, AJ and I were in the Public Defender's Office in the Bronx, New York—no high-paying, high-profile corporate firms for us. We had ideals about the future of the species. But it seemed we were condemned to a career of getting the guilty off on technicalities.

LISA: Meant you were good at what you did.

AARON: Confused us, though, as we still had this quaint notion vested in the Code of the West that right was right and wrong was wrong.

LISA: You have to learn to compromise your ideals.

AARON: You think so?

LISA: No. D'you?

AARON: I don't know. . . . Anyway, we came west, hand-carrying our remaining faith in the future of the species, to work for the Apaches who were trying to reacquire ancestral lands.

AJ: *(Entering)* We admire your faith in individual strength and responsibility. And I especially admire your respect for women. We hope you'll trust us.

AARON: But they didn't. Until two things happened. One, we began to develop a case President Chato thought they might actually win; and two, AJ and I got bombed one night and did a tap-dance routine in a bar near the reservation.

(Slides: Indians)

AJ: Five, six, seven, eight.

(AJ and Aaron do a lively tap routine, AJ quietly calling out the steps, "directing," along with the following)

AARON: They went wild—whole bar full of Apaches. Between the first number and the encore, Mr. Joel Chumazo, Vice-president of the Tribal Council, invited us to his home for dinner. Never so nervous in my life. I imagine magical drinks, some ancient peyote stew, full of visions of our shared humanity and oneness with the land.

AJ: Come on, Buster.

AARON: We dress in clean jeans and workshirts, bind our hair in leather thongs, load on the turquoise jewelry, eat a pack of Clorets. But when we get there, the Chumazos greet us in their church clothes: baggy polyester slacks and rayon dresses, tennis shoes and Hush Puppies.

(The dancing has ground to a stop)

AJ: *(Whispering)* Buster, you're staring.

AARON: For dinner they serve frozen stuffed bell peppers and a Sarah Lee cheesecake.

AJ: *(Whispering)* Buster, eat.

AARON: Frozen stuffed bell peppers and a Sarah Lee cheesecake. Afterward, instead of the ritual pipe, of visions of truth and shared oneness, we watch a Bob Hope comedy special at which the Chumazos—and the very pragmatic AJ—laugh uproariously.

AJ: Isn't this great!

AARON: And then Sammy Davis comes on.

(Aaron and AJ look at each other—they know what's coming)

Our vice-presidential host commands, "Yawl do that dancin with Sammy."

(Aaron and AJ hit the boards again)

You see, I was schmuck enough to actually see myself as integral to the salvation of those people. As a prospective hero who would, by regaining their lands, somehow resuscitate a purity of tradition that had been crushed. The next night we went before your Farm and Ranch Association and I packed it in.

AJ: I have never been so disappointed in another human being in my life.

(AJ goes. Laredo starts to awaken. Slides: Out West)

LISA: Hey, ya know it's only one of your lives and some of us have to be the people nobody wants to be. The thing is, though, you're not allowed to just give up and accept your fate.

(A chill shakes Aaron)

Cold?

AARON: Yeah.

LAREDO: How bout a song t'warm ya up, pard?

(Laredo's guitar flies in on cow horns as Lisa puts the blanket around Aaron. They look, touch. During the song, they disappear into the blanket together as they kiss. Laredo sings . . .)

Once upon a sunset day
In a time not very far away
There rode a man in black and white

Who believed in keepin justice
And makin wrong things right.

(Checking Aaron and Lisa out)

Lose sompin there, pard?

AARON: *(Popping out)* Huh?

LAREDO: I say, help ya look for sompin there?

AARON: No, we got it, here it is—thanks, Laredo—nickel, we got it, thanks a lot though. *(Aaron disappears)*

LAREDO: *(Singing)*

He rode a silver pony
And he had a saddlepal

(Sound of pleasure from Aaron)

She harmin you, buckaroo?

(Aaron waves Laredo off)

LAREDO: Got'cha covered, pard. *(Singing)*

He rode a silver pony
And he had a saddlepal
Lived his life only
For the rescue of a gal—

(Seeing Billy sneaking in) Uh-oh, grizzly! Pard? . . . Pardner? Pard . . . Pardner!

(Billy crouches on his haunches at Aaron's head. Aaron pops out)

AARON: Laredo, for—

BILLY: Hey there, Mr. Weese, you all right, buddy?

LISA: *(Popping out)* Billy, what are you doing here?

(Billy grabs Aaron by the throat)

LAREDO: Be calm now, pard, he's jist gonna try 'n scare ya in this scene.

AARON: Ah. Well, I think it's working.

LISA: Billy, don't hurt him!

(Aaron takes a nice sized bite out of Billy's arm. Billy screams and lets go. Aaron is on his feet)

BILLY: Son of a bitch *bit* me!

LAREDO: Ya *bit* him? Pard, the hero never bites anybody.

BILLY: That's the way they teach you fellers to fight out east, is it, Weese?

AARON: Out east, Judge, they teach us to fight any way we can. They also teach us to get a tetanus shot afterward.

LISA: What do you want, Billy?

BILLY: Well, I'd just like to inquire if I'm s'pose to share you with this turncoat, this cabron, this cat-eye curly wolf no good son-of-a-bitch book nurse of a yellow-tailed pisspot?

AARON: Oh shoot, Judge, you can just call me Aaron, no need to get formal.

LAREDO: Now yore gittin the hang of it.

LISA: Billy, may I speak to you privately?

BILLY: Shore thing, Leesey. *(Lisa and Billy move aside)*

"Where trust is greatest," Leesey — so Mr. Dryden warns us — "there treason is in its most horrid shape."

LAREDO: *(Taking Aaron aside)* Don't you never, ever bite a feller again, pard.

AARON: Guy's strong as an ox.

LAREDO: Don't matter. You trick him if you have to, but ya don't bite. Pretend yore not listenin to 'em. Whistle.

(Laredo whistles, Aaron listens. Billy's attention to Lisa is very gentle)

BILLY: I've always been there when ya needed me, Leesey.

LISA: I know, Billy, and I love you for that; as for the rest, though, let's just be friends.

BILLY: I can't go backward, puppy dog, I just can't. You do sompin like this to me, I'm jist liable to . . . *(Their voices become inaudible as they continue privately)*

LAREDO: Now this polecat's tellin her to steer clear a ya or there's gonna be big trouble. The more trouble the better, huh?

AARON: Bring on the trouble!

BILLY: *(Breaking from Lisa)* Welp. Night, night now. *(To Aaron, privately)* As the cat said to the skunk after they'd made love: I've enjoyed this, but I've enjoyed bout all of it I can stand. I'm gone be outta town coupla weeks.

AARON: Well, I'll miss you.

BILLY: I git back, we'll settle this.

AARON: Don't forget that tetanus shot.

BILLY: Yawl, take good care.

(Billy goes)

AARON: That was sure nice of the ole Judge to come all the way out here just to do a little chiropractic work on my neck . . .

LISA: He's my friend.

AARON: I get the impression there's more than friendship between you.

LISA: Look, I'd like to get back under the blanket and pick up where we left off.

AARON: I'd like nothing better, but I'm not interested in being a casual stand-in for the judge.

LISA: Far as I'm concerned, we can be as serious as ya like. *(She kisses him)* You let me know.

(She exits)

LAREDO: You bit 'im, pard.

AARON: Learned as a kid to put up a tough front — with my mouth, with words, and when that didn't work, like tonight, with my teeth or anything else that kept me from getting my ass kicked.

LAREDO: Don't say that word, pard. Say caboose.

AARON: But the truth is—physical violence scares the shit outta me.

LAREDO: And don't be sayin that word neither. You say dukey.
Okey-dokey, lookee here now, I'm gonna show ya how to
fistfight so ya never git whupped again.

AARON: I know how to fight, Laredo.

LAREDO: Shore didn't look like it. Show me whut ya kin do.

AARON: I wouldn't want to hurt you.

LAREDO: Hurt the Laredo Kid? Say I come up to ya in the saloon.
Yore drinkin a glass of milk. *(Rinky-tink piano music starts)* I take
it and pour it over your head. Whudduya do?

*(Aaron suddenly knees Laredo in the nuts. The music stops and Laredo
stares at Aaron a moment, then doubles over with a howl)*

Are you loco, buckaroo? That ain't the way ya have a fistfight!

AARON: You all right?

LAREDO: Course I'm all right! Now, lookee here, you take a swing
at me—come on—'cept ya aim right here and just when yore
fist comes awhizzin past m'chin, ya say THOCK . . .

AARON: Say what?

LAREDO: THOCK.

AARON: Spell it.

LAREDO: T-H . . .

AARON: . . . O-C-K.

LAREDO: THOCK.   AARON: THOCK.

LAREDO: That's what I said. C'mon now, do like Laredo tells ya.

*(Aaron takes a swing at Laredo, Laredo reels as if belted. Slide sequence:
cowboy fistfights, changes on each "thock")*

That's it—but don't fergit to say *(Laredo belts Aaron)* THOCK.
Now I go backward over the bar. Now, grab that bottle and
hide it behind your back. Shoot, if fellers really hit each other

in my pi'tures there'd been broken jaws and noses and blood and eyeballs hanging out and teeth all over the floor.

AARON: *(Shattering the bottle on Laredo's head)* SMASH.

LAREDO: Ow, that hurt. Yore whupping me. Ya got me on the run . . .

AARON: THOCK.

LAREDO: Yore beatin me bad.

AARON: *(Imaginary chair over head)* CRASH.

LAREDO: Ya think ya won it . . . Now, you refill your glass of milk, ya make the mistake of turnin yore back . . . THOCK.

AARON: FOOSH.

LAREDO: THOCK, THOCK, THOCK, WOMP, THOCK.

(Laredo blows Aaron down. End of fight. Music and lights change abruptly when Aaron hits the ground. Back to the old scene)

That's the way ya have a fistfight. Okey-dokey now, I gotta go somewheres — might take me a coupla weeks. Don't do nothin till I git back — 'cept work on yore quick draw. Hasta la vista, buckaroo.

(Laredo sweeps offstage)

SCENE 6

Lisa returns. She and Aaron fix on each other across a distance.

LISA: You didn't call. Thought maybe your phone was outta order. So I called you. You answered though, so I hung up. Hate for ya to think I was pursuin you if ya didn't wanna be pursued. Then I figured: Couldn't be sure ya didn't wanna be pursued unless I asked. So here I am.

(They come together and hold each other)

There's an exhibit up at the college of die-stamped metal powder flasks. Didn't know if ya went in for western memorabilia but thought I'd inquire.

AARON: I feel like Columbus setting out for the East Indies only to discover America.

LISA: Told ya we've met in another life.

(The lights shift as . . .)

SCENE 7

The doorbell rings and Lisa slips on an apron.

AARON: I got it.

LISA: Don't be silly—I got it.

(She moves to the "door." AJ faces her)

Oh, hello, you're Ava Jean.

AJ: AJ.

LISA: I'm Lisa.

AJ: Ah.

LISA: You want to see Aaron.

AJ: Please.

LISA: He's right in here. . . . Can I get you anything?

AJ: No, I don't believe so.

LISA: *(To Aaron)* I'll leave you alone. I'll be in the kitchen if you need me.

(She goes to the kitchen area and mimes cooking)

AJ: Is that a transient?

AARON: Wouldn't think that would be of any interest to you. What can I do for you?

AJ: We've gotta get our case into court. We hear there's some big eastern money about to complicate matters. How bout gettin your ass up to the reservation this weekend and go through your research for President Chato and me. Or would that be infringing on your "time out"?

LISA: *(Reentering)* Excuse me. Would you like to have dinner with us?

AJ: Oh, I don't know—what are you having?

LISA: A salad nicoise, wild asparagus and charcroute garni.

AJ: Charcroute garni—couldn't you just call it hotdogs and sauer-kraut and be done with it?

LISA: I guess you could—if it was real important to someone to call it that.

AJ: I've seen you somewhere.

LISA: At the Farm and Ranch Association meeting last month.

AJ: You a landowner?

LISA: Yep.

AJ: Well well well.

LISA: But Aaron isn't working with us.

AARON: Don't defend me, please.

LISA: Sorry.

(AJ exits angrily)

You got a look on your face sour enough to pucker a hog's rectum.

(She takes him to her, begins to rub his face. Music into next scene)

AARON: Don't massage. Just hold.

SCENE 8

The road box becomes a desk. Billy enters in his judicial robes, an old book in hand.

BILLY: Weese, thanks for comin over, buddy. Come in.

AARON: Happy to have the opportunity to talk, Judge.

BILLY: Siddown, buddy, siddown.

(Billy pulls his handgun out of his waistband, placing it obviously close by)

Ya know, Weese, I was all set to fergive and fergit when I heard you give up that craziness with the Apaches. Then I go out east, come back to find you livin with my gal.

AARON: I didn't come to talk about Lisa, Judge. I came to ask you what you can tell me about this eastern concern trying to—

BILLY: Been aglancin at ole Mr. W. Sumner here. "Property," he notes, "is dear to men not only for the sensual pleasure it can afford but because it is the bulwark of all they hold dearest on earth." M'self, I wouldn't be a'tall surprised— ya took a survey— as many men been killed over a piece a tail as over a piece a ground.

AARON: Judge, I have too little respect for myself right now to be frightened by threats on my life.

BILLY: How bout a ci'gar?

AARON: No thanks. What can you tell me about this eastern concern trying to buy up land in the valley?

BILLY: Senator friend of mine has 'em made by Cuban refugees— smooth as a milk cow's tit.

AARON: I'm getting the distinct feeling here you don't wanna discuss this—so maybe I just oughta mosey . . .

BILLY: Brain Boy, we ain't in court here, I ain't on the stand, and as I understand it, you ain't a lawyer no more. Havin hung up yore guns, I'd shore stay indoors and outta other folks' business. Now help me out here, amigo. Not bein an educated person such as yourself, I was wonderin if it'd occurred to you that my gal's taken up with you to make me jealous and not cuz she cares jackshit about you? That little dickens tried the same thing once before, taunted me with the first great love of her life. Course I'm sure she's told you all about him.

AARON: Actually she hasn't, but the way I see it, if she—

BILLY: Hasn't told ya bout ole Hum Pace?

AARON: Hum Pace? Who's Hum Pace?

BILLY: Lisa's told ya bout her momma, surely, the four times married Clara Scott Belmondo Edgar Pace Keene.

AARON: Lisa was in love with her mother's third husband, the gourmet cook?

BILLY: Uh-uh. His brother. The brain-damaged vegetable.

AARON: Brain-damaged vegetable . . .

BILLY: 'Fraid so. Like to know why we called him Hum?

AARON: Sure.

BILLY: Cuz he wouldn't speak. He would only hum.

AARON: Wouldn't speak, huh?

BILLY: That's right.

AARON: You should have called him Mum then. Not Hum. Mum Pace.

BILLY: Uncle Hum got his brain scrambled in the same accident that killed his wife and daughter. My Leesey, she took it on herself to come home from the college ever'day and act as her uncle's companion. At first, she endeavored to take the place of Uncle Hum's daugher—hell, she'd had a procession of daddies, what was one more. But she ended up, in all but ceremony, takin the place a Uncle Hum's wife. Things got complicated after Leesey's momma and Hum's brother busted up. Ole Clara, she pulled out, left Lisa with this cripple, a ranch to run, school. . . . I hadn'ta stepped into the pi'ture, she'da been up a Shit Creek without your proverbial paddle. I did it cuz I care about her, and don't let her kid ya, she cares about me. I own her just like I'll eventually own whatever else I want in this valley. Now I'm gonna give you till sundown this evenin to get my Leesey outta your apartment. . . . You try one a these cigars, cousin—I'm tellin ya, they make a feller feel bout ten feet tall.

(Billy bangs the cigar he's been smoking into Aaron's mouth, hovers a moment, then goes, leaving Aaron with his hand to the pain in his gut)

SCENE 9

Lisa "cooking" dinner, Laredo with arms full of scripts and an empty canteen draped across his chest. Sound of "Laredo Kid Movie" on TV. Laredo crosses to watch "TV." Aaron enters. AJ and Billy create the movie sounds in the background.

LISA: Hi, honey!

AARON: Hi.

LISA: Dinner's almost ready.

AARON: Good. *(He pops the cigar into his mouth)*

LISA: Ah, I see you're helpin Billy with the Cuban refugee problem. You need a breath mint.

(She takes the cigar and goes to the "kitchen." Slide sequence: old movie scenes)

LAREDO: Hi, pard!

AARON: Hi.

LAREDO: I'm back, 'n have I got news fer you!

AARON: Great.

LAREDO: But first, c'mere, you ain't gonna believe whut's on TV!

AARON: Right with ya.

LAREDO: *Parched.* Ran outta water.

AARON: Grab a Perrier. *(To Lisa, as she enters with a glass of wine for him)* Say, I hear you had an affair with your uncle, the humming vegetable. . . . Perhaps I didn't phrase that as well as I might.

LISA: I wondered when Billy'd start firing the big ammo. Uncle Luke and I shared a great deal.

AARON: I don't mean to make light of this, but shared a great deal how — musically?

LISA: He hummed at my mother and Billy. He spoke to me.

AARON: What happened?

LISA: Samsara, Aaron — we live many lives.

LAREDO: Sam Sara ain't in this pi'ture. Lookee here!

AARON: My God, Lisa, what are *you* carrying around inside? Uncle Luke when I don't even understand what's going on with Billy.

LISA: Please, let's just share this incarnation.

AARON: What are you hiding?

(Lisa walks away, into the "kitchen")

LAREDO: You gonna quit jawin at her and lookee here.

AARON: *(Focusing on Laredo for the first time, though still a good bit absent)* What happened to you — where you been?

LAREDO: Rode out to Hollywood to git a copy of *Carpetbaggers of Stoney Rock.* Dust storms and tornadoes the whole way. And wouldn't ya know it — after all that, it's on TV this very afternoon. Yore jist in time fer the showdown. Now watch this, then we got work to do. Oh, I betcha they thought they had ole Laredo fooled. Whu'chu been doin?

AARON: I went to see Billy.

LAREDO: Alone?

AARON: Why not?

LAREDO: *Why not?* Cuz you don't know what yore doin! I got the script.

LISA: I think I remember where I met you before. In one of these old westerns. You were the seemingly weak and naive drifter who turned out to be the hero who saved my land. Seriously.

LAREDO: Less'n you follow the script, yore gonna turn out to be dogmeat that saved nothin. Now, lookee here, there's the judge with one a the eastern blue bellies. Thock!

LISA: You know what really irks me about these movies, though?

AARON: Mm.   LAREDO: *(Quietly)* Thock!

LISA: The movie makes the woman capable as the dickens . . .

AARON: Uh-huh.   LAREDO: *(Quietly)* Whomp,
                                              thock!

LISA: . . . but too dumb to recognize that the mild-mannered drifter is really the hero in the mask and black duds.

AARON: Mm.

LISA: That way they won't have to get married, ya see. Because of course ya couldn't have the woman in distress in the next movie saved by the man who married the woman in distress in the last movie. So this guy just sings his way badly from movie to movie, rescuing towns fulla weak sops and leaving behind a trail of drooling but undefiled beauties. *(She turns TV off)* If ya ask me, what would be a tad more useful today would be: They get married and have children, and you have a series of movies about a family facing the challenges of ranch life together.

LAREDO: Lord amighty, pard, sometimes I think she don't got enough brains to wad a shotgun. Straighten her out, buckaroo.

AARON: Those guys, like the Laredo Kid, they gave up dreams of marriage and family . . .

AARON: . . . in order . . .   LAREDO: . . . in order . . .

AARON: . . . to rescue and redeem the lives and property of others.

LAREDO: She think I was doin it fer *fun?* Don't move, I'll be right back.

(He hustles off)

AARON: And besides that, men are less interested in families and children today than they were when this movie was made. Families and children are out. Indulgence and selfishness are in.

LISA: I miss families.

AARON: Mother married and divorced four times, your closest living relation a humming vegetable — I can see where you would.

(Lisa exits to "kitchen")

LAREDO: Now try to follow what I'm gonna say to ya here. We're not dealin with jist any bad feller in this Finlay. Ya know whut he's gone and done? Take a guess.

(Laredo has marked different spots in different scripts. He starts to organize as . . .)

You don't start payin attention to me, she ain't gonna have no ranch to be a rancher lady on!

AARON: She's making me crazy — trying to sell me exactly what I'm afraid I wanna buy!

SCENE 10

Aaron has moved away. Laredo goes after him.

LAREDO: Pard, yore drivin *me* loco. Whut is the matter with you, young 'un?

AARON: What's wrong is I think I've actually come together with someone I feel I could be happy with the rest of my life.

LAREDO: If ya feel so goldarn great with me, stop wastin—

AARON: Her. Lisa.

LAREDO: Huh?

AARON: But how can she trust me? Finlay hates me, the people in the valley hate me, the Indians hate me, my only friend thinks I'm the scum of the earth. I spent seven years in school preparing for a profession I'm not in. Every ideal I've believed in since I was nine is in the toilet . . . *(He starts for Lisa)*

LAREDO: C'mere, where ya goin? She just *thinks* she don't trust ya cuz ya ain't slipped into yore Majestic Kid duds yet and come to her rescue.

AARON: She thinks I'm too weak to share the load with her.

LAREDO: Share the—Ya don't *share* the load, pard. Ya carry it alone.

AARON: I'm not that strong. I'm just gonna tell her.

(He heads for Lisa. Laredo leaps on him, forcibly restraining him. Slides: Many saddlepals)

LAREDO: Pard, pard, pard, pard, pard! You cain't be sharin yoreself with some *gal.* Lord, son, yore the Majestic Kid! That's whut the hero's got his saddlepal fer. Exactly whut I had ole Snuffy Greenbush fer through a hunnerd and nine films. Whut Cisco had Pancho fer. Jehosafat!—ya think Tim Holt wouldn'ta been a goner without Chito? Red without Little Beaver? Lone Ranger had Tonto. Durango had Smiley. Wild Bill Elliot had Frog.

AARON: Ken Maynard had Frong. Wild Bill Elliot had . . . *(Short beat)*

AARON: . . . Cannonball.   LAREDO: . . . Cannonball.

AARON: Wild Bill Hickok had . . .

AARON: Jingles.   LAREDO: . . . Jingles.

LAREDO: Gene had Gabby.

AARON: Roy had Pat Brady.

LAREDO: *And* the Sons of the Pioneers — 'member them?

> *(They sing the phrase, "Tumblin along with the tumblin tumbleweeds.")*

Ain'cha never had yoreself a saddlepal?

AARON: AJ.

LAREDO: There ya go? What happened to him?

AARON: AJ didn't wanna be a saddlepal anymore.

LAREDO: Didn't wanna be a . . . !

AARON: AJ wanted to be the hero.

LAREDO: Uh-uh, no siree, the saddlepal cain't never be the hero. Cuz he always got hisself a pox — like he's big 'n fat or he's a redskin or he plays a harmonica — he jist ain't heroic, jist like a gal ain't.

> *(Laredo's guitar flies in on the cow horns)*

Help me out here on this one, pard'nuh . . . *(Singing)*

The truth about a gal
Is she cain't never be a . . .

AARON: Pal.

LAREDO:

Imagine talkin rescue 'n redemption
With the object a yore . . .

AARON: Intention.

LAREDO:

> A buckaroo'd seem mighty strange
> If ya found him on the range
> Sharin a pot a beans and a piece a
> God's earth with a feller name a . . .

AARON: Lisa.

LAREDO/AARON:

> Saddlepals, saddlepals
> The truth about gals is
> They don't make good . . .

(Aaron heads for Lisa)

LAREDO: Pard, where ya goin?

(Aaron and Lisa fix on each other)

LISA: I'll try to be whatever you need me to be.

AARON: That's not what I want. I want you to be whatever you need to be. *(They clutch each other)*

LAREDO: After the song I just sung ya . . . !

SCENE 11

BILLY: *(Entering)* Knock, knock. Hey, yawl love birds. Anybody to home?

LAREDO: Well, this jist serves ya right.

AARON: Don't you believe in ringing the bell, Billy?

BILLY: I said "knock, knock." Nobody didn't say nothin, so I come on in.

AARON: The door was locked. *(Instinctively, Aaron looks to Laredo, but Laredo's peeved)*

LAREDO: Don't look at me.

BILLY: Thought I smelled smoke. Used this little do–dad the po–lice gimme, opens doors there's a fire behind 'em.

LISA: Is there a problem on my ranch, Billy?

LAREDO: Oh now don't compound the mess ya made by lettin *her* ask any questions.

AARON: What can we do for you, Billy?

LAREDO: *I*—what kin *I* do fer ya?

BILLY: Welp, sun's been gone bout an hour here—thought I'd best pay a little call on yawl both.

LISA: You had no right to tell Aaron about Uncle Luke. Why don't you go ahead and tell him the rest. Go ahead. Aaron, Billy's got something to tell you.

BILLY: We got us a statute in this county says it is a second degree misdemeanor fer two unmarried folks to share the same dwellin place when the intent of that union is the practice of fornication and sodomy. You were an attorney at law, Weese—figured shore you'da knowed that.

LAREDO: *(Diving into the scripts)* Jist a second, pard, I'll look fer a sodomy scene—whatever that is.

BILLY: Welp, yawl, a complaint's been filed in Magistrate's Court and as Magistrate's Judge—

LISA: Complaint filed by whom, Billy?

BILLY: Lemme see here. Why . . . by me.

LAREDO: Lord, pard, I cain't find where he is. Legal talk! Stall him with lawyer know-how.

BILLY: Care to comment, Brain Boy?

AARON: Yeah. As Magistrate's Judge, you have no jurisdiction in morals complaints. That's a municipal matter. Even if you did have jurisdiction, needless to say you couldn't represent your own complaint. Now, I'll ask you to leave our apartment before I file a complaint of forcible entry with the police.

BILLY: *(Grabbing Aaron by the neck)* Listen to me, fuckstick: Don't you tell me what I can or can't do in my county!

(Suddenly pulling his revolver with his free hand and sticking it under Aaron's nose)

LISA: Billy!

BILLY: And you try some gutless East Coast trick like bitin me again and I'll blow your goddamn brains all over the Southwest.

LAREDO: No bite, pard, no bite.

LISA: Billy, may I speak to you a moment?

BILLY: Shore thing, Leesey.

(Billy and Lisa step aside)

LAREDO: Now smile at him like this, pard — look — so he don't think he scared ya one eensy-weensy l'il bit.

(Laredo demonstrates the smile; Aaron mimics him somewhat tensely)

Ya see whut he's done, pard? He's made hisself up from *Carpetbaggers of Stoney Rock, The Man From Forked Tongue,* and about half a dozen *other* pi'tures I found so far. So whut we gotta do is . . . *(Laredo whispers to Aaron)*

LISA: What do you want, Billy?

BILLY: Puppy, I'm doin somethin of great importance. For you. I can't tell ya just what it is, but ya gotta please stop makin me miserable while I'm accomplishin it for ya.

LISA: Billy, you're not involved in something illegal, are you?

BILLY: Leesey, you gotta leave him. Ya love me.

LISA: You've changed, Billy.

BILLY: No, maybe a teensy bit — when *he* come into our life.

LISA: No, I told you months before I met Aaron I wasn't gonna marry you and you got mean.

BILLY: Cuz I was afraid a losin ya, doggy.

LISA: You've lost me as a lover, Billy — don't lose me as a friend.

BILLY: Damn you, puppy dog. *(A beat)* I hope ya believe I never, ever intended it to come to this. *(He whispers to her)* I'll expose you if I have to. I'll do injury to him, kill him if I have to. Find out what he knows about the Apaches' case.

(As this is going on . . .)

LAREDO: Okay, here—skip the sarsaparilla in the face scene, skip the singin at the church social. You play poker?

AARON: Golf.

LAREDO: Golf?

BILLY: *(To Lisa)* Ya gotta understand, I wanna give ya everything you want cuz you're everything I want.

(Billy and Lisa break. Billy fronts Aaron)

LAREDO: Uh-oh, Lord knows which scene he's gonna throw at ya now.

BILLY: I'm through screwin with you, pigsnout.

(He exits. A beat)

SCENE 12

LISA: Lemme check on dinner.

(Laredo and Aaron look at each other)

AARON: Excuse me, Lisa, but what did you just tell him?

LISA: Not a whole heckuva lot.

(She returns from the "kitchen." Aaron stares at her until . . .)

I just told him if he didn't leave us alone, I'd remove his testicles with a blunt instrument. Except I didn't put it that politely.

AARON: You mean you're cleaning up your language so as not to offend my delicate sensibilities. You know how that makes me feel, Lisa—you constantly taking him aside to protect me? Not good. Not masculine and not terribly useful.

LISA: I'm sorry.

AARON: Boy, me too.

(She goes to the "kitchen" again)

LAREDO: Whut's that mean—remove his sompin with a sompin sompin?

AARON: Near as I can figure, she threatened to chop his balls off.

LAREDO: *(A beat)* Like I was sayin, whut we gotta . . . You don't think our l'il gal said that, do ya?

AARON: Na.

LAREDO: Course not. Okay, what we gotta—

LISA: *(Returning)* Aaron . . .

LAREDO: Oh, Lord amighty, now whut?

LISA: . . . it's not that I think you can't take care of yourself.

AARON: Oh, that's good. What is it?

LISA: Lot of men out here, men like Billy, they have their own code of ethics.

LAREDO: Feller makes hisself up from half a dozen movin pi'tures— she kin say that agin.

AARON: What happened to the Code of the West? "Do unto others as you would have others do unto you"?

LISA: The code Billy abides by, Aaron, is this one: You piss in my trough, I poison your well.

LAREDO: What west is she talkin about?

AARON: What west are you talking about?

LISA: What west are *you* talking about?

AARON: What west *am* I talking about?

LAREDO: *My* west!

AARON: *(To himself)* What am I talking about, *period?*

LISA: Just watch yourself, okay?

AARON: *(To himself)* *Why* am I talking?

LAREDO: Tell her to watch *her*self.

AARON: *(Overlapping)* I should shut up.

> *(Lisa moves to "kitchen" to get dinner)*

LAREDO: And listen to me! I went outta yore life, you been lookin all over tarnation fer guidance and ya turned into this little wimpy scaredy-cat that cain't make up his mind bout nothin cuz nobody's remindin ya the one thing ya gotta always 'member: There gotta be Majestic Kids or you're all of ya *dead.* You gonna countenance a world like that? You wee-wee in my trough, I poison yore well! No! Now, she wants her land saved, she wants to be rescued when the showdown a this dadburn pi'ture comes she just better watch her*self.*

(Lisa reenters with imaginary tray)

LISA: Come on, let's eat.

LAREDO: Yeah, tell her to jist keep her big yap shut 'cept to say, "Come on, let's eat."

LISA: Beef Carbonada Criolla in Pumpkin Shell — I think you're gonna like it.

(Lisa removes imaginary casserole lid)

AARON: I'm really not hungry.

LAREDO: Now dadburn it, you gotta eat, buckaroo — you got lives and property in *crisis!*

AARON: *(To Laredo)* Stop putting so much pressure on me!

LAREDO: Pressure's our middle name, pard.

LISA: Really should be eaten now.

AARON: *(To Lisa)* And you stop trying to *please* me so much!

LISA: Why should I, though?

AARON: Because you're driving me crazy!

LAREDO: Okey dokey now, pard, gentle down, huh. This is no time to —

LISA: Maybe you'd like to make a list of things I *can* do for you.

LAREDO: First thing we oughta do, pard, is make a lista all the scenes Finlay might —

AARON: You can't try to satisfy my every need and sympathize with my every idiocy — that's for starters. I'll work through my problems alone.

LISA: What on earth for?

LAREDO: Cuz he's a *feller.*

LISA: Because you think that's what I'm doing to you? Working through my problems alone?

AARON: Stop trying to have a rational conversation with me.

LAREDO: Let's git some grub in our jaws, pard — we'll feel a heap —

AARON: *(To Laredo)* No! *(To Lisa)* And you can't cook these spectacular meals every night and you can't iron and vacuum and scrub so passionately.

LAREDO: Whoa now, buckaroo, that's her job, jist like yores is rescue and —

AARON: It's not her job — women are different today.

LAREDO: Gals. And this 'un ain't.

LISA: So you're saying cleanliness is an issue?

AARON: It's just part of the big picture.

LAREDO: The western pi'ture, pard.

LISA: Fine — the place'll turn back into a pigsty like it was when we met.

AARON: I am a perfectly adequate housekeeper — it wasn't a pigsty.

LISA: Well, it wasn't as clean as it is now.

AARON: No place in the history of architecture has *ever* been as clean as this place is now.

LISA: So?

AARON: So you're a contemporary woman, Lisa, you shouldn't be ironing my socks!

LAREDO: She irons yore socks?

AARON: I mean socks, Lisa—when you puts socks on, they become smooth, no wrinkles.

LISA: The socks don't know that.

AARON: Socks have feelings now?

LISA: All right, I didn't—

AARON: Which eastern philosophy is that?

LISA: You've got me so upset—

AARON: And which socks? All socks?

LISA: You've made your point, Aaron!

AARON: Argyles? Black orlons?

LISA: The ones I made you for our first month anniversary! *(Short beat)*

LAREDO: Aw, God love ya, l'il gal. Gosh darn it, pard, ain't she sompin! How bout a song? What am I doin? Now ya got *me* crazy!

LISA: I feel like a spectator at my own execution and I don't know which crime I'm bein executed for. That I love you, that I want you to recapture your ideals; it can't just be Billy or Uncle Luke or that you resent that I can't share with you yet what I can't share with you.

AARON: I really think, Lisa, that we have to terminate our relationship before I start to hate your guts because I can't fathom you.

LISA: You have to trust me and give me time to—

AARON: No. I can't. I'm not currently that big a person. I'm going to go up to the reservation tonight to go through my research with AJ and President Chato; when I get back, I'd appreciate it if you would have your things moved out.

(A beat. Lisa runs off. Aaron doubles over, his gut killing him)

LAREDO: Whut's the matter, pard—he gut-shoot ya? *(Aaron shakes his head no)* Tummyache? *(Aaron nods)* Ya know, I had me a tummyache once like to brought me to m'knees. Crushed me up some yellow root and oatmeal, made me a poultice. Slapped 'er right up against m'gut, said this Arapahoe chant: *Hi*-yah, hi-hay, *hi*-yah—

(Grip comes on with phone and does ringing sound. Aaron answers)

AARON: Hello.

(Sound: Billy does rough and resonant voice humming Rachmaninoff agitatedly and badly)

What number are you calling, please?

LAREDO: Who is it, pard?

AARON: Someone humming Rachmaninoff.

LAREDO: No, now I tangled with him in *Pardon My Winchester*—he wasn't in *Carpetbaggers of Stoney Rock*. Whut's goin on here?

AARON: Oh no.

LAREDO: You sure he ain't talkin Mexican?

AARON: Look, I don't mean to sound impertinent, Uncle Hum— Mr. Pace, excuse me—but I don't feel this is any of your damn business so I'm hanging up now. *(Aaron hangs up. Billy stops humming)*

LAREDO: He must be out on parole—Rachmaninoff.

(Sound: Rachmaninoff . . . becoming "Indian" music)

SCENE 13

Lights change as the grips arrange road box for AJ's apartment. AJ enters.

AARON: Stuffed bell peppers and cheesecake, anyone?

LAREDO: Cheesecake? Well, shoot—*(Seeing who it is)* Oh no, not her agin! Don't eat *nothin* she offers ya, I'm gonna git your six guns and look around. This smacks of an ambush. *(Laredo goes off)*

AARON: It's good to see you. Really need to talk to you. You look good. Must have a new fella.

AJ: Dr. Edgar Farnsworth—comes up three days a week. Problem is, I think I like the four days he's not here better . . . We need you here, Buster.

AARON: I'll go through the research with you.

AJ: And that's it? Before you answer, let me catch you up on our current thinking. Now, this may be a little startling at first, and you're gonna think President Chato's sold out, but you're wrong—he's just decided to fight fire with fire.

(She begins to undress casually during the following)

If we win the suit and reclaim the valley, the Apaches are going to build a resort hotel and spa.

(Aaron looks at her)

Hear me out now—I reacted the same way. Condominiums, championship golf course, Indians running the whole place, looking extremely historical but totally unthreatening. The perfect place for the white man to do his penance painlessly and for the Indian to become a part of the economic mainstream.

(She has begun to undress him now. He stops her)

What's the matter?

AARON: Monogamy.

AJ: What?

AARON: Fidelity. Trust.

AJ: What about them?

AARON: Nothing. Doesn't matter. Ridiculous concepts. Go on, this is fascinating.

(She does—with the undressing and the talking)

AJ: Then President Chato wants me to bring suit against the federal government to permit gambling on what I think I can establish is sovereign Apache land beyond the control of the state or the feds.

AARON: It sounds like Las Vegas with local extras, AJ. You're kidding, right?

AJ: The hell we are, babe. I read some damn government report recently that noted that "cognatic consanguineal bonds and affinal ties used to be the anchoring points of the Apache network of social relations." Well, maybe they used to be, but *this* Apache tribe is about to reunite in pursuit of Anglo bucks. The new Little Big Horn's gonna be fought right on the plains of Capitalism.

AARON: " . . . cognatic consanguineal bonds and affinal ties"—what does that mean, AJ?

AJ: Lie down here.

(They climb on the road box)

It means that the family and the family's dependence on other families is no longer the center of Apache life.

AARON: The family's no longer the center of anybody's life! Ouch! Don't bite people, AJ, for chrissake!

AJ: Sorry—let Mommy fix. It's worse for the Apaches because the white man has methodically eviscerated the family tradition so—

AARON: —So let's reunite the Apache family in Apache Las Vegas! Can we anticipate the resurrection of Apache family life through an amalgamation of tap and war dancing?

AJ: Would you prefer we were still slaughtering the Indians and they were scalping us?

AARON: In a way, I think I would.

AJ: Look, could we make love first and fight this out later?

(They come together)

Make sure that your little friend understands you're only on loan, that we always come back to each other, to share the other's burdens.

(He freezes)

What happened? Did I bite you again—I'm sorry—Where? *(A beat)* What?

AARON: I told her to move out.

AJ: Good. You're tired of her—what'd you expect?

AARON: It's not good, and I'm not tired of her. I'm *sick* of her —
there's a difference. I'm sick of her *not* sharing the other's burdens, sick of her protecting me.

AJ: Look, shall we get dressed? It's cold.

AARON: Ya know, that's something I've always hated about our
relationship.

AJ: What?

AARON: We could make love, we could not make love — it never
really mattered. We could sleep with other people, come back
to each other, sleep out some more, come back again. Ya know
what? I'm really not in favor of promiscuity. I think I've been
meaning to tell you that for about fifteen years but I was afraid
you'd belittle me for being moral or something.

AJ: Buster, what in God's name are you talking about?

AARON: In God's name — nothing. When was the last time either of
us talked about anything in God's name? I would *love* to talk
about something in God's name, go to a synagogue, a *dinner*
party — anywhere where there was a conspiracy of faith. Not in
God, though — no, that's not it. A sense of community, of something larger than any of us — farmers, ranchers, Indians, me me
me. But I think it has to start with the other.

AJ: What other?

AARON: The family.

AJ: Times have changed, Buster.

AARON: "Times have changed"? People change times. We're people;
we can change it back. Jesus, I see that's always bothered me
about our relationship — it's so free of obligation. It's full of
dexterity —

AJ: Buster, you're really pissing me off!

AARON: And why have I always broken my ass not to piss you off?

AJ: All right, Buster, I'm going to become calm now and you're
going to tell me what the hell you're talking about!

AARON: I don't know — I'm confused . . .

AJ: No—really?

AARON: . . . confused about what I'm going to be when I grow up. Except I'm grown up and I don't know what I *am.* C'mere a second, Ava Jean.

AJ: Don't you dare call me Ava Jean.

AARON: Just for a second, let me hold you like I'm the boy and you're the girl.

AJ: Mister, you just start interpreting these damn notes and then I want you the hell out of here until you—

AARON: Okay, we'll both be the boy but let's just hold each—

(She starts to dress. He grapples with her; they topple to the ground, wrestling. Laredo hustles in)

LAREDO: I knew it! Jist in time! Thock her in the jaw, pard!

AJ: Buster, stop it!

(AJ flips Aaron over her head. Music on flip)

LAREDO: Geez.

AJ: If I'm not "girl" enough for you, Buster, it's because you've never been *man* enough for me. *(She takes off)*

LAREDO: Pard, let's git outta here, this place is crawlin with redskins. They got us smack dab in the middle a *Die, Apache, Die.*

(The lights become dreamlike around Aaron. Billy and Lisa hover over the supine Aaron. Billy carries Lisa's suitcase)

LISA: Go away, Aaron. Go on back out east. Go home.

BILLY: I don't want you near me, my land, or my gal again, Weese. Ever.

LAREDO: Oh, that's good, pard, that whupped dog look.

(Billy leads Lisa away)

Laredo thrusts Aaron's guns at him.

AARON: Something's badly amiss here.

LAREDO: Yessir! So put your guns on.

AARON: They're capguns.

LAREDO: Put 'em on or you're gonna hate yoreself yore whole life long.

AARON: I already hate myself.

LAREDO: Ya gotta follow the script, pard.

AARON: Script's all screwed up. What's goin on here?

LAREDO: Ya gotta rescue the gal.

AARON: From what?

LAREDO: What're you, some kinda dumb cluck?

(Sound: theme music)

LAREDO: *(Singing)*

> The Majestic Kid, ya know
> He rides a righteous trail

AARON: Laredo—no!

LAREDO: *(Singing)*

> Bearin all he can
> A other folk's travail.

AARON: Somethin's wrong. What's she hiding?

LAREDO: *(Singing)*

> Reapin justice and redemption
> All along the way

Leavin to the pure of heart
A sweeter, better day.

AARON: What if he's blackmailing her somehow? All right, OK.
Time in. The Majestic Kid to the rescue.

THE COMPANY: *(Singing)*

Ride, Majestic, ride . . . !
Ride, Majestic, ride . . . !

AARON: Hang on Lisa. Here I come!

ACT II

~

The Finlay spread. Slides: Trees. Night sounds. Other actors making noises like dogs, owls, cows, etc. as Laredo leads Aaron in the moonlight. Pantomime: snake, crossing stream, confronting bad dog, mean cat. They become lost.

AARON: I thought you said you could track a woodpecker across the Pacific.

LAREDO: You sayin I'm lost?

AARON: You're not?

(Howl. Aaron ducks down. Laredo points gun over his head)

LAREDO: Mm-mm—jist smell that manure.

AARON: Cowshit.

LAREDO: Don't you call it that—they're the same thing.

AARON: No, no, that's where you're wrong. Manure is when you're nine years old and on vacation at a dude ranch with your mommy and daddy. This is cowshit.

(Sound of hoot owl. Aaron and Laredo look up. Laredo whips off his hat)

LAREDO: Lookit what that hoot owl done to my hat!

(From behind, Billy sticks his rifle between Aaron's legs)

BILLY: What the hell you doin on Finlay land, mister?

AARON: Huh?

BILLY: Grab the sky, goatroper!

LAREDO: Use yore noggin now, pard. Yore the Majestic Kid.

BILLY: What the hell you doin on my land?

AARON: Uhm . . .

BILLY: Choke it up.

AARON: *(Affecting a hero-of-the-Old West voice)* Talk.

BILLY: Talk? What kinda talk?

AARON: Good talk, nice talk.

BILLY: Bout what?

AARON: Uhm . . .

LAREDO: Cows.

AARON: Cows. Buy. *Cattle.*

BILLY: You wanna buy cattle? What kinda cattle?

AARON: Heifers—

BILLY: What?

AARON: Hoofers.

LAREDO: Herefords!

AARON: —Herefords!

BILLY: Hey, you turn around here, citizen. *(When Aaron turns, Billy unmasks him)* Well well well. As the right Rev. C. Simmons pointed out hunnerd years ago or so:—

LISA: *(Entering)* Leave him alone, Billy.

LAREDO: Lordy, don't let her protect you agin, pard.

BILLY: *(Turning to Lisa)* Feller comes onto a man's land wearin a mask after he's been told— *(Aaron pulls his capgun when Billy turns and sticks it to his head)*

AARON: All right, drop it, Judge.

BILLY: Fergit it.

AARON: *(To Laredo)* He's not dropping it.

LAREDO: Say it like ya mean it and use his last name.

AARON: Drop it, Finlay. *(Billy drops it)* It worked.

LAREDO: Grab the sky, sodbuster.

AARON: Grab the sky, sodbuster. *(Billy grabs some sky)*

LISA: Aaron, what are you doing?

AARON: You're gonna tell me what's going on and you're gonna tell me the truth.

LISA: You think this is some old cowboy movie, Aaron? Coming out here with a capgun, when this man is capable of—

LAREDO: Oops.

(Slides: cowgirl with gun)

BILLY: What kinda gun?

LISA: I'll handle this, Billy . . .

AARON: Real gun!

LISA: . . . you go on up to the house.

AARON: Peacekeepers!

LAREDO: —makers!

AARON: Winchester . . .

LAREDO: Colt . . .

AARON: Colt . . .

LAREDO: . . . Peacemakers.

AARON: . . . Peacemakers. *(Billy has the drop on Aaron)*

BILLY: Up with 'em, dickhead!

AARON: *(To Laredo)* Now what?

LAREDO: How bout a song?

LISA: *(Yanking the rifle from Billy)* Gimme that, Billy!

LAREDO: Get that thing, pard!

AARON: *(Grabbing the rifle from Lisa)* Give me that thing, Lisa!

BILLY: *(Grabbing it from Aaron)* I'll take that, Brain Boy!

LISA: *(Grabbing it)* Give me that!

LAREDO: Get it, pard!

AARON: *(Grabbing it)* Lisa, let me have that!

BILLY: *(Grabbing it)* Gimme that damn thing!

(Aaron and Billy wrestle for the rifle. It is wrenched out of Lisa's hand as . . .)

LISA: Stop it! Stop it before someone gets—

(The rifle suddenly comes free into Aaron's hands and discharges, striking Lisa in the shoulder. She is thrown into Billy's arms.)

LAREDO: Dear Lord, buckaroo!

AARON: Oh my God—Lisa!

BILLY: You shot her!

AARON: It was an accident.

LAREDO: How'd that happen?

BILLY: You shot my gal!

AARON: We were wrestling . . . the gun went off . . .

LAREDO: Don'cha worry none, ma'am, ever'thin's gone be all right.

AARON: It just went off.

(Billy scoops Lisa into his arms)

BILLY: You're under arrest, Weese—you run for it, I'll hunt ya down and kill ya! *(Billy bears Lisa offstage in his arms)*

AARON: Lisa! *(To Laredo)* Oh my god!

LAREDO: Okay now, okay, so sompin that ain't in no script happened. Okay . . .

AARON: My god, you see? You've been telling me how there's always a bad fella the gal's gotta be rescued from . . . ? Well, I'm it, I'm him, I'm the fella!

(Aaron takes off screaming, running, Laredo following)

AJ!

LAREDO: Where ya goin?

AARON: AJ!

(AJ enters in her batbrobe)

AARON: AJ!

AJ: Buster, what are you doing here?

LAREDO: AJ! I thought ya said AJ was yore saddlepal?

AJ: What are you doing with that rifle? *(Aaron thrusts the rifle at her)*

LAREDO: Pard, whut are you doing? Don't give her the —

AJ: My god, what's happened?

LAREDO: You lame-brain!

AJ: Talk to me, baby.

LAREDO: Don't tell her nothin!

(Aaron drops to his knees, presses his head into the folds of AJ's robe)

AJ: Tell me what you need, baby.

AARON: Rescue.

LAREDO: Whut!

SCENE 2

Aaron, under an Apache blanket, seemingly asleep. Laredo above him, wadding up a "scene," throwing it away. There's wadded paper strewn about.

LAREDO: I'm not a writer! We always had a writer, I jist did the fightin 'n ridin 'n rescuin! And you—you shoot the gal yore s'posed to rescue and come crawlin fer rescue to the gal's in cahoots with the redskins. You had a destiny. To uphold justice, to defend the American Spirit. Lookit you, snorin away— ya didn't even say yore now-I-lay-me-down-to-sleeps.

AARON: I'm not snoring and I'm not asleep.

LAREDO: Then git up and do sompin.

AARON: What?

LAREDO: I'm testin *you*; *you* tell me.

AARON: I don't know what to do . . . and neither do you.

LAREDO: Yore sayin the Laredo Kid don't know whut to do?

AARON: Yes.

LAREDO: I know what to do, believe you me.

AARON: What?

LAREDO: Believe you me, I know.

AARON: What?

LAREDO: Stop sayin "whut"! How can a feller think with somebody all the time sayin "whut," "whut"?

(AJ enters. Aaron sits up. She has a bag of groceries)

AARON: AJ.

AJ: What, what?

AARON: What'd you find out?

AJ: Finlay's trying to prime every landowner in the valley to shoot you on sight.

AARON: *Lisa,* AJ, what about *Lisa?*

AJ: Stable condition. So, in spite of the sentiments of the townsfolk, you're not lookin at a murder rap yet.

AARON: You think I tried to kill her?

AJ: I'm your attorney, Buster, I want to believe whatever you tell me.

AARON: That's very reassuring, AJ. *(AJ shows him a newspaper)*

AJ: It says here you were reported last seen in the airport boarding a flight for Mexico City.

LAREDO: Where'd they git that?

AARON: Where'd they get that?

AJ: I phoned it in last night. I picked up some salami and what passes for rye bread out here.

AARON: We don't need food, I'm— *(Aaron throws off blanket and heads for "kitchen")*

Oh, no, my chicken tetrazini! *(He checks his chicken)*

AJ: You're cooking chicken?

AARON: Yeah.

AJ: But *now?*

LAREDO: Cookin chicken?

AARON: Ya hungry?

LAREDO: Well, shore, but . . . *yore* cookin chicken?

AARON: Okay, egg whites ready . . .

AJ: Buster, Finlay's issued a warrant for your arrest . . .

AARON: . . . salad . . .

AJ: . . . his friends are no doubt loyally combing the countryside . . .

AARON: . . . vegetable, need a vegetable.

AJ: . . . I'm guilty of harboring you, and you're cooking chicken. Does that make sense to you?

AARON: Sense? Of course it doesn't make *sense.* Who's talking sense? I'm trying to fathom someone whose actions I do not comprehend. Peas with pearl onions okay with you?

AJ: No! This is no time to eat!   LAREDO: No! This is no time to eat!

AARON: I'm cooking it, we're gonna eat it.

LAREDO: Pard, I swear sometimes you'd make a saint mad 'nough to stomp a porcupine barefoot! We got to write new scenes! We got to clear yore name 'n rescue the gal from Finlay!

AARON: *(At AJ)* My god, what if it turns out I accidentally killed someone I loved and you're stuck with trying to get me off on a technicality.

AJ: I don't believe you loved her. She aroused your pity for her frailty, then she dumped on you. You're hurt and —

AARON: It's all right for you to have been in love with other men, though, right?

AJ: Hey, let's clear up this little fugitive from justice matter, then go ahead, marry her, have a kid! What do I care — I've had a child all my life — you! — it's not gonna bother me to see you somebody else's problem.

(AJ lights a cigarette; Laredo fans the smoke away with his hat)

LAREDO: You pile a stew meat, you gonna let her talk to you like that?

AARON: Hand me that bowl.

AJ: Now what?   LAREDO: Now whut?

AARON: Cake. Gotta fold my egg whites into my batter.

AJ: Buster, I beg you, forget the cake.

LAREDO: Oh, pard, I do too.

AJ: Let's figure out what to do.

LAREDO: Right. Now put that goop down, huh, pard.

AARON: Don't touch my egg whites! What's that smell?

AJ: Something's burning.   LAREDO: Sompin's burnin.

AARON: Oh, no — Lisa's chicken!

AJ: It's her recipe?

AARON: Of course it's her recipe. How am I gonna fathom her if I don't cook her recipes?

AJ: You know, I think if all else fails, we can cop an insanity plea.

AARON: Look at this.

AJ: Is it ruined?

AARON: Yes!

AJ: Good! I'm gonna wash up; then I am going to start making decisions — with or without you. *(She goes off)*

AARON: I killed her chicken.

LAREDO: Pard, forget the chicken. We gotta swing into action. Don-'cha think? Huh? Shore.

AARON: There's nothing I've done more frequently in my life than swing into action, Laredo. I've swung into more action than anybody I know — except AJ; nobody in the history of the planet has swung into more action than AJ — but the thing about all the action I've swung into over the years, Laredo, is none of it has resulted in even the minutest alteration in anyone's perceptions or a sense of satisfaction that I achieved anything of any real —

LAREDO: I don't know whut yore talkin about! Gals are runnin yore life, ya cook chicken and bake a cake . . . !

AARON: It's not considered unmasculine nowadays to let your female side out, Laredo.

LAREDO: Say agin.

AARON: I've been cooking and sharing the housework since AJ and I went off to college. Come to think of it, you weren't so different. You always played a mild-mannered drifter who was ineffectual and damned with a sensitivity we associate with femininity. You just didn't address the fact that that was your female side.

LAREDO: That was jist *pretend.* That wasn't me. Me was the guy who put on the black duds and mask and rode a white horse to the gal's rescue.

AARON: I always found that very confusing.

LAREDO: Whut?

AARON: Why did you have to change into black duds and hide behind a mask?

LAREDO: Shoot — black's s'posed to make a feller look thinner, that's all; and the mask was so's them that wasn't s'posed to know who I am when I'm not me won't know I'm the same feller as the other feller they're not s'posed to know I am when I'm him. Wasn't meant to confuse you l'il fellers none.

AARON: The way you explain it, it makes perfect sense. But I don't think women today have a whole lot of respect for men, they don't see men as heroes anymore.

LAREDO: And you think that's good?

AARON: I think it stinks.

LAREDO: So don't listen to 'em! Nobody ever has before! They don't know whut they want, they don't know whut's good fer 'em, whut's good fer *civilization*! Don't listen to no stupid, snivelin, drip-nose, stinkpot of a gal. *Be* a hero! Please, pard.

(Grip enters with phone — makes ringing sound. AJ enters)

AARON: Don't answer that.

AJ: What if it's for me?

AARON: Answer it. If it's not for you, pretend you're someone else and hang up.

LAREDO: Oh, that's good, pard.

AJ: *(Answering)* Hello.

(Sound: Billy humming "Swan Lake")

I don't think it's for me.

AARON: Who is it?

AJ: Someone humming.

LAREDO: Rachmaninoff!

AARON: Rachmaninoff?

AJ: No.

LAREDO: She's lyin.

AARON: Angry? Wagner?

AJ: Oh no — very romantic.

AARON: Tchaikovsky, Schumann . . . ?

AJ: Tchaikovsky, I think.

LAREDO: No such person — not in all hunnerd 'n nine pi'tures. Gotta be a trick — tell her to hang up.

AARON: Hang up! *(AJ hangs up. Billy stops humming)*

Tchaikovsky . . . ! Trying to make me think all is forgiven.

LAREDO: You git on the phone, he knows where yore hidin, tells Finlay —

AJ: Buster . . . ?

AARON: This guy calls me, see, hums threatening music. Guy named Lucas Pace.

AJ: Lucas Pace?   LAREDO: Lucas Pace?

AARON: Lisa's uncle, brain-damaged person who's in love with her, sees himself as her protector.

AJ: The same Lucas Pace, brother of your little friend's mother's third husband, who owned the Toyota dealership in town?

AARON: I don't know — I guess, yeah. What've you been doing — spying?

AJ: "Spying?" I've been doing my homework, Buster. In any case, you're saying this Lucas Pace calls you and hums threateningly.

AARON: Right.

AJ: From where, Buster?

AARON: From where what?

AJ: Is Lucas Pace calling you?

AARON: From where he lives, I guess. Long distance, I hope.

AJ: Ah — long distance. Well, that would explain it. I mean, it would have to be very long distance, as Lucas Pace has been dead for two years. *(A beat)*

AARON: Dead?

AJ: Murdered.

AARON: By whom?

AJ: Unsolved.

AARON: Unsolved!

LAREDO: Finlay!

AARON: I'll tell you who did it: Finlay!

AJ: Why would he kill a man whose land he already owned?

LAREDO: Because Pace knew what no-good use Finlay wants to make a the land.

AARON: *(Just a beat behind)* Because Pace found out that Finlay planned to misuse the land. Wasn't he a suspect?

AJ: No.

LAREDO: Had to be. In *Carpetbaggers of Stoney Rock,* it was —

AARON: *(Hearing something)* What's that?

AJ: Someone's coming. Hide behind the bed.

LAREDO: *(As he follows Aaron behind the bed)* This is it, pard — this is where she turns on ya; be ready to "thock" yore way outta here.

(Aaron and Laredo hide, Aaron in the road box, Laredo behind it . . . as Billy enters)

AJ: Judge. Come in.

BILLY: Lady. Don't have to remind you, I'm sure, that I got no legal jurisdiction on the reservation here; so just consider this a social call. Somethin smells mighty good.

(AJ begins to absently stir Aaron's cake mix. The road box moves closer)

AJ: Why, thank you, Judge. Just burning some chicken. What can I do for you, Judge?

BILLY: Welp, word is your friend's long gone for May-heco, but it crossed my mind that if ya happened to be in touch with him, ya might tell him I wanna make an arrangement.

AJ: What kind of arrangement?

BILLY: Man to man.

AJ: Ah, one of those. Well, I don't expect to see him, but if I do I'll tell him. *(When he lingers)* Is there something else?

BILLY: I'm told you been doin a bit a nosin round my affairs.

AJ: I'm curious about your relationship to an eastern concern which I believe to be interested in securing land in this part of the country for the purposes of toxic waste disposal.

LAREDO: Purpose of whut?

BILLY: Sister, lemme give you a little piece of advice.

AJ: Fire away.

BILLY: You get your nose one little bit further into my affairs and ya know what I'm gonna do?

AJ: Nope. Sure don't.

BILLY: I'm gonna yank it off your face. *(Billy starts to go, Aaron sneezes)* Bless you.

AJ: Thanks.

BILLY: Tell Weese he knows where to find me.

(Billy goes. Aaron and Laredo come out from hiding)

AARON: AJ, why didn't you tell me you'd made a connection between Finlay and this eastern concern?

AJ: You checked out on us, Buster—wasn't any of your business.

(Grip brings phone to AJ)

AARON: Who're you calling?

AJ: President Chato. *(She dials and has a conversation we don't hear)*

LAREDO: Whut's toxic waste whutever she said? In *Carpetbaggers of Stoney Rock,* the eastern blue-bellies are buyin up land fer—

AARON: Stop talking to me about cowboy movies! This is my real life! *(A beat)*

LAREDO: Yore sayin my pi'tures ain't real life?

AARON: I'm almost thirty years old . . .

LAREDO: That whut yore sayin?

AARON: . . . How can I still be in the clutches of a way of life that —

LAREDO: Whut I stand fer ain't important no more — that whut yore sayin? Cuz yore gonna be thirty years old, preservation a the land, right 'n wrong, doin unto others what you'd have them do unto you ain't important no more? THAT WHUT YORE SAYIN TO LAREDO? . . . No. Course it ain't. Cain't be. Was, there wouldn't be no hope fer no one nowhere in this republic.

(Aaron bends over, holding his gut)

Still got that tummyache, don'cha, huh? Cramp in the gut kin make a feller say things he don't mean, cain't it? You make a poo-poo today?

(Aaron shakes his head)

You take another l'il piece of advice from Laredo, concernin certain functions that don't become the hero. Now me, I never moved m'bowels in m'life, even when I had that rip-snortin tummyache that one time. Know why? Huh?

(Aaron shakes his head)

Cuz the Laredo Kid cain't be crouchin behind no mesquite bushes with a fist fulla leaves. What would all you children think if ya thought yore idol was out there makin poo-poo 'n pee-pee? I figure the same thing could be true fer the Majestic Kid he behaves hisself huh? Shore. Now here's whut I think we gotta do —

AJ: *(Hanging up)* All right, here's what I think we've gotta do. We turn you in to the police. I go before Magistrate's Judge Finlay to seek bail. He denies bail and I file an affidavit to have him disqualified. A coupla days I've got you out, you go back to Chicago while President Chato and I try to get to the bottom of this. Any luck we'll never have to take you to trial. *(She grabs her coat and briefcase)*

LAREDO: Be the hero, pardner. Send her on a wild goose chase while you go see the l'il gal and find out what she knows. In *Carpetbaggers of Stoney Rock* the gal knew whut the judge was up to and he blackmailed her to shut her yap.

AJ: All right, I'm ready, let's go.

LAREDO: Pard . . .

AJ: Buster, come on, move it, baby.

AARON: *(Swinging into action)* Disguise! I need a disguise!

LAREDO: Good, a disguise.

AJ: Why?

AARON: To get into the hospital and find out what Lisa knows.

LAREDO: Good, good.

AARON: An Indian outfit!

LAREDO: What?

AARON: Call President Chito back . . .

LAREDO: Chito?

AARON: . . . ask him if I can borrow —

AJ: I'm sorry, Buster — what did you say?

AARON: What?

AJ: You called President Chato President Chito.

LAREDO: Chito?

AJ: That's some kind of corn chip — Chitos.

AARON: You want me to act — I'm ready to act; you think I'm gonna stop for a round of ethnic slurs?

AJ: Your behavior of late, Buster, has been just a bit erratic.

AARON: Fine — then let me clarify that I think you mean Fritos, Ava Jean, not Chitos.

AJ: Don't call me Ava Jean.

AARON: Okay, look . . .   LAREDO: . . . Tim Holt.

AARON: Thank you. Chito used to ride with Tim Holt, okay?

AJ: It's okay with me.

AARON: Remarkable friendship . . .

AJ: I'm deeply touched.

AARON: . . . Anglo and Mexican united against the forces of injustice.

AJ: Make your point!

AARON: Let's not fight. Let's work together, like in the old days.

(Slides: Gal and hero together)

LAREDO: Oh, that's good, pard, makin her think she's yore saddle-pal again.

AJ: Ah, now you're all reason and strength, huh, and—don't tell me—you'll be the hero and I'll be the sidekick.

LAREDO: Na!

AARON: Absolutely not. Equals. Now, what have you got for a disguise?

AJ: *(A beat)* I've got Dr. Edgar Farnsworth's medical bag, coat, and glasses.

AARON: Perfect, I'll take 'em.　　　LAREDO: Perfect, we'll take 'em.

AARON: *(As she goes for the stuff)*　　LAREDO: *(Overlapping)* Now lis-
Now, listen to me.　　　　　　ten to me . . .

AARON: I'll go to the hospital and find out what Lisa knows. You contact the newspaper and the TV stations, tell them—

AJ: I'm not the sidekick! Tell them what? Drop a little hint that maybe one of their leading citizens is in the process of buying up their land to turn the valley into a gigantic cesspool?

(They head off, Laredo with them, happy as can be)

AARON: Right.

AJ: Damn good idea, Buster. *(Stopping)* You're back with us, aren't you?

AARON: I'm here to do what I　　LAREDO: I'm here to do what I
can, ma'am.　　　　　　　　can, ma'am.

(Sound: Laredo theme)

SCENE 3

Billy enters. Laredo slips in and follows Billy. Billy goes upstage. Laredo listens at floor for approaching danger. Billy returns.

BILLY: Raymond, don't you be sniffin round them nurses now. You keep your both eyes open. Gonna call the State Police, see if they got anything for me.

(Billy goes off, Laredo waves Aaron on. Aaron, in coat, scrub hat, and scrub mask pushes Lisa—on the road box—center as she stirs)

AARON: *(Italian accent)* Ah, signorina, buona sera. You are wakin up—good.

LAREDO: Why you usin that Mexican accent? You tryin to sound like Cisco?

AARON: I have to find out what she knows, right—without her knowing who I am. Right?

LAREDO: Right.

AARON: So I'm using an Italian accent.

LAREDO: Italian? Sounds Mexican to me. *(Bad Mexican accent)* Italian accent, she sound like this: Hey, mild-mannered drifter, you wanna meet my sister?

AARON: Come sta, signorina, how you are feeling?

LISA: My shoulder hurts, but I'm feeling much better.

AARON: Ah—good that is the best news of my life as a doctor of medical science. I am so sorry that you were injured, signorina. I want you to know that I hurt in my heart that you hurt *any-where* on your entire person.

LAREDO: Okay already, find out whut she knows.

AARON: Signorina, I am examine you more early in the evening and you seem to be, how you say, delirious. You keep mumbling something sound like "Hum, Hum, Billy kill Uncle Hum."

LISA: Aaron?

AARON: Oh great, I'm sure I'm gonna fool Billy.

LAREDO: Don't panic, pard.

LISA: Get away from me! Nurse! Help—

LAREDO: *(Panicking)* Shut her up!

AARON: *(Clamping his hand over her mouth)* Now, I am scared to death — you understand? — but you have to trust me — like you didn't trust me with the fact that Billy killed your Uncle Luke and is blackmailing you somehow to keep you quiet. Why didn't you tell me?

LISA: Because you're wrong! I love Billy!

(He clamps his hand back over her mouth — doesn't want to hear that, unclamps)

I wanted to make him jealous and I did and you tried to kill me, and get out of here!

AARON: *(Clamping)* I would never do anything to intentionally harm you. Never.

(She tries to speak against his hand)

LISA: *(Muffled)* I would never do anything to intentionally harm you either.

LAREDO: Whut'd she say?

AARON: She said she would never to do anything to intentionally harm me either. *(To Lisa)* Then why won't you trust me?

LISA: Oh, Aaron, what if things were reversed? Tryin to handle it alone would be all right, cuz you're a man.

AARON: I'm not a man. I'm just an aging boy adapting badly to a world run amok.

LISA: But you think you have a right to treat your struggles like some holy crusade that I don't.

AARON: I don't know what I think. I know what I *want* to think.

LAREDO: Not now, pard, huh?

AARON: I want to think people can share the burden of each other's struggles, without the question of who's the male and who's the female having anything to do with it.

LAREDO: Don't you start that "sharin" twaddle agin.

AARON: Now let's stop this. Just tell me what you're keeping from me — whatever it is, it won't change the way I feel about you.

LISA: Billy didn't kill my Uncle Luke.

AARON: If he didn't, who did?

LISA: Me. I did. *(A beat)*

LAREDO: What'd she say?

AARON: She said she killed her uncle.

LAREDO: What movie is this?

AARON: How? Why? You loved him. He must have *asked* you to put him out of his misery. Did he ask you to do it?

BILLY: *(Entering)* Begged.

LAREDO: Uh-oh.

BILLY: Begged her to put him out of his misery — yes, he did.

LISA: Oh Aaron, you see . . .

BILLY: So she gave him the greatest gift she could. Twenty-five cc's of an animal euthanasia serum in the saphenous vein of his ankle. Held his head in her lap while he convulsed and died. But then she come to realize she didn't have anyone to share the burden with. Her momma'd run off, she was tryin to take care of this vegetable and run a ranch and go out to the college . . . You figure you could tender the support for that load? She needed a real man. And she required a man who could take an act of love that could be misconstrued as murder and make it disappear.

LAREDO: I don't quite understand what he's —

AARON: Then why are you using it against her now?

LAREDO: Fine question, good question.

BILLY: Cuz I do not fail to accomplish what I set out to. Cuz I love her. Cuz I gotta have her.

(Laredo whispers in Aaron's ear)

AARON: Wouldn't have anything to do with wanting to get your hands on her ranch.

BILLY: No, sir, not one thing.

AARON: I don't believe you.

BILLY: Then you got shit for brains, boy,

AARON: So I can assume Lisa knows what you're conspiring to do with this eastern concern. Tell her what you're planning to use the land for, Judge.

LISA: What's he talking about, Billy?

AARON: He's not buying up the valley to preserve it.

LAREDO: Darn right. Tell her.

AARON: He's buying it up to sell for God knows how many times the amount he's paying for it so folks back east can bury their poison out your way. How bout it, Judge, care to comment?

LISA: Billy?

BILLY: The government, Lessey, got no alternative but to send those folks back east out here with their troubles. Puppy dog, the valley's terminal, it's just a question of when the obituary hits the papers. Listen to me carefully: I'm workin with folks in positions of power in this republic that'll spin your eyeballs in your head like a slot machine, I mean, doggy, I'm tellin 'em, you're gonna hafta jump to get what I got, and they're saying, just tell us how high, Judge.

LAREDO: How could *he* be workin with the government? He's the bad guy.

LISA: But the land. You always said you'd —

BILLY: Leesey, someone was destined to make a fortune comin face to face with the future and I decided it was gonna be me . . . *for* you. Everything you ever dreamed of.

LAREDO: Huh?

LISA: All I've ever dreamed, Billy, is to ranch my land and bear children in clean air and wide space and share the struggles of life with a family!

BILLY: I know I hurt ya, doggy, but we'll go anywhere in the world ya want. We'll have it all — the land, the family . . .

LISA: I don't want them with you!

BILLY: *(Suddenly pulls Lisa to him)* Yes ya do! Damn you, Brain Boy, let's go, you come along with me — we're goin out to my barn, I wanna talk to you.

LISA: Aaron . . .

AARON: Are you nuts? I'm not going anywhere with you.

LAREDO: That's good. Tell him where yore goin.

AARON: I'm taking Lisa out of here and I'm turning myself in to the police in the presence of legal counsel, then I'm going to suggest to the Attorney General of this state that he investigate your —

BILLY: Investigate my nothin! Because *I* am the law of this county.

AARON: You're not the law and somebody's gotta stop you from abusing it.

LISA: Aaron, please don't get yourself killed to prove to me you're a man.

BILLY: *(Leaning over Lisa)* Oh Lord, look here, you're bleedin right through your dressin.

AARON: Where? Lemme see. Get outta the way!

LISA: Watch out, Aaron!   LAREDO: Duck, pardner!

(When Aaron swings his attention to Lisa's shoulder, Billy slaps the blood pressure belt around Aaron's throat, quickly pumps it up, cutting off a good portion of Aaron's breathing)

BILLY: You don't quit makin speeches, I'm gonna detonate your head.

LISA: Billy, if you hurt him, I don't know what I'll do to you!

BILLY: Please, Leesey, *pelase* stop talkin like that. Cuz ya know what? Huh? Cuz in a coupla hours I'm gonna come on back here and I'm gonna giddy-giddy-git you, my little puppy dog.

(Billy leads Aaron away, Laredo beside them)

LAREDO: New scenes, pard, we need new scenes.

LISA: Billy, *no* . . . !

SCENE 4

The lights shift. Laredo enters, followed by Billy and Aaron. Billy puts Aaron on the road box, ties his hands behind his back, ties his feet.

BILLY: I never been able to understand why folks that don't understand other folks' way a life always feel what they gotta do is make those other folks like them, 'steada just mindin their own damn business. Why is that, Brain Boy?

AARON: Some misguided sense of what's right, I suppose.

LAREDO: Okay, that's good, pard, make him think ya agree with him, uh-huh.

BILLY: Gonna offer ya an arrangement, Weese. Ya don't take it, I'm gonna kill ya and dump ya on the reservation, make it look like your Indian brothers killed ya for runnin out on 'em. *(A beat— Aaron and Laredo look at each other)*

AARON: That's ridiculous.

BILLY: Don't doubt me, boy, cuz I assure you that I am the law in these parts. And I assure ya what I want is worth the risk to me.

LAREDO: Whut he wants, pard, is the gal's land—that's it!

AARON: What he wants isn't the gal's land. I think what he wants is just the gal.

LAREDO: He's sayin he'd kill ya for a *gal*? He's lyin, call his bluff.

BILLY: I want you to gimme your word as a man you'll pack it up and go on back to wherever ya come from. Just walk away, don't never make contact with her again and you 'n me are clear.

(A noise: AJ snaps twig, then exits. All attention to the sound. Billy pulls his revolver, goes off carefully)

LAREDO: All right, pard, now listen to me, here's whut ya do.

AARON: Pretend to agree to his terms, he unties me, I "thock" him in the jaw.

LAREDO: Now yore learnin!

AARON: Right. What I should do, Laredo, is I should agree to his terms, go back to Chicago, get a degree in Computer Science and dedicate my life to machinery.

LAREDO: Buckaroo, I'm startin in to think maybe you jist don't have it to be me. I'm thinkin maybe you remind me more of a saddle-pal, of 'fraidy-cat, turnip-brain Snuffy Greenbush. You play a harmonica?

AARON: Ukelele, as a matter of fact.

LAREDO: Yeah, well whut I think you oughta do, pardner, is you oughta jist give up this dreamin bout bein the hero, this Majestic Kid I ain't never even got a eensy-teensy glimpse of and you oughta jist git on to bein a parta the multitude. Go back east, marry some l'il gal and cook chicken and raise ya some l'il babies and ya jist pray to the Good Lord that when ya git yoreself in trouble — and you will — that there's someone like me around to come to yore rescue!

AARON: I wonder if it *is* possible to achieve Grace that way.

LAREDO: Grace? Oh no ya don't, no sir! You stay away from Grace. Yore gutless enough to go 'n git yoreself hitched, then you ain't never to have nothin to do with no other gal, buckaroo. "Thou shalt cleave unto that runny-nose wife only and be but one flesh." *(A beat, Aaron staring at Laredo)*

AARON: Laredo, you mind if I ask you a question?

LAREDO: Yore runnin low on time, pardner, ya better make it fast.

AARON: What do you know about women?

LAREDO: *(An expansive subject)* Whut do I know about women . . . Well —

(Slides: Women)

AARON: My god, you don't know anything about women. "Cleave unto thy wive only and be but one flesh" — you know what that means?

LAREDO: Course I know whut it means. It means some goony gal takes yore name, becomes a . . . a disciple of the feller whut takes her as his lawful, wedded wife, cooks fer him, cleans his —

AARON: It also means to fornicate.

(Slides: Men and women)

LAREDO: Whut kinda cake?

AARON: Not cake. Cate—cate—

LAREDO: Oh—cate.

AARON: —fornicate!

LAREDO: Oh—fornicate.

AARON: How do you think those little babies get made?

LAREDO: Shoot—there's the stork that comes in the winder, he—

AARON: But why did I *expect* to learn anything about women from you? Who were you always with? Who was always riding with all you conquerors of injustice?

LAREDO: You know who was at my side. Snuffy Greenbush.

AARON: Another *guy.*

LAREDO: Course another—I don't believe I follow ya here, buckaroo.

AARON: And so I lurched into adolescence steeped in the male-male and the male-horse relationship.

LAREDO: You start castin aspersions on Lightnin and you 'n me gonna tangle here.

AARON: And shallow dipstick that I was, I failed to comprehend the obdurate indifference all you guys displayed toward women.

LAREDO: We weren't indifferent to them gals! We put 'em on a pedestal!

AARON: You never got near 'em.

LAREDO: We worshipped 'em from afar. And I saved one from disaster in ever' last dang pi'ture I was in!

AARON: What good is that to someone like me who just wanted to learn to . . . to touch and be touched?

LAREDO: Don't touch 'em! *(A beat)*

AARON: What?

LAREDO: Well, I mean with all the rectifyin of wrongs I was doin, all the disasters I was savin 'em from, when did I have time to go on a date?

AARON: *(Hops over to Laredo)* No—oh no. No, no, no—they scared the crap out of you. All you "kids." The Durango Kid, Ringo Kid, Cisco, Sundance, Billy *the* Kid. The Laredo and Majestic Kids. Little boys scared to death of having to meet a woman face to face and deal with her, not as a *gal,* but as a woman, and protected from her by a hundred and nine scripts with the same plot.

(Aaron hops back to box and plops himself back on it)

LAREDO: I oughta "thock" you right in the jaw! I am the Laredo Kid! Children don't talk thataway to me!

(Slides: Fireworks)

AARON: Whudduya know . . .

LAREDO: Whuddo I know *whut?*

AARON: I don't have to be a hero. *(A beat)* Laredo, I wanna lay my ass on the line.

LAREDO: Don't say that word—I thought ya jist said ya don't hafta be the hero.

AARON: Right.

LAREDO: Then I don't understand whut yore sayin. Could ya say whut yore sayin so's I kin understand it jist maybe one time?

AARON: Something AJ said to me coupla months ago. Plant our feet. Might be the last stand. Some of us have to stand firm. I don't have to be a hero, just a decent man who's willing to risk his life for what's right. I think I know what I want to be when I grow up, Laredo.

LAREDO: Oh Lordy, I'm afraid to ask whut.

AARON: I gotta get outta here, get the police, bring this sucker Finlay down.

LAREDO: Attaboy!

AARON: Untie me.

LAREDO: You know I cain't do that. But you kin do it, cuz you *are* the Majestic Kid. You jist had a spell there, huh? Shore. Yore okay now, ain'cha, pard?

AARON: Actually, Laredo, I think I'm in deep, deep shit, pardner, but fact is, yeah, yeah I'm okay.

LAREDO: That's m'buckaroo! How bout a song, buckaroo, 'fore the showdown? Huh? You 'n me—little tune to—

AARON: Why don't we hold off on the song just now, Laredo.

LAREDO: Oh—oh sure, pard. So whut's yore idea fer the new scene?

AARON: Haven't got a clue.

(Billy enters with AJ slung over his shoulder, her wrists and ankles bound. He carries her to the road box and sets her down next to Aaron. Slides: Men tied up)

SCENE 5

BILLY: Got a little present for ya, Brain Boy.

AARON: AJ!

LAREDO: Now whudduya figure *this* is about?

BILLY: I'm gonna give ya ten minutes, Weese, to make your friend here a complicitor in our arrangement . . . or what'll remain of both of ya is a corpus delicti. *(Billy goes off)*

LAREDO: A whut?

AARON: Dead body.

LAREDO: Why doesn't he just call it that?

AARON: AJ, what are you doing here?

AJ: I was worried about you. Do I understand correctly that if we don't meet some condition, the good judge is threatening to kill us?

AARON: He wants us to go away—permanently.

AJ: Fine. Let's agree. Swear to it on a *Bible* on our honor as gentlemen, whatever he wants.

AARON: And walk away?

AJ: You do what you want. I don't walk away. But neither am I anxious for death. The newspapers and TV stations, though dubious about what I told them, are nevertheless going to have him splashed all over the news in the morning. We agree to anything we have to to get free — once the news breaks, the Attorney General's in it, Finlay won't dare touch us. *(A beat. They look at each other)*

AARON: Why do I think he's too smart to believe we'll walk away.

AJ: We have to be very convincing, very gracious in defeat, very . . . *(A beat. They look at each other)* Jesus, maybe we should enhance the odds and just get the hell outta here.

LAREDO: Pard, in *Masked Vengeance* —

AARON: Try to get up — c'mere. *(He helps her up, they work at untying each other as . . .)*

(Slide: Horse trick)

LAREDO: In *Masked Vengeance* I whistled for Lightnin and he did this trick where —

AARON: Please — sshh.

LAREDO: But . . .

AARON: Shh.

LAREDO: But . . .

AARON: Shh, shh!

AJ: Buster, you're too calm; you're not gonna panic on me, are you?

AARON: Do I seem like someone about to panic?

AJ: No, that's what scares me.

AARON: Ya know, it's really nice to see you a little unnerved, AJ. Makes you kinda . . . cute.

AJ: Oh Jesus Christ.

AARON: Don't be scared. I'm gonna figure a way out of this.

AJ: Oh baby, I've known since we were nine years old that you couldn't rescue me. How ya gonna do it now?

AARON: My fingernails are too short. Lie across my lap.

(She does. He works with his teeth and fingers)

AJ, why is it that since childhood I have always felt I could never live up to your expectations?

AJ: Buster, I am not having this conversation with you now.

AARON: I'm going to stop trying to free us until you answer my question.

AJ: Buster, I would dearly love to have a serious conversation about our relationship, but not now.

LAREDO: Pard, I shore agree.

AJ: Try your teeth again.   LAREDO: Try yore teeth agin.

AARON: There will be no more teeth until I get an answer. Now, who are you that I should never disappoint you?

AJ: Buster, I would have to be crazy to demand that you *never* disappoint me.

AARON: Who are you that I should *rarely* disappoint you?

AJ: I am someone who wants you to be the best you can be. Now, may we start trying to save our lives again?

LAREDO: Sink those choppers into that rope, pard.

AARON: Based on whose view?

AJ: Whose view of what?

AARON: Whose view we're talking about when you say you want me to be the best I can be.

AJ: My view. It's the only one I can have.

AARON: I don't think our relationship would work if I became as strong as you.

AJ: Are you crazy? This little sabbatical aside, you've *always* been strong!

AARON: But you've always been a little stronger. Ya know what I'm most sorry about, AJ?

AJ: What?

AARON: That all these years you didn't want a family because I hadn't grown into someone yet you would want to have one *with*.

AJ: Oh Buster.

AARON: AJ . . .

AJ: Yes.

AARON: Two more things. First — I love you. Second — stop calling me Buster. Now, let's get out of this together.

(Laredo during the above, has gone agitatedly to stand lookout. He hustles back)

LAREDO: He's comin, pard. Now here's exactly whut I think ya should do.

AARON: Don't tell me.

LAREDO: *(Trying to show Aaron a script)* But I got the plan. I 'membered this scene from *Two-Fisted Stranger* where I was tied up 'n the bad feller wanted me to leave town.

AARON: Sshh — please, I'm gonna wing it.

(AJ's hands suddenly come free from Aaron's efforts)

AJ: You did it!

LAREDO: Pard, ya did it!

AARON: Of course I did it.

AJ: We're not out of this yet, Buster.

LAREDO: Don't call him Buster.

AJ: I mean Aaron.

(She unties Aaron's hands. They untie their own feet and are about to make a run for it)

Let's get the hell outta here!

LAREDO: *(Overlapping)* Let's git the heck outta here. That way.

AARON: This way.

SCENE 6

. . . when Billy enters. A beat.

AARON: *(Genially)* Hi, Bill.

BILLY: Seems yawl've come to some sorta decision. So, gimme a clue — you kids wanna live?

AARON: Given the alternative, Bill, I would have to say we do.

BILLY: Then I assume you're ready to pack it in and leave town. We never hear from or lay eyes on either of ya again. We're not in agreement on that, I gotta make it look like you killed your friend here and the . . .

BILLY: . . . Apaches killed you.   LAREDO: . . . redskins killed you.

LAREDO: Here we go — *Two-Fisted Stranger.*

AARON: Nope.

BILLY: Nope what?

AARON: Nope, we don't agree to pack it in and leave town. I have no intention of giving up Lisa or AJ or the Apaches.

AJ: What are you doing, Buster?

AARON: Don't call me Buster.

LAREDO: Pard, ya gotta trick him into —

AARON: Sshh. *(To AJ)* What I am doing is telling this geek he's not scaring me off and that I'm not going to lie to him that he *is.*

AJ: Oh, Jesus, Aaron, not principles now! Are you crazy! Of course lie to him! Who is he that he shouldn't be lied to?

LAREDO: Pard, could I —

AARON: Laredo, I have everything under control. It would be most helpful if you'd stop interrupting me. 'Kay?

LAREDO: *(Indicating script)* Shore, pard, I'll jist hold this in case . . .

AARON: *(To Billy)* Come on, Bill, what's holding you up? Shoot AJ with your revolver, then shoot me and stick the revolver in my hand. You're the law in these parts — people'll be happy to believe whatever you tell them, right? . . . Are you nuts! There are decent people all over this valley. They're not gonna hold still for you murdering two innocent people, you addle-brained jackass! . . . Let's go, AJ.

(Billy sticks the rifle up Aaron's nose)

BILLY: Well well well, that was pretty darn good, Brain Boy. *(Billy slams rifle butt into Aaron's gut)* But ya see, dependin on me to have a conscience or to be too scared, when it comes right down to the doin, to kill you folks cause a how my more decent neighbors might respond, well that's just an error in judgment on your part. What I want to accomplish means everything to me. You, in particular, ethics, in general, don't mean dogshit.

AARON: You piss in my trough, I poison your well, huh?

BILLY: You piss in my trough, I kill you and *take* your well.

LISA: *(Entering, her arm in a sling)* Not yet ya don't, Billy.

LAREDO: Oh Lordy, now whut?

AARON: Lisa!

AJ: Lisa — come on in!

BILLY: Leesey, what're you doin out here, baby?

LISA: *(As Billy starts for her)* Stay where you are, Billy.

BILLY: Gotta get you back to the hospital, Leesey.

LISA: Damn you — stay where you are!

BILLY: Sure, darlin.

LAREDO: Pard, 'scuse me, I'm really sorry to interrupt the showdown, but this is all wrong — it cain't possibly happen this way.

AARON: The thing is, though, it is . . . it is happening this way.

LAREDO: But it cain't.

AARON: But it is.

LAREDO: But it cain't.

AARON: Laredo, you're impeding the showdown. Is that really what you want to do?

LAREDO: I never-what-ever-you-said-a showdown in my life.

AARON: Laredo, you're in the way.

LAREDO: You! You're the brain-damaged vegetable!

(Laredo exits, stands off the stage altogether, close to the audience)

LISA: I'm takin them outta here, Billy. Aaron, you and AJ come this way.

BILLY: Stay right where ya are, Brain Boy.

AJ: He's got a revolver in his jacket, Lisa.

LISA: Oh, I hope he's well armed, because this isn't gonna be capguns at twenty paces.

BILLY: You got a gun, sweetheart?

AARON: Lisa, do you have a gun?

AJ: Jesus Christ, I hope she's got a gun.

BILLY: My gal wouldn't come out here with a gun.

(Lisa pulls a revolver from her sling)

Gimme that, Lisa.

LISA: You think about comin at me, Billy.

AARON: What are you doing out here alone, Lisa?

LAREDO: *(To audience)* Whut's she doin out here at all?

AARON: You should have brought help.

LISA: I *am* the help, Aaron. I got all of us into this, I gotta get us out.

BILLY: You know what kinda trouble you're causin your Billy here, Leesey?

LISA: Threats don't mean anything anymore, Billy. No more threats.

AARON: What threats?

LISA: That day in our apartment, he told me if I didn't leave you, he'd do injury to you . . . or kill you if he had to.

BILLY: I didn't want to. You forced me.

LISA: And I'm damned if I could convince myself he didn't mean it! I got myself trapped!

BILLY: Trapped! Leesey, I'm offering you the world.

LISA: Now, before anything worse happens, let us walk out of here and we'll forget that you —

BILLY: Can't do it, Leesey.

(Billy puts the shotgun on floor, but still keeps the revolver in his belt)

I am just not given to losin you gracefully. Now what are you gonna do? *(Billy moves toward her)*

LISA: I'm gonna count to three, Billy. You either step aside or use that thing in your belt. One . . .

AARON: Lisa . . .

LISA: Stay out of this, Aaron. I know you want to help, but you can't.

LAREDO: *(To audience)* He cain't let *her* do it.

LISA: . . . two . . .

BILLY: I couldn't shoot you, Leesey. So you come ahead on, you git on to three, puppy dog, and you take me out.

AJ: Do it, Lisa, I can get you off!

LISA: . . . three.

(Lisa extends the gun at Billy. For a moment it's steady, then begins to shake . . . and Billy takes it from her hand)

AJ: Oh Jesus.

(Billy takes Lisa in his arms, sits her down, as . . .)

BILLY: We've shared too much. There are bonds 'tween us that nothin can break.

LISA: *(To Aaron and AJ)* I'm sorry. So sorry.

(AJ and Aaron connect. During the following, they slowly start moving)

BILLY: Leesey, you remember with me the wisdom of Mr. R. Perry who said: "Ignorance," puppy dog, "ignorance deprives men of freedom." Ya know why? "Because the ignorant do not know what alternatives there are." An intelligent feller, doggy, he defines his own freedom. *(Billy stops Aaron and AJ)* All right, Brain Boy, this is your last chance to agree to my terms.

AJ: We agree.

AARON: I don't.

AJ: Buster . . . !

AARON: Don't call me Buster, AJ. AJ agrees, Bill. Let her go, shoot me.

BILLY: You think I won't.

(Lisa and AJ connect)

AARON: Let's find out. As I don't smoke, I request that I be permitted the customary last words.

BILLY: Keep it brief.

AARON: One sentence on the subject of freedom.

BILLY: Fire away.

AARON: "The only freedom worth possessing is that which gives credence to virtue."

BILLY: Pure, unadulterated horseshit. Who said that?

AARON: I did. Me. A. Weiss.

AJ: Finlay!

(Slide: Hero)

LISA: Billy!

(As Billy glances at the women, Aaron charges, clutching the hand with the revolver in it and tearing the revolver free from Billy's grasp)

LAREDO: Yay, pard!

AARON: Don't move!

(Aaron cocks the pistol. Billy starts moving)

BILLY: What if I move?

LISA: Don't make him kill you, Billy.

LAREDO: Oh, don'cha worry, l'il gal—the hero don't kill no one in my pi'tures; he whups the bad feller senseless now and carts him off to the—

AARON: Damn it, Finlay, stay where you are!

LAREDO: Whut's he doin, pard?

(Billy has kept moving, is now behind Lisa, puts his arms around her. The gesture is loving; it also shields him a great deal from Aaron and the pistol)

BILLY: You got a .357 Magnum there, Brain Boy—reasonable chance at this distance, bullet'll pass through her and take me.

AJ: This is how you show your love for her?

BILLY: I'm not here, I wouldn't want her here; she's not here, I don't wanna be here. Course, we could play that one, two, three thing again.

(Billy's hand flies out of his belt, holding his own revolver. The two men face off, revolvers pointed at each other)

AJ: Ya gotta kill him, Buster.

BILLY: One . . .

LAREDO: *(To audience)* He cain't *really* take another feller's life.

BILLY: . . . two . . .

AJ: Kill him!

BILLY: . . . three.

AARON: I can't!

(A shot . . . and Billy's gun flies out of his hand. He cries out and clutches his hand. Slide: Indian warrior)

LISA: My god. You did it.   AJ: Holy Christ . . .

LAREDO: *(To audience)* He shot the gun out of his hand! He did it!

AARON: Wasn't me.

AJ: What?

AARON: I didn't fire.

LISA: *(Pointing off)* Look—there! Someone running!

AARON: AJ, look, it's—

AJ: *(Shutting Aaron up)* Aaron!

> *(AJ picks up Billy's rifle, his revolver, and takes the Magnum from Aaron as she says to him, quickly, quietly)*

It was no one . . . no one we recognized. *(A beat)*

LAREDO: Pard, who was that? It looked like a . . .

AJ: Did you recognize that person, Lisa? *(A beat)*

LISA: No. Sure didn't.

AJ: On your feet, Judge. We'll get you to the hospital. *(When Billy hesitates)* You test me, Your Honor, you're gonna lose.

LISA: *(Touching him)* Come on, Billy. *(A beat. BLACKOUT)*

SCENE 7

Aaron and Laredo, Laredo deeply disturbed. AJ on the phone, inaudible.

AARON: Get you something to eat, pardner?

LAREDO: Huh? Me—no, no thanks, pard, I'm not really hongry.

AARON: What's the matter? You can tell me.

LAREDO: I'm sorry I called you a brain-damaged vegetable. I never called no one a name like that in my life. It was jist all wrong out there, pard. All wrong. And sompin happened to me out there never happened to me before. I was . . . Aw, shoot: I was scared fer you 'n them gals, pard, cuz I knew I couldn't do nothin to help ya. There! And I seen, when it come right down to it, you couldn't do nothin neither. And then that Injun chief comin to your rescue that wasn't even *in* the pi'ture. One a the most important rules was always whoever's gonna be the hero, ya hadda meet him in the first fifteen minutes. Rescue and redemption didn't jist *show up*. And when it did, it wasn't never an Injun.

AARON: President Chato was following AJ, Laredo. He was protecting AJ, but that kind of last minute intervention by a character we've never seen is an old trick. Just hasn't been used a lot since the Greeks.

LAREDO: Well, I don't recall I ever seen one a their pi'tures and I don't care to! I bet they're stinky pi'tures. Pard, I'm startin to wonder if . . .

(Lisa enters)

AARON: 'Scuse me a minute, pardner.

LAREDO: Oh shore, go on, pard, I ain't in no big . . .

LISA: I'm gonna go on home now. You be all right here alone?

AARON: Oh sure. You?

LISA: Oh yeah. *(A beat)* No. You?

AARON: No.

AJ: *(Hanging up)* Hot damn! Attorney General's coming down from the capital tomorrow. Now, we'll see what we can do about that toxic waste disposal.

LISA: Just you and us now, I guess.

AJ: I guess.

LISA: You can tell President Chato and the tribal council that I'd like to sit down with them and talk about sharing my land. But only in terms of preserving it, farming and ranching it.

AJ: I'm afraid the Apaches aren't interested in farming and ranching this valley, Lisa.

LISA: Well, if as rumor has it, they wanna put a hotel down here, they'll have to fight me through every court in the land before they do it.

AARON: And me too, AJ.

AJ: Don't believe I follow you, Aaron.

AARON: If Lisa will have me, I'll be her attorney through every court in the land.

AJ: Oh, boys and girls, get your dreams in line! You think you can go back to innocence from here? If the Apaches want to build a hotel in this valley . . . *(A beat)* Okay. *(A beat. To Aaron)* What am I gonna do without you? I might miss you, ya know.

AARON: You're the best friend I've ever had—I can't imagine my life without you.

AJ: You may have noticed . . . we always seem to come back to each other. *(They come together)*

AARON: Tell President Chato if he changes his mind and wants to talk, we'll bring the cheesecake. *(A beat)*

AJ: Time out's over. See ya in court, counselor. Goodbye, Lisa.

LISA: So long, AJ.

(AJ goes off. A beat)

Thought you didn't wanna be a lawyer anymore.

AARON: I'm not sure I wanna be a lawyer, but I know what I wanna be when I grow up.

LISA: Tell me.

AARON: I want to be someone who helps people without hurting other people . . . and I want to marry you and have children and share the challenges of ranch life together.

(A beat. They come together in a fierce embrace . . . and then Lisa goes off leaving Aaron and Laredo)

I'm sorry—what were you saying, pardner?

LAREDO: Oh, nothin, I was jist . . . Pard, 'pears maybe you kin, but me, I don't know if I kin live in a world where folks don't seem to know or care whut's right 'n whut ain't, maybe even includin folks in the government of the republic out in Washington. I don't know if I *wanna* live in a world where the good guys and the bad guys are the same guys. So I'm thinkin, ya know, maybe

I oughta jist . . . *(But he just can't say it)* Well, shoot now, buckaroo—say, how bout a song, huh?

AARON: Laredo, I really ought to . . . sure, sing me a song. *(The guitar flies in on the horns)*

LAREDO: That's whut I'm hankerin fer, is a tune. Shore! *(Singing)*

Funny how time's got a way
Of testin us from day to day
I may never git this here chance agin
So I'll tell ya now while yore alistenin
I'm yore pardner now
And I'll be there when
There's no one around
To call yore friend
Take care of yourself, pardner
Take care of yourself
You got somebody who cares a heck of a lot fer you
Take . . .

(Unable to finish) Aw, whut's gonna happen to me, pard? You don't need me no more.

AARON: Time for both of us to get on to other dreams, Laredo.

LAREDO: Whose? L'il fellers today, they don't even know who I was—I mean, who I am. I mean . . . *(A beat)* I'm lost, pardner.

AARON: But thanks to you, pardner, I'm not. *(A beat)*

LAREDO: Welp.

AARON: Well.

LAREDO: Which way's that sunset?

(Aaron directs Laredo into a glorious sunset. The Big Guy heads off)

AARON: Hey, Kid . . . *(Laredo goes for his gun, only to turn and find that Aaron has for the first time beaten him to the draw with his finger. Laredo nods, tips his fingers to his hat, and is gone. Alone, Aaron looks after Laredo a moment . . . then turns to us, raises the gentle fingergun, twirls and holsters it)*

(BLACKOUT)